AFTER BREXIT AND OTHER ESSAYS

Andrew Gamble

BRISTOL
UNIVERSITY
PRESS

First published in Great Britain in 2021 by

Bristol University Press
University of Bristol
1-9 Old Park Hill
Bristol
BS2 8BB
UK
t: +44 (0)117 954 5940
e: bup-info@bristol.ac.uk

Details of international sales and distribution partners are available at
bristoluniversitypress.co.uk

© Andrew Gamble 2021

British Library Cataloguing in Publication Data
A catalogue record for this book is available from the British Library

ISBN 978-1-5292-1709-4 hardcover
ISBN 978-1-5292-1710-0 paperback
ISBN 978-1-5292-1711-7 ePub
ISBN 978-1-5292-1712-4 ePdf

Cover design: Liam Roberts
Image credit: Liam Roberts
Bristol University Press uses environmentally responsible
print partners.
Printed and bound in Great Britain by CMP, Poole

For my grandchildren

Joni, Nye, Louis, George, Ceinwen, Ivy
and Emyr

Contents

Preface

These two volumes of essays would not have happened without the patient encouragement and sound advice of Stephen Wenham at Bristol University Press. I must also thank for some very useful comments on the original plan Helen Thompson, Ben Clift, Simon Griffiths, Colin Hay, Magnus Feldman and Ben Rosamond.

So many people have helped and shaped me over the last sixty years. Many of them are mentioned in the pages which follow but by no means all. One of the greatest influences upon me has been my students, both research students and undergraduates, as well as my colleagues at Sheffield and Cambridge, and in the wider academic community and the public policy world. Most of the essays collected here had their origins in those engagements over the last forty years.

My family has supported me in so many ways through this time, and these essays are dedicated to them, and in particular to my grandchildren.

Introduction: Historical Contexts

This book contains a selection of my articles and papers on political economy and British politics. They have appeared over the last forty years and illustrate some of the main themes of my writing in this field. The companion volume to this one, *The Western Ideology*,[1] covers political ideas and ideologies. The themes covered in the two books at times overlap but they are intended to be self-standing. The essays in this book range from my essay on 'The free economy and the strong state', first published in 1979, to 'After Brexit' and 'The Anglo–American world view', which were both first published in 2019.

Any selection of essays for a book such as this faces a dilemma. Is it better to concentrate in depth on one or two themes, or is it more important to cast the net more broadly, choosing pieces that are representative of work done in different periods and addressing many different topics? I have for the most part selected pieces which had some impact at the time, but there are a few which have been forgotten and are rarely cited. All of them I hope stand alone as contributions to particular debates and themes in political economy and British politics.

Like all academic work these essays belong to particular times and contexts, and there are things in them which I would express differently today. But I hope they are still of some interest. I have mostly left the texts as they were, only correcting obvious anachronisms, and explaining certain references which were familiar enough at the time, but which will now be obscure to most people, for example the activities of the Clegg Commission in 1979. I have also removed some passages discussing scenarios which have since been overtaken by events. This Introduction is followed by brief notes on the themes of each essay. At the end of the book is an epilogue which reflects on the contexts in which the original essays were written and on what has changed since then. Some of my judgements and analyses have lasted quite well, others not so much.

The title essay in this collection, 'After Brexit', has been chosen as the title essay because it reflects on the historical contexts which have shaped the British political economy and its external relationships in the decades of European engagement and non-engagement since the Second World War. The European issue has been central in British politics in the last forty-seven years, since Britain first entered the European Community in 1973, but it reaches back before that, to Churchill's identification of Europe as one of three circles of key external relationships in which Britain was involved (the others were the Empire and the United States) and to Britain's refusal to become involved in the first steps towards European collaboration after the Second World War and in the 1950s, followed by the two failed attempts to join the Common Market in the 1960s.

When Edward Heath finally secured entry in 1973 he intended Europe to provide a new national purpose and to give Britain a new role in the world, following the withdrawal from Empire. It was regarded as a watershed moment in Britain's post-war development and a decisive recalibration of Churchill's three circles, giving top priority (for the first time) to the European circle. In the same way, the decision to withdraw from Europe after the 2016 Referendum has the potential to be a major watershed which some of the leaders of the Leave campaign are hoping will recalibrate the three circles again by giving priority to the United States and the wider Anglosphere. To the extent that this occurred, it would reshape British politics in many different areas – its political economy, its role in the world, its party system and its constitution.

Britain was often a reluctant member of the European Union, but supporters and opponents of the European turn in British policy assumed that Britain's membership of Europe was permanent and most unlikely to be reversed despite the presence of a strong and vocal anti-European minority. Europe was always an issue of low importance for most British citizens, but it was a vital matter for parts of the political class, as the virulence of the civil war in the Conservative party attested. Both main parties were divided about the merits of integrating with the rest of Europe and the priority to be given to Britain's relationship with Europe over its relationship with the United States.

'After Brexit' provides a frame for thinking about how the increasing Europeanisation of Britain's laws and institutions and policy-making processes and its regulatory regime over the four decades of membership intersected with other domestic issues and debates, including the response to the relative decline and poor performance of the economy, the character of Britain's hybrid Anglo–liberal model of capitalism, the reshaping of the post-war Keynesian welfare state, the rise and fall of Thatcherism, the transformation of both the Conservative and Labour parties, the relationship between Britain and the United States, the new regulatory state, and the changing constitutional order with the devolution of power to assemblies and parliaments in Wales, Scotland and Northern Ireland. These issues have their own time-frames and internal dynamics which have to be understood in their own terms. The essays in this book approach these issues in a variety of ways. They were written at different points in Britain's European odyssey, which shows no signs of ending any time soon, because although Britain is now *after Brexit* it will never be *after Europe*. Much as some Brexiters might like to weigh anchor and sail off into the Atlantic, Britain's oscillation between engagement and non-engagement with the rest of Europe will remain a fundamental part of British politics.

Whether Brexit turns out to be a major watershed in British political history and in the British political economy is unclear at the moment, and will depend on the choices which British governments make in the next ten years. Will Britain after ten years be as close to the EU as Norway or Switzerland, or will it find a new role as 'Global Britain' outside the EU orbit altogether? Watersheds are hard to identify with certainty at the time, and Brexit has several other recent events to contend with, including the 2008 financial crash and the 2020 COVID-19 emergency.

Looking back over the sixty years I have been studying and writing about politics, and reading again some of my earlier writings, I am struck by some of the continuities but also by what has changed, and by what I left out. From this distance it is much easier to see the political contours of the last six decades, the decisive breakpoints and watersheds, and why events unfolded as they did. But hindsight has its own pitfalls. Outcomes are never inevitable, at the time there are always different possibilities and one of the difficulties of writing enveloped by the fog of events is understanding which paths are more likely to be taken. The role of contingency in human affairs constantly contradicts our yearning for order and rationality and for the fulfilment of our hopes. Some of these essays describe paths which were never taken, scenarios which were never realised, doors which were never opened.

Another difficulty in writing about contemporary politics is that events in any one national territory like Britain are not shaped by just one context but by many different contexts, with different time-lines which only occasionally overlap. For the seventy-five years which have elapsed since 1945 these contexts have included all the usual domestic ones, such as the economy, elections and the political parties, the Union, and external relationships, but also international contexts, including the geopolitical, the economic, the security, and the environmental. It is hard to pay adequate attention to all these at once. The degree of complexity is too great. What everyone does is to simplify. I have long thought that the real value of theories in political economy and political science is not to provide certainty and all-encompassing explanations but to act as searchlights which illuminate particular aspects of a problem. It follows that we need many searchlights to understand something as complex as politics, from as many different perspectives as possible.

The frame I have relied on most in these essays is a set of overlapping historical contexts focused on problems of British politics and political economy, using a concept of political economy still understood as Marx or Hayek or Adam Smith would have understood it. The first context is the end of the post-war settlement, both national and international. It runs from the early 1960s to the late 1970s, from the 1961 pay freeze and the Cuban missile crisis through the final stages of decolonisation and end of empire, and the entry of Britain into the European Community, to the end of the Bretton Woods system and the first questionings of US power, the inflation crisis and the industrial conflict which that provoked, the 1976 IMF (International Monetary Fund) bailout, paving the way to monetarism, and Margaret Thatcher's election victory in 1979. This is the period which saw the challenges to the post-war gains of the Labour movement, the discrediting of Keynesianism, the economic crisis of the 1970s with its novel combination of high inflation and slow growth, the polarisation of politics, and the rise in Britain and elsewhere of a new politics of the right. My work was shaped in this period by the debates on the economic crisis and the specific crisis of British capitalism, debates on the new Conservatism, and debates on British decline.

The second context, from the mid-1970s through to the early 1990s, is the neo-liberal turn. This was made possible by the wider international context – the reorganisation of the US dominated international order under Ronald Reagan, and the second cold war with the Soviet Union, which at first involved a ratcheting up of nuclear tensions, and then the period of 'perestroika' and 'glasnost' under Gorbachev, which ended with the opening of the Berlin Wall in 1989 and the collapse of the Soviet Union in 1991. Another key context for Britain was now the European context, the progress of EU integration towards monetary union with the creation of the Exchange Rate Mechanism (ERM) in 1979, and the establishment of the single market, over which Britain had much influence. It is within these contexts that the Thatcherite project in UK unfolded, assisted by the normalisation of neo-liberal doctrines and policies throughout the western world. It ends with the opening of the Berlin Wall in 1989 and the subsequent collapse of the Soviet Union, and in the UK the forced ejection of the £ sterling from the ERM. My work was shaped in this period by major debates on Thatcherism, on economic policy, on the new cold war, on the acceleration of technological and cultural changes, and on the beginnings of the new era of globalisation.

The third context, from the early 1990s to the late 2000s, is the new world order. The boundaries of this period are unusually distinct since it began with the proclamation of a new world order by US President George H. Bush, the third post-war phase of US hegemony, and ended with the 2008 financial crash. This was the era of globalisation and the Third Way, of renewed economic growth and western prosperity, and the beginnings of a massive geopolitical shift with the economic and political rise of China, India and Brazil, as well as the development of new regionalist associations in many parts of the world, and the growing strength of the European Union. The Kyoto Agreement on the urgent need to tackle climate change was signed in 1997 and the UN formulated its Millennium Development Goals in 2000 to counter inequality and promote sustainable development. My writing in this period responded to debates on the Third Way, on neo-liberalism, on European integration, on reforming capitalism and on regionalism and world order.

The fourth context is the crisis of neo-liberalism. It lasted from the financial crash up to the COVID-19 pandemic. As with Brexit, we do not yet know whether this is a watershed or whether the disorder of the last twelve years will continue. It was a time of austerity and a very weak economic recovery from the recession which followed the financial crash, growing challenges to the international rules-based order and to multilateralism, and the rise of populist nationalism and the return of great power rivalry. This took place against increasing challenges, particularly around nuclear proliferation and the environment. But the fragmentation of political authority and the withdrawal of the US under Donald Trump from the kind of leadership role it used to play accelerated the fragmentation of the world into increasingly hostile blocs, with growing strategic competition between the US and China.

In reading these essays the different contexts in which they were written needs to be borne in mind. One of the easiest things to do is to write history with hindsight. One of the hardest is to reconstruct the contexts and the choices which individuals actually faced at different times. Some of these essays look back at how particular debates or events unfolded. Others seek to understand the contexts which shaped the perceptions which individuals held and the choices they made. The question of what I got wrong and what I got broadly right is taken up in the Epilogue.

Notes on the Essays

There are four main themes.

Theme 1: Britain's political economy

   1 After Brexit (2019)
   2 Explanations Of British Decline (1999)

Theme 2: Europe and America

   3 The European Disunion (2006)
   4 The Anglo–American world view (2019)

Theme 3: Thatcherism

   5 The Free Economy and the Strong State (1979)
   6 Thatcherism and Conservative politics (1983)
   7 Economic Growth and Political Dilemmas (1983)
   8 The crisis of Conservatism (1995)
   9 The Thatcher myth (2015)

Theme 4: The British constitution

  10 Theories of British politics (1990)
  11 The constitutional revolution in the UK (2006)
  12 What's British about British politics? (2016)

Many of these essays employ a political economy approach to the study of British politics. It is an approach developed in four linked books which I have published over the last thirty years: *The Conservative Nation* (1974), *Britain in Decline* (1981), *The Free Economy and the Strong State* (1988) and *Between Europe and America* (2003). They attempt to understand the shifting agendas, issues, outcomes and debates in British politics through an analysis of the political economy of the British state, exploring the historical, institutional and ideological contexts which have shaped it. This work has had a particular emphasis on the Conservative party and its central role in British politics, but I have always had a wider interest in British politics and comparing it to other political systems. The essays in this book have been chosen to illustrate these different aspects of my writing on British politics and its political economy.

Theme 1: Britain's political economy

'After Brexit' (Chapter 1) was a contribution to a book edited by Colin Hay and Daniel Bailey, *Diverging Capitalisms: Britain, the City of London, and Europe* published by Palgrave-Macmillan in 2019. It was written after the Referendum result but before it was clear what kind of Brexit the May Government was seeking to deliver. I have updated the essay to reflect the replacement of May by Johnson (although at the time of writing it is still not completely clear what the Johnson Government is aiming for or will deliver). The essay examines the historical contexts which shaped the UK economy and its particular model of Anglo–liberal capitalism, the political discourse of economic and imperial decline which took hold particularly after 1945, the yearning for Anglo–America rather than Europe as the focus of British identity and interests, and the distinctive and persistent characteristics of the UK model of capitalism. This is set in the context of the wider debate on models of capitalism, and why membership of the EEC was attractive partly because of the different models of capitalism which had developed in Europe and were for a time regarded as superior to that of the UK. The trajectories of the development of the UK political economy from 1942 to 2017 are traced, in order to identify the major shift in direction which took place under Thatcher and Blair. The essay concludes by analysing the tension between US and European models of capitalism in the thinking of the British political class, the impact of Brexit, and the different futures for the UK which Brexit has made possible.

'Explanations of British decline' (Chapter 2) was written twenty years before 'After Brexit'. It was a contribution to a collection edited by Richard English and Michael Kenny, *Rethinking British Decline*, published by Palgrave-Macmillan in 1999. This is a reflective look back at the debate on British decline which had consumed the political class for several decades, particularly in the 1960s and 1970s. This debate became one of the main lines of research I pursued in the 1970s, resulting in *Britain in Decline*, first published in 1981 by Macmillan, which went through four editions.

Decline has many meanings and has always been a contested term. The essay distinguishes between absolute and relative decline, and imperial and economic decline, and explores the different debates which have emerged over relative economic decline during the last hundred years and the various political programmes on right and left to overcome it. Imperial decline came to be accepted as inevitable in a way that relative economic decline was not. The varying accounts of the economic decline hold different national peculiarities responsible. The essay analyses the debates around an anti-industrial culture, the size and role of finance, the distractions of empire, the absence of a developmental state, and the organisation of industry.

Theme 2: Europe and America

'The European disunion' (Chapter 3) was published in *The British Journal of Politics and International Relations* in 2006, and won the prize for best article in the journal that year. Like the next essay it takes up themes laid out in *Between Europe and America* (2003). Britain's vexed relationship with the European Union, culminating in Brexit, has been a major theme in my work. This essay analyses the strains within the European Union and the competing visions and strategies imagining different futures for the EU. It explores the state of the UK debate on Europe following the rejection of the constitutional treaty by France and the Netherlands in 2005. It examines the conflict between the intergovernmental and supranational conceptions of the EU which lay at the heart of the constitutional treaty, various scenarios that had been proposed as to how the EU might develop, and different overlapping images of Europe which defined the European debate. The contradictions in Britain's attitude to the EU are spelled out. The British remained strongly attached to an intergovernmental conception of the EU and rejected any further pooling of sovereignty, while at the same time they were strongly attached to the virtues of a liberal world order, requiring constant subordination of national sovereignty to achieve it.

'The Anglo–American world view' (Chapter 4) was published in *The Anglosphere: Continuity, dissonance, and location,* which was edited by Ben Wellings and Andrew Mycock, and arose from a British Academy conference in 2018. It examines the various terms used to characterise the relationship between Britain and the United States, particularly Anglo–America and the Anglosphere. It argues that the substance of

Anglo–America was the cooperation which developed between the two states in creating and sustaining a hegemonic conception of world order. It examines the ideas and institutions which were crucial to this project, and the differences between the hegemony which Britain exercised in the nineteenth century, and the hegemony which the US exercised in the twentieth, and traces the stages by which the collaboration between these two states came about. The Anglosphere is the latest narrative of Anglo–American hegemony and the essay concludes with a discussion of how it is faring in the era of Brexit and Trump.

Theme 3: Thatcherism

'The free economy and the strong state' (Chapter 5) was published in *Socialist Register* in 1979, when it was edited by Ralph Miliband and John Saville. It appeared shortly after the Thatcher Government took office. It is the first of five essays in this book written at different times on the political phenomenon of Thatcherism. This essay highlights the intellectual revival which had been taking place on the right, the novelty and ambition of the ideas that were being advanced by supporters of Thatcher within the Conservative party, and the depth and seriousness of their critique of post-war Conservatism, Keynesianism, social democracy and the post-war settlement. They were seeking a break with the Keynesian social democratic order and proposing a radical shift in the direction of the UK political economy. Behind these ideas lay a revival of liberal political economy as a dominant discourse which was taking many forms but owed a great deal to Friedrich Hayek. Along with Milton Friedman, Hayek had emerged as a key authority for this new radical project of the right to overturn the post-war political settlement between capital and labour. The phrase 'free economy, strong state' was used by Alexander Rüstow, one of the key thinkers who developed a new form of economic liberalism in the 1930s which influenced Hayek and other Austrian economists and later became the foundation of Ordo-liberalism.

'Thatcherism and Conservative politics'(Chapter 6) draws on two articles which were commissioned by Martin Jacques for the monthly journal, *Marxism Today*. It was published in 1983 in *The Politics of Thatcherism*, edited by Stuart Hall and Martin Jacques. It was written before Thatcher's second election victory in 1983, but after the Falklands War. It represents a first attempt to make sense of the drama and turbulence of the first two years of the Thatcher Government and to assess its prospects. It discusses the novelty of the Thatcher project in the history of British Conservatism, and the precariousness of the

Conservatives' position after they returned to government in 1979. It examines the formidable obstacles Thatcherism faced in maintaining electoral support in the face of an economic slump and the imposition of unpopular policies, the similarities and differences between Thatcher and her predecessor, Edward Heath, the relationship of Thatcherism to traditional Conservatism, the rise and different components of the new right in the party, and the difficulties the Government was encountering in delivering its radical agenda.

'Economic growth and political dilemmas' (Chapter 7) was a contribution to a collection in honour of Fred Hirsch, entitled *Dilemmas of Liberal Democracies* and published in 1983. It was edited by Adrian Ellis and Krishan Kumar. This essay looks at Thatcherism from a different angle, the nature of the post-war Keynesian social democratic settlement, its unexpected success in the 1950s and 1960s, the reasons for its unravelling in the 1970s and the insights provided by Fred Hirsch into this process, specifically his analysis of the political dilemmas confronting affluent consumer societies. Hirsch's analysis was very different from Hayek's, and offered very different political remedies. He argued that the way economic activity is organised in a capitalist economy undermines the non-economic political conditions which must be sustained if capitalism is to survive. The essay examines post-war policies in Britain on full employment, economic growth and redistribution, and pinpoints the difficulties which governments of both parties experienced in managing the strains which emerged, particularly in the form of inflation and its consequences, and how this helped create the intellectual and the policy context for Thatcherism.

'The crisis of Conservatism' (Chapter 8) was published in *New Left Review* in 1995, five years after the end of Thatcher's premiership. The Conservatives were still in power and continuing many of her policies, but support for the party had collapsed after Black Wednesday in 1992, shortly after their fourth consecutive general election victory, and a Conservative defeat at the next general election was widely anticipated. The essay assesses the long-term effects of Thatcherite radicalism on the Conservative party by analysing the pillars of Conservative hegemony in the past – state, union, property and empire – and how all of them were undermined by the policies which the Thatcher Government pursued in the 1980s, creating the conditions for a deep electoral and political crisis for the party which was triggered by the manner of Britain's exit from the ERM in 1992. The essay discusses the civil war which had erupted in the party over Europe and the ratification of the Maastricht Treaty, drawing on findings from the ESRC project 'Conservative Parliamentarians' attitudes to the EU', a collaboration with Steve Ludlam, David Baker, David Seawright, and Imogen Fountain. It highlights the seriousness of the schism which had opened up in the party over Britain's future relationship with Europe and the project of European integration, comparing the schism to earlier schisms in the party over the Corn Laws and tariff reform.

'The Thatcher myth' (Chapter 9) was published in *British Politics* in 2015, in a special issue devoted to Thatcher's legacy. Margaret Thatcher had died on 8 April 2013, and had been ill and out of public life for a long time, but for ten days, after her death was announced, it felt as though the 1980s were back. The passions of that era were suddenly reawakened. This essay reflects on what was true and what was false in the way she was being remembered, and on the power of her myth, the heroism of the warrior leader, both for her admirers and for her detractors, and gives an assessment of her tumultuous years as leader of her party after 1975 and Prime Minister from 1979 to 1990, highlighting a number of episodes such as the Falklands War and her economic policy. It examines her political character, particularly her willingness to take risks on big issues but also her caution and pragmatism, the role of structure and agency in politics, and what her legacy has meant for her party and for British politics.

Theme 4: The British constitution

'Theories of British politics' (Chapter 10) was published in *Political Studies* in 1990, right at the end of Thatcher's premiership. It examines the assumptions underlying the Westminster model of politics and why this has been such an important operating ideology for the British state. The traditional theory of British politics emphasised the unique character of the British political tradition and the interrelationship of ideas and institutions. Its three main elements were a constitutional doctrine, a theory of the state, and a theory of history. New theories and perspectives, often influenced by American and European political science, have challenged the assumptions of this Westminster model because it excluded too much and explained too little. The study of British politics has become more fragmented, with no single dominant perspective. This essay discusses theories in five main research areas – ideology, the constitution, public policy, political economy and political behaviour – as well as the prospects for more interdisciplinary and comparative studies.

'The constitutional revolution in the United Kingdom' (Chapter 11) was published in *Publius* in 2006, when Tony Blair was still Prime Minister. It reflects on the devolution of powers brought about by the Blair Government since 1997. These changes to the territorial constitution were extensive, but there was no agreement on their long-run significance, opinion being divided as to whether the changes were substantive or cosmetic, and whether they represented the conclusion of a process or the start of a new one. This essay connected these arguments with historical debates on the nature of the British state and its distinctive constitution and multiple identities, in order to assess whether the devolution process of recent years signals continuity, rupture or reform of UK institutions. It concludes that some of the changes have introduced quasi-federal features to the constitution, and mark a historical watershed, although progress towards full federation remains limited.

The final essay, 'What's British about British politics?' (Chapter 12), was a contribution to *Developments in British Politics 10*, edited by Richard Heffernan, Colin Hay, Meg Russell and Philip Cowley and published by Palgrave-Macmillan in 2016. It ranges across all four themes in this book, asking what has made Britain distinctive as a polity from other European states with similar population and resources in the last seventy years. It discusses whether British politics is unique or whether it is a variation on a common pattern found in liberal democracies. It examines some of the main features of the British state which are said to make British politics distinctive – its multinational union state, its highly centralised institutions, its uncodified constitution. It argues that understanding how politics in a particular place is constructed through both identities and institutions is the key to understanding British politics.

1

After Brexit[1]

In the referendum held on 23 June 2016 the British people voted by a narrow margin (52 per cent to 48 per cent) to leave the European Union. 37 per cent of the total electorate voted Leave. The result introduced great uncertainty into the future path of British politics and the shape of its political economy. The debate has been shaped by partisan perspectives. Some have called it the most disastrous peacetime event in British history, the greatest act of self-harm ever inflicted,[2] others have described it as a liberation from a corrupt and failing organisation which allows the British people to take back control and Britain to be Britain again.[3] The result has placed the long-term future of the UK union in doubt, since both Northern Ireland and Scotland voted Remain, and it raises questions once again about the UK's place in the world, particularly the nature of its relationship with the United States and its future defence and security cooperation with its European allies.

The UK had endured three difficult decades after 1945, adjusting to the loss of empire and world power. After the Suez debacle it tried and failed twice to join the European Economic Community (EEC), finally succeeding in 1973. The decision was then ratified by a two-thirds majority in a referendum in 1975. Joining the EEC was not the economic panacea for the many ills of the British economy which some of its advocates had hoped, partly because it occurred during the major recession and prolonged crisis of the 1970s, but it did appear to many observers that it had settled Dean Acheson's concern ten years before that Britain had lost an empire and not yet found a role. Membership of the European Economic Community gave Britain a role at the heart of the European project for economic integration which complemented and supported the parallel structures of NATO for defence and security. For forty years, membership of the EU was a crucial anchor of British policy, and although the UK was often reluctant to back deeper integration, it was enthusiastic in its support for the creation of the single market, and then for the enlargement of the EU after the collapse of the Soviet Union in 1991. The single market bound the UK ever more closely to its European partners and encouraged increasing convergence of the UK economy with other European economies.

Empire and decline: the peculiarities of the Anglo–liberal model

The UK's political economy and the peculiarities of the Anglo–liberal model were shaped by the role Britain has played in the global economy in the last three hundred years. Britain became first a successful entrepreneurial and commercial society, an expanding colonial and naval power, and then partly as a consequence the first significant industrial society. By the middle of the nineteenth century Britain had become the world's leading commercial, industrial and imperial power. Many of the peculiarities of the Anglo–liberal model became set in this period and have proved very hard to reform. Some of the features which made the UK distinctive in the nineteenth century, such as Britain's industrial lead and the size of its urban working class, have disappeared as other countries have caught up and industrial economies have converged. But there remain some important features of British capitalism which mark it out from development elsewhere.

One of the most important of these is the size and weight of its financial sector. One million people currently work in financial services in the UK, as many as worked in the mines in the 1920s. The City of London has an economic and political weight that is greater than in any state of equivalent size. The financial sectors of some other countries such as Switzerland are even larger in relation to their host economies, but their populations are much smaller. In the nineteenth century the City became the leading centre for financial, shipping, and insurance services for the rest of the international economy. It formed its own 'industrial district'. This cluster of expertise survived long after the disappearance of the economic and military power which made it possible. Having weathered the collapse of the gold standard and the Great Depression, the Second World War and the post-war social democratic settlement, the City experienced a remarkable renaissance starting in the 1960s with the development of the Eurodollar market.[4] British governments allowed the City to behave as if it were an offshore financial centre, free of many of the regulations which other jurisdictions, including the US, imposed on their financial centres.

In the neo-liberal era the City became once again one of the world's leading international financial centres. One of the most significant reforms of the Thatcher Government was the deregulation of financial services in 1986, the 'Big Bang', removing restrictions on the entry of foreign banks into London.

A second distinctive feature of the British economic model is the legal framework governing its labour markets, trade unions, and companies. For a time in the twentieth century trade unions appeared powerful actors, but they were never fully incorporated as part of the governance of the economy, and their powers were granted as privileges, exemptions from the provisions of the common law. In the 1980s these privileges were revoked. Similarly UK corporate governance has always treated the company primarily as a private association rather than as a public corporation, in contrast to European law.[5]

A third distinctive legacy from the British *Sonderweg* is the size of the British state, and its relationship to civil society and the economy. This is reflected both in the relatively small size of UK public expenditure compared to those in some other European member states, and the corresponding low fiscal base, and also in the relative lack of success of the British state in recasting itself as an entrepreneurial state in the manner of Germany, France, Japan or even the United States. This liberal conception of the state is paralleled by a liberal conception of the household, reflected both in the emphasis on consumption rather than production in the Anglo–liberal growth model, and the importance placed on self-reliance and independence, which has shaped attitudes towards welfare.

In the nineteenth century Britain became the world's most modern and advanced economy, the economy which, as Marx noted, showed every other economy the image of its own future. But this was not true in every respect. Many aspects of the British model in time came to seem anachronistic and no longer modern. Britain was surpassed by other major powers. As British power waned the British model began to be questioned. Its shortcomings were exposed, and numerous prescriptions offered as to how it might be reformed. Many of the projects for reversing British decline recommended learning from the more successful models of some of the UK's competitors in Europe, East Asia and North America. The widespread perception of Britain as the 'sick man of Europe' reached a peak in the 1970s. Britain it seemed had the wrong kind of capitalism, the wrong kind of state, certainly the wrong kind of unions and was rapidly moving to the abyss. As Sir Keith Joseph, one of Margaret Thatcher's closest allies, put it:[6]

The visible signs of Britain's unique course – as it slides from the affluent Western World towards the threadbare economies of the communist bloc – are obvious enough. We have a demotivating tax system, increasing nationalisation, compressed differentials, low and stagnant productivity, high unemployment, many failing public services and inexorably growing central government expenditure; an obsession with equality, and with pay, price and dividend controls, and immunities for trade unions; and finally, since 1974, top of the Western league for inflation, bottom of the league for growth.

Yet within eight years these problems had been miraculously dispelled. The 1987 Conservative party manifesto proclaimed:[7]

Remember the conventional wisdom of the day. The British people were 'ungovernable'. We were in the grip of an incurable 'British disease'. Britain was heading for 'irreversible decline'. Well, the people were *not* ungovernable, the disease was *not* incurable, the decline *has* been reversed.

This triumphalism proved slightly premature and was quickly followed by a severe recession between 1989 and 1992, which saw unemployment rise again by 1.5 million, the collapse of the housing market, plunging many house owners into negative equity, and the Exchange Rate Mechanism (ERM) debacle. But following the exit from the ERM and a substantial devaluation, growth resumed, and by the start of the new century, decline as a theme in British political discourse had almost disappeared. The condition of the economy was no longer at the centre of political debate. Triumphalism had reappeared. In his 2004 budget speech Gordon Brown declared:[8]

For decades after 1945, Britain repeatedly relapsed into recession, moving from boom to bust ... since 1997 Britain has sustained growth not just through one economic cycle but through two economic cycles, without suffering the old British disease of stop-go – with overall growth since 2000 almost twice that of Europe and higher even than that of the United States. Indeed in the Pre-Budget Report, I told the House that Britain was enjoying the longest period of sustained economic growth for more than 100 years ...

I have to apologise to the House. Having asked the Treasury to investigate in greater historical detail, I can now report that Britain is enjoying its longest period of sustained economic growth for more than 200 years – the longest period of sustained economic growth since the beginning of the Industrial Revolution.

Something of a sea-change had taken place in Britain's economic fortunes. The pessimists had been proved wrong. Britain in 2004, the Chancellor announced, had 'the lowest inflation for 30 years, the lowest interest rates for 40 years, and the highest levels of employment in history'. The inflation peaks in the last three recessions of 27 per cent in 1975, 22 per cent in 1980, and 9 per cent in 1990 were a distant memory, as were the three million unemployed of the 1980s, and high interest rates (17 per cent in 1980 and 15 per cent in 1990).

Had the performance of the British economy improved? At the time many still argued that it had not, or at least that the improvement was only superficial, and that the fundamental problems of the British economy remained unresolved. The economy only appeared to improve because expectations about British economic performance had been lowered so much. As David Coates argued:[9]

The UK had spent the first four decades of the postwar period locked in a process of cumulative economic decline caused by inadequate levels of investment in plant and equipment, and that growth trajectory remained firmly in place at century's end ... [positioning] the UK as predominantly an off-shore warehouse economy, where a low-paid, underskilled and now poorly unionised workforce depended for the attraction of foreign direct investment on the economy's role as an assembly pad within the tariff boundaries of the EU for the export of medium-tech mass-consumer goods into the more prosperous heartlands of corporatist Europe. The UK economy remains disproportionately a service-based economy, internationally competitive in financial services, but otherwise centred around low-paid service provision to a slowly growing domestic market.

Others, however, maintained that the 1987 Conservative manifesto had been essentially right but premature. A combination of the institutional reforms pushed through by the Thatcher Government in the 1980s and structural changes in the global economy had altered the trajectory of the British economy and created a set of conditions which had enabled first the Major Government and then the Blair/Brown Government to maintain financial stability and steady growth. A new consensus on economic policy had been established which all parties were content to work within, and which had created the conditions for addressing long-term problems of low investment and skills shortages. Typical of this point of view was Geoffrey Owen, a former editor of the *Financial Times* who argued:[10]

> For the first thirty years after the war, the political climate militated against the single-minded pursuit of industrial efficiency and international competitiveness. The tide turned in the 1980s, when two powerful forces came together and reinforced each other: external economic pressure and domestic policy reform. By the end of the 1990s Britain had found a role for itself as a medium-sized industrial nation, well integrated into the world market.

From this standpoint Britain's decline from its nineteenth century dominance had now come to an end. The adjustment had been hard, but since the 1980s a new chapter had opened, in part as a result of the changes introduced by Margaret Thatcher, consolidated and extended under John Major and Tony Blair. The policies which the Blair Government pursued were a sign that something had changed permanently in the British political economy, and UK capitalism was back in business.

Models old and new

The performance of the British economy was certainly different at the beginning of the twenty-first century than it had been in the 1970s, but was it a new model, or the old model, suitably patched up? And from where did the inspiration come? In the 1960s, 1970s and 1980s, the British looked to models of capitalism from France, Germany, Sweden and Japan. But in the 1990s the US model gained in attractiveness again, as the performance of other models faltered, and the strategic choice facing Britain tended to be posed more starkly as a choice between Europe and America,[11] which was bound up also with attitudes towards Britain's membership of the European Union and the military alliance with the US. The rival charms of the Anglo–American shareholder model of capitalism and the European stakeholder model increasingly set the terms of this debate.

Critics of models of capitalism argue that these models presuppose a unity that does not exist. National economies are a construct of national governments; many economic relationships are transnational and cannot be neatly contained within national boundaries. Each national economy in any case is normally a hybrid, with different models in different sectors, rather than a single model throughout. Nevertheless despite these qualifications the concept of models is hard to dispense with entirely, even if as some argue the space in which such models could exist and thrive is now fast shrinking, and the logic of competition and accumulation are forcing all national models to converge[12] On this reading it was the US model which had emerged once more in the 1990s as the leading edge model, and the European social model which was underperforming.

In their seminal analysis Peter Hall and David Soskice distinguished between two basic models of capitalism – liberal market economies and coordinated market economies. This distinction runs right through the political economy literature: market led/state led; market based/ trust based; bank based/credit based; individualistic/communitarian. It seeks to isolate the mechanism by which an economy is coordinated and the different ways in which successful long-term businesses are built. Hall and Soskice argue that in a liberal market economy firms coordinate their activities primarily through hierarchies, competitive market arrangements, and formal contracting. The exchange of goods and services is coordinated through price signals, which leads agents to adjust their behaviour. In a coordinated market economy firms depend more heavily on non-market relations to coordinate with other actors. Contracting tends to be relational and incomplete. Networks are much more important for the exchange of private and privileged information, and collaborative arrangements are more common than competitive ones.

From this perspective what is important are the different national regulatory regimes, which provide the institutional foundations of comparative advantage. From an institutionalist perspective there is no reason to expect institutional foundations to merge into one best model. On the contrary, the shifting circumstances and opportunities of the global economy ensure that different models will thrive at different times. The ascendancy of the Anglo–American model in the 1990s was as shortlived as the ascendancy of the French, German and East Asian models in earlier decades. But that does not mean it is easily replaced in the countries where it is established. As Hall and Soskice put it:[13] 'So many of the institutional factors conditioning the behaviour of firms remain nation-specific.'

The trajectory of British capitalism, 1942–2016

1942–1956: The relaunching of the UK model

In the plans for reconstruction during and after the war the priority of the British political class was to reestablish the old UK model of capitalism, based on the trading and financial links of Britain's territorial and commercial empires built up over the previous three centuries, through which so many successful British businesses had been established. At the same time there was growing acceptance that the institutional conditions of the model had to be revised to permit a political settlement with organised labour, along the lines set out in the influential 1942 Beveridge Report.[14] The report offered a compelling vision of a Britain in which the social security needs of all citizens would be met through flat-rate contributions to a general fund, with additional services such as family allowances and a national health service being met by general taxation. The plan would be underpinned by government pledging to make the maintenance of full employment the prime objective of its economic policy. These proposals were implemented by the Attlee Government, in addition to a substantial enlargement of the public sector through nationalisation of core utilities, as well as the introduction of new planning powers, and the restoration of legal immunities for trade unions (removed by the Conservative Government after the 1926 General Strike). By 1950 Britain had one of the most advanced welfare states in the world, one of the pioneers in combining liberal capitalism and democratic citizenship.[15]

The enlarged state and widened conception of citizenship which the Attlee Government bequeathed to the Conservatives in 1951 survived through the 1950s and 1960s largely intact. The Conservatives concentrated their energies on assisting the networks, both industrial and financial, which British capital had built up in the nineteenth century, and which had been so badly disrupted during the war and its aftermath, to reestablish themselves.[16] The reopening of the markets of the City of London and making sterling convertible in 1958 were major steps on the way to reestablishing the distinctive British form of capitalism and its associated businesses that had flourished so much in the past. The liberal and global character of British capital and the importance of sterling and the financial networks around it were reaffirmed. In 1951 the British economy was still the third most important after the US and the USSR, and had leading edge industrial sectors, particularly in the defence field.[17]

1956–1992: The crisis of the UK model

The crisis developed in stages, as successive programmes of modernisation were launched to overcome Britain's economic problems. The mood at first was optimistic, but the failure to improve British economic performance gradually created a mood of despondency about Britain's prospects and the intractable nature of its problems. This came to a head in the 1970s, with the discrediting of the political centre, increased polarisation between right and left, and talk of ungovernability and overload.[18] This time of stalemate and drift was ended with the election of the Thatcher Government, which set out to reverse the collectivist and social democratic framework of policy and restore key elements of the old liberal economic model.

Fundamental to this period of crisis was the acceptance by a majority of the political class of two unpalatable facts – that the debacle of Suez meant that Britain could no longer act independently without the support of the US, and that therefore disengagement from the Empire should be speeded up. The second was that Britain could no longer stand on the sidelines of the new European union that was in the making. 1956 was the year of both Suez and the negotiations which led to the Treaty of Rome. British governments had refused to participate in the new European institutions, believing that Britain could remain an independent power between Europe and America, linked to both but absorbed by neither. In the aftermath of Suez and the establishment of the Common Market, the British position began to seem untenable. At the same time, it was becoming clear by the late 1950s that Britain was being outperformed by the other economies of western Europe. The first big inquest into the failings of post-war British economic policy began.[19]

One of the most important features of this period, which began with Suez and the setting up of the EEC in 1956 and ended with the forced exit of Britain from the ERM in 1992, was that Europe became the focus for many of the economic and social programmes of modernisation that were proposed. This was so in two senses. Membership of the European Community came to be seen as essential for Britain's future economic prosperity; at the same time European models of capitalism, particularly the French, the Swedish and the

German began to be widely studied and discussed in Britain, and many of their features were incorporated in the new policies which were put forward. The French model of indicative planning in particular became highly fashionable in the early 1960s and directly inspired the setting up of the National Economic Development Council (NEDC) and the devising of a National Plan, as well as (unrealised) plans for remodelling the British civil service along French lines. Many of the interventionist agencies which the first Wilson Government established, such as the Industrial Reorganisation Corporation (IRC), the forerunner of the later National Enterprise Board (NEB), were justified by the need for the state to play a much more proactive role in organising innovation and raising investment, and in reorganising British industry by arranging mergers and creating national champions which could compete with the rest of the world.[20]

The attraction of the French model of capitalism for the British was at its strongest in the 1960s; later the German, Swedish, and Japanese models became more influential. Britain finally joined the European Community in 1973 and the emphasis shifted from establishing a more *dirigiste* form of state to plan the British economy, to reorganising the basic social relations of British capitalism, particularly the production process, the education system and industrial relations. But the basic premise of most of the remedies for decline in this period was that what Britain required was a developmental state which could intervene to modernise the antiquated institutions and structures of British capitalism, and make it a capitalism able to compete again with the rest of the world.[21]

The developmental state argument was further developed in the 1980s, at a time when the ascendancy of Japan was at its height and both the US and the UK were perceived to be in decline. The Anglo–American or Anglo-Saxon model was contrasted unfavourably with European and East Asian models. Yet the decisive turn in British politics was not towards the alternative models of capitalism on offer. Instead the Thatcher Government elected in 1979 appeared to go in a quite contrary direction, aiming at the restoration of the UK model as it had existed before the entrenchment of the rights of labour and of welfare in the post-war period.

The Thatcher Government could not restore the Empire, but it did seek quite consciously to open the UK economy to international competition, through ending exchange controls, encouraging foreign direct investment both outwards and inwards, and setting its face against protectionism (at that time being strongly canvassed on the left). The consequence of this stance, combined with the adoption of a strict monetary policy which pushed up sterling, was to deepen the recession into which the UK plunged in 1980 and 1981, leading to a wave of bankruptcies in manufacturing industry and a doubling of unemployment to over three million. This shakeout of industry was accompanied by a progressive tightening of trade union laws which removed the legal immunities trade unions had enjoyed, and hampered their freedom to call strikes by among other things outlawing secondary action.

Whether the Thatcher Government intended the shock to be as severe as it turned out to be is doubtful. But once it had occurred it was quick to seize the opportunity to argue that a watershed had been crossed and that the British economy needed to be restructured as a free market economy with a smaller public sector and much weaker trade unions. Deregulation, the reduction of taxes on high income groups and business, privatisation of state assets, and marketisation of public services all followed. Much of this was bitterly contested in Britain, and little of it was popular at the time. Yet although many of the grandiose ambitions of the Thatcher Government were never achieved, a new framework was gradually put in place which marked a decisive change in the UK political economy and steered it in the direction it is still travelling.[22]

This direction pointed away from the alternative European models of capitalism that were on offer, making it less likely that Britain would participate more fully in European integration. The European social model was increasingly perceived by many Thatcherites as the model they did not wish to copy. The consequences of the Thatcher period and the type of capitalist modernisation that Britain underwent was to move Britain further away from Europe not closer to it, because during it the UK model was substantially reconstructed, and the kind of business environment the UK now sought to build owed more to the US model than the European.

1992–2016: The financial growth model

The shape of the new model economy which emerged from the travails of the 1970s and 1980s was broadly neo-liberal. Its institutional foundations were open and flexible markets, including foreign exchange and labour markets, a competition state, low marginal taxation, residual welfare programmes and monetary stability. Within these constraints, however, (and contrary to many accounts of the monolithic character of neo-liberalism) quite a wide variation of policies proved possible, and important political choices and emphases remained. In Britain political argument focused on such questions as membership of the Economic and Monetary Union (EMU) as against maintenance of a national currency, universalism as against selectivity in welfare, higher public expenditure as against lower taxation, employment protection as against employment flexibility, and stakeholder value as against shareholder value in corporate governance.[23]

What was undeniable, however, was that Britain had adopted a set of institutions for its political economy which precluded certain options – including planning, industrial intervention, protectionism, or corporatism. Britain after 1992 had a political economy which ensured financial stability, steady economic growth, low levels of strikes, low inflation, and high employment. What was different from what went before was the removal of many of the factors which led to intractable problems, policy failure and the cycle of decline.

The post-war UK political economy had severe structural defects, both external and internal. The chief external problem was the impossibility of maintaining a value for sterling high enough to sustain the global networks of British capital and military bases that had been built up during the British ascendancy.[24] The attempt to do so made the task of building strong competitive industries at home more difficult, and delayed effective modernisation of the industrial base, much of which eventually had to be written off in the recessions of the 1970s and 1980s. Unwinding the coils of empire and breaking free from the straitjacket of sterling took a long time, and many sterling crises, but by the middle of the 1990s after a last disastrous policy choice, when entry to the ERM was made at too high a rate, the transition appeared finally to have been made.

The chief internal problems were the incompatibility of combining the voluntarist system of industrial relations, based upon the principle of free collective bargaining, with social democratic aspirations to plan all aspects of the economy, including prices and incomes. The desire of the trade unions to remain independent of the state undermined the policies of Labour and Conservative governments in the 1960s and 1970s and created the climate for the successful onslaught by the Thatcher Government on the legal immunities of trade unions. The inability to bridge this divide meant that corporatism in Britain never achieved the degree of organisation or success that was common in many other European countries, and again opened the way for the thorough-going dismantling by the Thatcher Government of corporatist structures for managing the economy. The attitude of the trade unions towards the state and towards capital in Britain also meant that the Labour movement paid little attention to the question of how companies should be governed or managed. Apart from the abandoned proposals of the Bullock Report in the 1970s there were no moves to change the institutional relationship of capital and labour except through nationalisation on the one hand and the reinforcement of free collective bargaining on the other.[25]

Another internal problem was the set of principles on which the welfare state was founded. Flat rate insurance contributions to fund universal benefits, along with general taxation to fund a national health service and family allowances, failed to anticipate rising demand and rising earnings and expectations. As a result a huge chasm gradually opened up in the welfare state which came to a head in the 1960s and 1970s. Either there needed to be a move towards a much more generously funded system of welfare benefits on Scandinavian lines, to make good the original promises of the Beveridge Report, or there needed to be a retreat from universalism to a residual welfare state. The first required a substantial increase in general taxation to fund the welfare state. The latter required an increasing number of citizens to take out private provision. The inability to find a political consensus for either course, coupled with the weakness of the domestic economy and the problems of sterling, led to oscillations between sharp increases in public spending programmes, shortly followed by fiscal crises and forced public expenditure cuts. The Thatcher Government was at its least radical over the welfare state, and failed to reduce overall spending on it,[26] but it did succeed in slowing the growth of spending by introducing a number of significant changes, such as breaking the link between benefits and earnings, and abandoning the consensus on long-term pension provision. Over twenty years this had done much to transform the British welfare state in some areas, particularly pensions and housing, into a residual welfare state.[27]

During the Thatcher period many of the deep-seated problems in the political economy that so plagued the conduct of economic policy in the 1960s and 1970s were overcome or at least reduced. The Thatcher Government was able to pursue a strategy for smaller government, lower taxation, weaker unions, and stronger companies. It was not wholly successful, but aided by structural changes in the global economy it made sufficient institutional changes to permit the new financial growth model to emerge. This economy was not without problems, as many critics noted. Productivity and investment remained stubbornly low, there was relatively little improvement in the skill base, investment in infrastructure and science was seriously underfunded, along with most of the public services, and regional imbalances remained and were increased. But the new flexibility in many markets, along with a gradual revival of entrepreneurship, marked a major change.

The Labour Government which inherited the new model economy had a ten-year period of sustained success in managing it, while shifting some of its emphases, and consolidating its achievements, for instance by giving the Bank of England operational independence. The structural changes in the global economy which took place in the 1970s and 1980s, in conjunction with the institutional changes in Britain, made the British economy much easier to manage than it had been two decades before. The global shift from manufacturing to services shifted the balance of the British economy towards those sectors where it enjoyed some comparative advantage, and removed or downsized those sectors which had been the source of so much of the instability as well as poor performance of the British economy. At the same time a new low inflation, low interest rate international regime was established and sustained, again greatly reducing the external pressures on the British economy. Britain was not alone in enjoying low inflation, low interest rates, high employment. It was the common experience, especially of the English-speaking countries of the Anglosphere after 1991, and one of the chief reasons was the impact of the new emerging economies like China. It helped make British performance among the best in the OECD, whereas earlier it had regularly been among the worst. The weakness of the trade unions compared to their position in the 1960s and 1970s also helped insulate British economic policy-making from unwelcome pressures.

This good fortune did not last. The British economy was increasingly propelled by credit bubbles (in housing and equities in particular)[28] and was running very large deficits on the balance of payments. In addition, household debt by 2007 had practically reached its limit. The economy was very vulnerable to the pricking of any of these bubbles. The sub-prime crisis in the US provided the spark which led to a serious financial collapse, destroying Labour's reputation for economic competence. Its spending plans depended on growth continuing, and that prospect disappeared in the crash. The banking crisis precipitated a recession, and quickly became a fiscal crisis, leading to plans to cut the deficit through sharp increases in taxes and major cuts in public spending. Labour's electoral coalition fell apart and it ceded the political initiative to the Conservatives.

Before the crisis struck, the Labour Government had persisted with its plans to expand public spending. The result was, in public expenditure terms, the most successful social democratic government Britain had ever had. Resources for the public sector were increased more substantially than under any previous Labour administration. Spending on the NHS for example, which was £41 billion in 1997, was planned to reach £106 billion in 2008. From being below the European average for health spending Britain at the end of two terms of Labour Government was above and set to go higher still. Spending on the NHS, which was 4 per cent of GDP in 1950 and had risen quite slowly to 6 per cent of GDP by 1997, had jumped to 8 per cent of GDP in 2005 and was planned to be 9 per cent of GDP by 2008. The same broad picture was true of education. The 2002 plans aimed to raise education spending to £69 billion per annum by 2008 (from £36 billion in 1997). Labour chose to use the growth in the economy to increase public spending rather than to reduce taxes, and it put huge emphasis on increasing investment in human capital, particularly education and skills, through schools, training programmes and the New Deal youth employment scheme. It also invested heavily in other public services such as health, but still struggled to overcome the perception of poor public services bequeathed by two decades of underfunding.

Its other main strategy was to increase the competitiveness of the British economy, partly through regulatory bodies such as the Financial Services Authority (FSA), and partly through investment in science and technology to encourage innovation and an enterprise economy, focused around the industries of the new knowledge economy. There were some signs too that this had begun to pay off. A new generation of entrepreneurs and companies emerged in the UK in the 1990s, while traditional British strengths in sectors like aerospace and pharmaceuticals were retained.[29] There was no longer anything resembling an industrial strategy in the UK, and the British state no longer had the capacity, if it ever did, to manage industrial change. The shrinking of the manufacturing sector continued under Labour. Manufacturing by 2007 accounted for only 12 per cent of total employment, compared with 28 per cent in 1979 and 17 per cent in 1997. There was no longer any substantial body of opinion in the UK supporting the kind of industrial strategy aimed at fostering indigenous investment, still practised in many other capitalist countries. Before the crash, given the way Anglo-Saxon model countries had outperformed Germany, France, Italy and Japan since 1991, many wondered whether it any longer mattered.

Europe and America

Many critics of New Labour acknowledged that the alternative they preferred could not be delivered within the constraints of the political economy model Labour had inherited in 1997. It required the adoption of a very different model, such as the European social model of stakeholder firms, high taxation, high welfare benefits, buttressed by high levels of trust and cooperation. The British model in the 1990s appeared much closer to the US model, particularly its policies on welfare, on deregulation, on new public management in the public sector, on public private partnerships, on shareholder value, and on the encouragement of the knowledge economy. Gordon Brown was a strong critic of many aspects of the European model, particularly the inflexibility of its labour markets and its discouragements to business enterprise, and often contrasted Europe unfavourably with America. The very success of British domestic economic management encouraged a sceptical stance among British ministers to further European integration in the 1990s, particularly in regards to the euro. This approach was echoed on the Conservative side.[30]

Being more like America again and less like Europe is the heart of the UK model of capitalism. For several decades modernisers toiled to make the UK more like Europe, but as the voluminous literature on models of capitalism demonstrates, they have not had much success, and the counterattack launched by the Thatcher Government swept away many of the institutional supports on which a social democratic political economy might have been built in Britain. On the other hand there are many respects in which Britain remains unlike America despite its strong appeal to the British political class.[31] Many of the attitudes, for example on welfare, on tax, on fairness and social justice, on public spending, and on poverty are broadly in line with those found in other European countries. Repeated surveys have shown that British views on welfare and taxation are not Thatcherite.[32] The British welfare state has always been a hybrid, and quite hard to classify. Esping-Andersen sees Britain as belonging broadly to the liberal regime type of welfare state, and argues that it moved closer towards it in the Thatcher period, but at the same time acknowledges that there remain some strong social democratic aspects to the British welfare state, most notably its universalist features such as the National Health Service. Starting from a high base after 1950 Britain failed to move on to a full social democratic welfare state as Sweden and similar countries did in the 1960s, and had since slipped back, and in that sense had come to resemble more closely the US model. The change of direction signalled by New Labour did not survive the crash.

One way of reading the history of the British political economy over the last sixty years is that after the attempt to restore Britain's lost position in the world had been abandoned, successive governments sought to transform the UK into a coordinated market economy which could play its full part in the process of European integration. But these initiatives, although not as unsuccessful as sometimes suggested, nevertheless did not achieve their goal. This prepared the ground for the sharp turn of policy in the 1980s, abandoning the attempts to create either a coordinated market economy or a social democratic welfare state. Instead trust was placed again in the institutions and regulatory forms of a liberal market economy. By the end of the 1990s this was clearly bearing fruit, in the form of a political economy whose assumptions, including membership of the European Union, were accepted by all the leading political parties. British economic growth was not spectacular but it was steady. Critics still worried about the weakness of manufacturing, and the low wage, low skill syndrome in which Britain was caught. But the change in atmosphere and in performance from the 1970s and 1980s was marked.

The 2008 financial crash and Brexit

Since the crash a new phase has opened in British politics, and many of the achievements of New Labour have been rolled back. The political fall-out from the crash discredited the record of the Blair/Brown Government for economic competence, and its relegitimation of public spending and state action assisted the ascendancy of fiscal conservatism, and led to renewed attempts to shrink the state. Enduring features of Britain's liberal market economy have been emphasised once again. With the exception of some ministers in the Coalition Government such as Vince Cable, the Business Secretary, there was little political appetite to rebalance the British economy, to regulate the financial sector, to move Britain on to a different path or embrace a different model of capitalism.

The 2008 crash also marks a watershed in the development of the international market order. This international order has been extraordinarily resilient since the financial crash in 2008. Huge efforts were made to stabilise the international economy, and a new world depression was avoided, but the recovery was patchy and weak, the slowest recovery since 1945, and living standards for the majority continues to stagnate. Many incumbent governments in the western democracies lost elections after 2008, but they were replaced by governments who adhered to the broad terms of the neo-liberal consensus.[33] Events in 2016 changed that. The financial crisis started in the heartlands of Anglo-America, so it is perhaps appropriate that it was in the UK and the US that the first serious breaches in the neo-liberal political order were made.

Trump's victory in the US presidential election has been compared to the vote for Brexit but there are important differences. Both were driven in part by anger and despair among sections of the white working class, and their rejection of the liberal, cosmopolitan establishment, both neo-liberal and social liberal. Both were part of a wider populist rebellion against globalisation and the western international economic and political order. Populist nationalism in western democracies is a politics of *ressentiment*, fed by economic and cultural grievances. The economic grievances stem from the displacement of many workers from jobs in manufacturing. This is a process which stretches back to the 1980s and has seen the blighting of formerly prosperous industrial regions and the creation of long-term worklessness and dependency. At the same time wages have stagnated or risen only very slowly in many countries, particularly since 2000, so at a time when inequality was increasing and the wealth of the top 1 per cent was growing quite dramatically, many working-class and middle-income citizens saw little if any improvement in their standard of living and were increasingly reliant upon borrowing. The social wage in the form of public services and employment protection was maintained during the boom years, but has come under sustained attack in the austerity programmes implemented since 2008. These economic grievances are often blamed on globalisation. The rapid pace of change, the introduction of new technologies, competition from immigrant labour, the outsourcing of jobs to other cheaper jurisdictions, the weakening of trade unions, have all combined to reduce labour's share in national income and weaken labour's bargaining strength. Many workers have come to feel resentful at being left behind and ignored, and they have become as a result increasingly disconnected from mainstream politics and government.[34]

But there were also important differences between Trump's victory and Brexit. Trump's natural allies were to be found in UKIP rather than the British Conservatives. Many Conservative Brexiters like Daniel Hannan regarded Trump as an economic nationalist.[35] Trump wanted not just to curb immigration, and deport illegal immigrants, but also to protect US jobs by slapping tariffs on foreign imports, ripping up trade deals, and unwinding the production chains of US multinationals, ending outsourcing. Hannan insisted that the vote for Brexit was about *increasing* free trade not limiting it. Britain was to be a global power again with greater openness than ever before. Brexiters like him believe in 'Global Britain' and acknowledge that immigration will continue at a high level after Brexit because the UK economic model demanded it.

Britain's first post-Referendum government, led by Theresa May, was more ambivalent. It wanted strict border controls *and* free trade. Trump's position was more consistently nationalist – against free trade, against trade deals, and against immigration. It assumed that the US was a large enough economy to make the costs of going protectionist bearable. That was not an option for the UK after Brexit, because it relied too heavily on international trade for its prosperity, and lacked a large enough internal market to be a substitute. The problem for Conservative Brexiters is that while many of them were strong free traders, many of the people who voted for Brexit, particularly in the old industrial heartlands, were not. They did not want a global Britain but a closed Britain or at least a protectionist Britain. They wanted serious controls on immigration, regardless of whether this meant a contraction of trade. The May Government agreed with them. It indicated that controlling immigration was a priority. Trade deals came second. It accepted that there was no good Brexit, only a Brexit which limited the economic damage.

The May Government pursued a two-stage strategy. Falling in with the wishes of the EU Commission the Government accepted that it had first to clinch a deal over the divorce terms (the withdrawal agreement) and then move on to discuss trade. It set out its red lines for the negotiation in 2016, but its position was weakened when it called a general election in 2017 and lost its majority. It pressed on with negotiating a withdrawal agreement with the EU and succeeded, but it was then unable to get it approved by the House of Commons. The concessions it made to secure a deal were not acceptable to a powerful block of Brexiter opinion in the Conservative party. The result was an extraordinary period of parliamentary deadlock which lasted up until the election of 2019.

During this period there were four main possible outcomes of the Brexit negotiations: a No-Deal, a limited Canada-style free trade deal, a Norway-style deal, or a decision by Britain after a second referendum to suspend Article 50 and Remain. Almost all economic impact assessments of these options showed that, apart from the last, they would leave Britain significantly worse off but many Brexiters argued this was an acceptable price to pay to regain full sovereign control of borders, money and laws.

The outcome remained uncertain for two years, but after the third rejection of her withdrawal agreement by Parliament in 2019 Theresa May was ousted as Conservative leader and Boris Johnson, the leader of the Leave campaign in the Referendum, took her place. He conducted a sweeping purge of the Cabinet and the parliamentary party, ending the thirty-year civil war in the party over Europe, and won a general election in 2019 by uniting Leave supporters behind the Conservatives while the Remain vote remained split between several parties. Johnson's victory allowed his revised version of Theresa May's withdrawal agreement to pass in Parliament and Britain formally exited the EU on 31 January 2020. This removed two of the four options, Norway and Remain, from consideration.

At the 2019 election the Johnson Government presented itself as a new government with a radical new agenda. It was committed not only to making Britain 'Global Britain' once more, freed from the shackles of the EU, but also to 'Britain First', the pledge to level up and rebalance the economy, shrinking the inequalities which emerged so starkly as a consequence of the 'Global Britain' policies pursued by the Thatcher Government in the 1980s. The 'Britain First' agenda seeks to consolidate Conservative support in the 'red wall' seats won in 2019. The question for the Government was how it would seek to reconcile these very different agendas.

The May Government had signalled that it was aiming to remain as close as possible to the EU, to minimise economic harm. This would have left Britain in a sub-optimal but broadly similar position to the one it had before Brexit, where it was already semi-detached from significant aspects of European integration such as Schengen and the euro. The May strategy would have confirmed the EU as Britain's most important long-term trading partner, and that would have created at least some pressure for continued convergence between the UK and the European models of capitalism. The May Government had intended through its EU Withdrawal Bill to incorporate all EU legislation into UK law until such time as the UK Parliament decided to replace particular measures. It also recognised that there would be future pressure for the UK to adopt new regulations announced by the EU, so as to preserve its access to the single market. Under the May plan, the UK might have eventually achieved something close to an associate status with the EU, although not as complete as Switzerland and Norway, and like them with no influence over the content of new rules.

After the 2019 election the new choice was between No-Deal, now called an Australian-style deal, based on trading on WTO rules, which would involve tariffs on a wide range of goods and border checks, or a Canada-style free trade agreement, which would still have border checks but would be tariff-free. A more radical version of the

No-Deal option, as set out by Economists for Brexit,[36] was for Britain to declare unilateral free trade. This would be truly 'Global Britain'. This 'Hong Kong' or 'Singapore-on-Thames' option would see taxes and regulation pared back, and welfare provision made less generous, public expenditure reduced to no more than 25 per cent of GDP, and employment rights, social rights and environmental protection all reduced to make the UK labour market even more flexible. It would represent an extreme form of the Anglo–liberal model, and the divergence between the UK and the rest of Europe would be magnified. The viability of this model would depend very much on the ability to trade freely with the rest of the world, in an era of trade blocs and trade wars.

'Britain First' is at the opposite end of the spectrum. This vision for Britain's future after Brexit places primary emphasis on the national economy and the communities it supports rather than global or regional engagement. It draws on the heritage of social imperialism and protectionism from the 1930s and also on the protectionist traditions of the left, as expressed for example in the alternative economic strategy developed in the 1970s and 1980s. Such policies would have a profound effect on the UK economic model, giving priority to industry over finance, putting employment ahead of financial stability, and investment ahead of consumption. Depending on the left or right inflection of these policies, border controls might become very tight.

The 'Global Britain' agenda implied radical divergence from the EU, which government ministers frequently confirmed was their aim. The UK could not be a passive rule taker, so could not belong to either the single market or the customs union. It must have the freedom to pursue trade deals with non-EU states, signalling the end of frictionless trade with the EU, creating a difficult period of adjustment. The Johnson Government accepted that there would be winners and losers and that in the short term the economy would be smaller than it would otherwise have been. But it argued that in the longer run the economy could be larger and more dynamic if looser regulation and taxes stimulated higher rates of economic growth, particularly in new emerging sectors.

Many supporters of the 'Global Britain' agenda welcome the prospect of No Deal with the EU and the severe economic shock that might bring, forcing the disruption of many supply chains and a radical restructuring of the British economy. Those sectors of the UK economy which are highly dependent on trade with the EU will go under, shrink or be forced to diversify into other markets. New sectors such as AI will emerge. Such an economic shock is what some supporters of a No-Deal Brexit have always wanted, believing that as in 1979 what the British economy requires is the breakup of a particular model of the economy. The strategy has some big risks attached. The Johnson Government cannot know how large the losses might be in the short run, or how swiftly a new wave of enterprise and innovation can be unleashed, or whether trade deals with major non-EU markets can be negotiated quickly. A Canada-style agreement carries fewer risks, but in practice might mean the Government sticking more closely to EU rules than it would like. A minimalist free trade deal is less optimal than current arrangements but the costs and risks will be more manageable than No-Deal.

Even this version of 'Global Britain' will be hard to reconcile with the 'Britain First' agenda. The towns and regions which have suffered cumulative disadvantage in the last forty years are unlikely to be the cutting edge of 'Global Britain'. What they want is not more globalisation but less. They want economic security, infrastructure investment, better public services, and much less immigration. 'Global Britain' embraces free trade, a minimal state, and a capitalism which is more dynamic, open, cosmopolitan and inegalitarian. 'Britain First' embraces protectionism, an interventionist state and a capitalism which is more risk-averse, closed, communitarian and egalitarian. To meet its election promises the Johnson Government will struggle to deliver both free trade *and* protection, lower taxation *and* better public services, higher economic growth *and* a big reduction in immigration.

The UK is not a continental sized economy. Since the middle of the nineteenth century it has been dependent on trade. 'Global Britain' does not seek to abandon the Anglo–liberal model which has shaped British development for so long but to entrench it still further. 'Britain First' would move Britain in a very different direction, with major consequences for its politics and its political economy. The Conservatives might not necessarily be the long-term beneficiaries of this shift.

2

Explanations of British Decline[1]

Decline has no single meaning. It has always been a contested term and is dependent upon seeing the world and Britain's place within it in a particular way. It does not have a fixed or objective character and cannot be directly observed. It depends on a particular historical and political construction of evidence and experience, which is open to quite different interpretations.

Amid the mass of assertions and counter-assertions, decline often appears to have as many meanings as there are explanations for it. If a term can be as widely defined as this, does it have any objective reality at all? Like many other contested terms in social science, however, the diversity of meaning arises from the origin of the term in political experience and conflict. Contests over its meaning and its implications have been a key part of the discourse of twentieth-century politics. Decline is a concept which many British politicians, from Joseph Chamberlain to Margaret Thatcher, have used to understand the world around them and urge particular courses of action. Its different meanings are therefore closely tied to the various strategies for halting or managing it which have emerged at different times and in different contexts during the last hundred years.

Decline has become an inextricable part of Britain's political reality in the twentieth century and has engaged the attention of many leading historians, economists and political scientists as well as columnists and leader writers. It is hard to think of a major public intellectual who has not contributed in some form to the decline debate. It has produced a lively academic and journalistic literature on whether there really has been a decline and if so how it is best measured, and whether there are any policies which might reverse it.[2] Many of the disagreements about the meaning of decline are hard to settle, although that does not mean that rules of evidence and relevance which narrow the area of controversy cannot be established. But even if future historians were to agree that in some of the senses in which the term has been used Britain's decline was an illusion, it would still be necessary to ask why so many British politicians on both left and right viewed the world through the lens of 'decline' and advocated ambitious programmes to overcome it.

Absolute and relative decline

In assessing any particular piece of writing on decline, a good starting point is to establish what it is that is supposed to be in decline. Decline has been applied to morals, to the economy, to military power, to international influence, to culture, to standards of behaviour, and to democracy. Some writers treat British decline as part of the more general phenomenon of the decline of western culture and civilisation, others are only concerned with a much narrower topic, such as the performance of the British economy, or particular economic sectors.

In understanding how decline is used in any particular literature or context, a useful distinction is that between absolute and relative decline. Absolute decline signifies a permanent fall below a level that had previously been attained. Relative decline, by contrast, is derived from comparing the performance of the entity in decline with that of similar entities. Relative decline is therefore quite compatible with overall improvement. The distinction is particularly relevant to the discussion of British decline. Despite the apocalyptic tone of much writing on British economic performance, British living standards and productivity have continued to rise throughout the century. There have been absolute declines in particular sectors and the disappearance of entire industries, but the overall performance of the British economy in the twentieth century certainly does not show any signs of an absolute decline. On the contrary, the wealth it generates will be approximately three and a half times as great in the year 2000 as it was in 1900. If British economic decline exists at all, it is relative and depends on comparing Britain as a national economy with similar economic entities, estimating the extent to which the British economy grew more slowly and performed less well than economies of similar size and development.

In this 'league table' approach, Britain is typically shown to have progressively slipped down the table according to a variety of indicators, particularly in the 1950s and 1960s.[3] The decline is relative in respect of the particular indicators and countries chosen and in relation to the particular countries. Apart from the objections in principle – voiced most recently by Paul Krugman – to the propriety of treating national economies as though they were a single unit,[4] the data is also difficult to interpret because different indicators and comparators give different results. British performance looks very different in the league tables produced, for instance, by the World Economic Forum and the Institute for Management Development.

The key point is that whatever the final judgement on the performance of the British economy, there clearly has not been anything approaching an absolute *economic* decline. Where there has been an absolute decline is in Britain's position as a world power in the twentieth century. This imperial decline might also be considered a relative decline, since Britain's fall is measured against the rise of other states. At a certain point their power eclipsed that of Britain. What makes it an absolute decline is that Britain has demonstrably less power and influence at the end of the twentieth century than at the beginning. This decline has been a long-drawn-out process which is still not complete – Britain still retains some of the trappings of great power status, such as its permanent seat on the UN Security Council and the size and range of its military deployment. But there is no doubt, comparing Britain's position in 1900 with its position a century later, that there has been a qualitative and permanent change in Britain's status in the international state system. Compared to 1900, Britain no longer possesses a territorial empire or the world's top currency; after 1945 it became an important but subordinate partner in NATO and dependent on the United States for military technology; and after 1973 it agreed to pool its sovereignty in more and more areas through participation in the process of European integration.

The two declines are separable analytically but not politically, and in both popular and elite experience they have been joined together. But popular and elite experiences of decline have been different. Popular discourse has focused on the absolute decline of British power. The loss of Britain's colonial empire is much more readily communicable (the shrinking of the area of the globe coloured red) than the idea that increasing prosperity signifies decline rather than progress. Future historians may find it puzzling that so much of elite discourse was obsessed with the idea of economic decline at a time when the country was more prosperous than it had ever been. Martin Wiener, for instance, has called (economic) decline the most important problem of twentieth-century British history.[5] But if so it is mainly because it has been defined as such by the political class, which developed a discourse in which Britain was portrayed as constantly underperforming and slipping further and further behind its rivals. The majority of the population has enjoyed rising, not falling, living standards. The quality of life for the great majority of British citizens has improved in measurable ways during the twentieth century. But the British political elite has had a different experience. Its members no longer inhabit a state which is either the leading state in the international system of states or the dominant economy in the global economy, yet today's generation of leaders is constantly reminded in innumerable small ways of what has been lost.

To grasp the dynamics of the decline debate and its impact on British politics and popular opinion, this interrelationship between the two declines needs to be understood. The most potent populist characterisations of decline, such as social imperialism and Thatcherism, have always linked economic decline to Britain's place in the world and therefore with threats to British and more specifically English identity. In this way the loss of empire has resonated in popular experience and imagination, and influenced other perceptions. The tabloid newspapers have helped fuel new forms of English nationalism and xenophobia, particularly in relation to the European Union. Any reduction in British sovereignty is interpreted as a threat to national identity. In this way the performance of the British economy in the twentieth century has often been presented as a symptom of national decline because it cannot be associated with an unequivocal assertion of British power and self-sufficiency, and because other nations to which Britain has been accustomed to regarding itself as superior have had economies plainly performing better than Britain's.

More than any other concept, decline – in this double sense of economic and imperial decline – has been used to interpret Britain's political experience this century. It is not a concept which belongs exclusively to either left or right, but has been used and developed by both. The institutions and policies most favoured by one side have frequently been attacked by the other as the main contributory cause of decline. Decline should not be treated as a single continuous process. There have been different debates and different contexts, and although there has been some continuity in themes and concerns, there are also some quite radical discontinuities and breaks. Changes in the economic and political organisation of the world system have been dramatic in the twentieth century, revolutions and wars have made and remade the balance of power between states and the character of economic and political institutions. These seismic events have created the contexts which express the particular relationship between the political and the economic, between the absolute decline in world power and the relative decline in the national economy, within which the discourses on economic decline have emerged.

The debate in each period has always included competing strategic views of Britain's place in the global economy and the international system of states, and therefore how best to define Britain's economic and security interests and the options for safeguarding and advancing them. Moreover, the very notion of a national economy is itself a construction which depends on a particular view of international politics. In much of the secondary literature on economic decline the national economy is often treated in isolation as though it were a simple natural phenomenon which requires no further explanation. Yet, since no absolute decline has taken place, this national economy can only be said to be in decline as a result of a comparison with the performance of similar national economies elsewhere. Understanding British decline requires an appreciation of how the world system has evolved – both the global economy and the international state system.

Decline is therefore politically constructed and needs to be understood through the political debates which have taken place on its dimensions, its causes and its remedies. Three debates have been crucial, and each one is linked to a definite historical and political context which imposed particular constraints on external and internal policy, reflecting Britain's place in the global economy and the balance of interests and the climate of ideas within the state and civil society.

Debates on decline

The first debate, which lasted from the 1880s to the 1920s, was centred on the challenge of Germany and the United States to Britain's dominant economic and military position in the international state system. The key issue for the British political elite was how this challenge might be contained and how the basis of British power in the world – the Empire and Britain's commercial and financial supremacy – might be preserved.[6] The key political battle was fought over the merits of free trade and tariff reform. This was much more than just a dispute over the direction of Britain's trading policy. Free trade had become a symbol of Britain's external and internal policy, and its critics argued that it was leaving Britain seriously unprepared for economic and military competition with its new rivals. The attack on free trade became an attack upon the policy stance and liberal ethos of the British state and civil society.[7] The programme of national efficiency, supported by many on both right and left, made collectivism and individualism the key dividing line in internal political debate. At stake was the issue of how Britain might be turned into a modern state, and how preservation of its Empire was compatible with harnessing the forces of democracy and accepting collectivism without embracing socialism at the same time.

The second debate emerged in the aftermath of the First World War and lasted until the 1960s. Its context was set by the big shift in the balance of power between the leading states in the international system which the First World War signalled and the Second World War consolidated. For Britain the most important aspect of this shift was the rise of the United States to a position of undisputed hegemony, and the exposure of the increasing political and military incapacity of Britain to sustain its Empire or the position of sterling as the leading international currency. In this new environment the principal dispute on external policy within Britain was over how to deal with the United States and how to accommodate Britain to the anticipated loss of its power and status,[8] while the key debate on internal policy became how to modernise the British economy by adopting the best practice methods of American business and commerce and by changing the balance between the public and private sectors. The principal dividing line in political debate became the role of the state in the economy, the free market versus planning. This era saw enormous growth in the size and scope of the state, accelerated by the impact of two world wars, the development of collective bargaining and new forms of economic management.

The third debate emerged in the 1960s and early 1970s from widespread disillusion with the programmes of both left and right to modernise the British economy. These programmes appear in retrospect as the last attempt to create a successful British mass production, Fordist economy.[9] Its context was shaped by Britain's involvement in the development of European integration through the European Community and by the increasing tendencies towards a more interdependent global economy in the 1970s and 1980s. The main external policy issue became whether Britain should seek to advance European integration by participating in plans to form a single currency and a European defence and foreign policy or whether it should resist any attempt to make the European union more than a free trade area, a loose arrangement between sovereign states. The central internal policy debate focused on social democracy and how far collectivist institutions should be dismantled and the scope and scale of government redefined.[10] The key issue for economic decline was perceived to be national competitiveness, the kind of supply-side measures which government might introduce to boost the performance of particular sectors and equip citizens with the necessary skills and flexibility to compete in an increasingly uncertain global marketplace.

The issue was often posed as the conflict between an enterprise state and a developmental state.[11]

These three debates and their different historical contexts have made decline a long-running theme in twentieth-century British politics, and are the basis on which different explanations of decline have been formed. Ever since it became apparent that the dream of Joseph Chamberlain and the social imperialists was not going to be realised, absolute imperial decline has been treated as a painful inevitability. The British Empire was not transformed into a bloc in the world economy sufficiently integrated and powerful to compete with the newly emerging continent-based empires of Germany, Russia and the United States.

That option lingered on in a truncated form but the political elite gradually became reconciled to the need to manage an orderly decline of British power through the dismantling of the British Empire. Although there were always romantics (from Enoch Powell in 1948 urging Churchill to reconquer India by force, to the enthusiasts for the Commonwealth who wished to give it priority over the EEC in the 1960s), the realists among the political elite knew that at best the process might be delayed, but not reversed. Late imperial gestures, like the despatch of a task force to recapture the Falklands in 1982, did not contradict this assessment. The Falklands War itself had been preceded by British government attempts to negotiate a transfer of sovereignty to Argentina via a leaseback, and was followed by acquiescence in the return of Hong Kong to China in 1997 on Chinese terms. The props to British grandeur – the maintenance of a nuclear deterrent and a state-of-the-art military capability, the diplomatic service, the Foreign Office, the UN role, the secret service and special forces – are all still present at the end of the century, but much of the substance of British power has disappeared and the acceptance of Britain's middle-ranking status is all but complete.

This acceptance of the inevitability of Britain's decline as an imperial and a world power has been the essential backdrop against which explanations of the relative economic decline have been advanced. Some have rejected fatalism, arguing that if the weaknesses of the domestic economy had been tackled the decline in world power might have been arrested.[12] Certainly the social imperialist or Chamberlainite wing of the Conservative party always believed so, stressing the intimate connection between economic and military power. Britain proved unable to consolidate its Empire, partly because of a conflict in interest between the priority of maintaining a liberal global economic order and building a self-contained economic and military bloc. The latter was difficult to achieve logistically, and most parts of the Empire made it clear that it was not what they wanted. The settler states wished to exercise the autonomy they had been granted by being given dominion status while the rest of the Empire wanted independence from British rule. Britain lacked either the military or political capability to hold its Empire together in the twentieth century, and the realisation of this steadily sapped the political will of the political elite, and established a mood of resignation and fatalism.

Even if the absolute decline could not have been prevented, however, many have questioned whether Britain's relative economic decline was inevitable. Why could Britain not have prospered by shedding the costs and the burdens of being a world power in the way that Japan and Germany, defeated in war and stripped of their military machines and great power pretensions, had done? The focus of the first decline debate was whether Britain should reorganise its economic and political institutions in order to match the emerging power of the continental-based economies of Germany and the United States, and be prepared to abandon the rules of the liberal economic world order which had been the expression of Britain's nineteenth-century hegemony. The political class was not prepared to make that choice before 1914, and remained deeply ambivalent through the 1920s. National protectionism when it came was a defensive reaction to the collapse of the gold standard in 1931 rather than a proactive policy of national renewal.

The starting point of the second decline debate was this breakdown of the liberal economic world order and the rise of national protectionism. It focused on whether and in what ways the British economy could be modernised through increasing the role of the state. The superiority of American over British industry was now plain. Worries about Britain's relative decline at this juncture were largely about the growing gap between Britain and the United States. By 1945 this gap had become a chasm. But the rebuilding of the British economy after 1945 and the devastation of most other industrial economies by the war left Britain still in a relatively strong position. It was the economic decline which took place in the 1950s and 1960s relative to the performance of the reinvigorated economies of western Europe and Japan which became the new focus of the debate at the end of the 1950s on why Britain, despite achieving better growth rates than at any time in the last hundred years, was being outperformed by other industrial economies. This prompted a new bout of plans for the modernisation of British institutions mainly through the enlargement of the role and responsibilities of the state.[13]

It is the last phase of the debate around the theme of modernisation, as well as the third decline debate in the 1970s and 1980s around the theme of competitiveness, which have made relative economic decline so important in British politics in the second half of the twentieth century. Some of the decline literature argues that there was no significant economic decline until the 1950s, and that the prime focus of the decline debate should be on explaining British economic performance in the last fifty years, not in the last hundred.[14] This view has some merit, although it downplays the gap which emerged between Britain and the United States which was so much the focus of concern in the earlier part of the century. Competition from other countries, particularly Germany, was seriously affected by the outcome of the two world wars. Only when the absolute decline of Britain as a world power became plain did relative economic decline emerge as the central concern.

There are many analysts of economic decline, however, who, even though they accept that there has not been a continuous economic decline since the 1880s, do not believe that post-war economic decline can be satisfactorily explained without taking into account its historical roots in the peculiarities of British institutions and British development. The most important dividing line is between explanations which accept that the concept of a national economy is a valid one and that the statement that a national economy can be in decline has meaning, and those which believe that talk of national decline, national competitiveness and national economic performance are fictions. The debate on economic decline can be seen in this respect to be the product of the era of national protectionism, when the formulation of the concept of a national economy for purposes of state policy was very important. Such explanations of economic decline either trace it to particular policies or regard it as deriving from the peculiarities of British capitalism. The latter are the more interesting and the more tenacious. Proponents disagree strongly among themselves as to which peculiarities are actually the most significant ones, and they have to contend with alternative theories of British economic development which analyse the British economy in the context of the processes and trends of the global economy, and argue that if there is any reality to the phenomenon of British decline it has to be understood within these parameters and not as something which has been generated from within Britain.

Those explanations which seek to uncover the roots of decline in particular British economic and social institutions all accept the idea that there is such a thing as a British national economy, that it could be in decline in relation to other states, and that there might be measures which could reverse it. The main peculiarities which appear in this literature will be summarised here under the headings of culture, finance, Empire, state and industry. Sometimes explanations of decline which fall under these headings are just seeking scapegoats and offer little theoretical or historical depth. Sometimes they concentrate on making a precise but narrow point about some particular institution or policy. The explanations considered here are those which provide more ambitious general accounts. They reconstruct and reinterpret the past in terms of their favoured *explanans* and point to particular remedies. They have always been contested, empirically, theoretically and politically, and many of them have informed current political debates.

National peculiarities

Culture

This thesis is known by some of its detractors as the declinist thesis[15] and has become one of the best-known of all explanations of decline. It argues that the principal cause of British decline is to be found in the formation and transmission of an anti-industrial and anti-enterprise culture through the schools, universities and professions. Key occupations for a modern industrial economy, particularly engineering and industrial management, lagged in status behind the professions, the public sector and the City of London. For some of its critics, this 'gentlemanly capitalism', which was averse to industry and technology, was further reinforced by the ascendancy of liberal welfarism over the British establishment and led, especially after 1945, to greater priority being given to policies of fiscal redistribution and the provision of a welfare safety net than to productive efficiency.[16]

The cultural thesis concentrates mostly upon the British upper class, which is implicitly contrasted with supposedly more capitalist and entrepreneurial elites in other countries. The thesis has been extended to explore the deep conservatism of all sections of the British people and their aversion to change, the lack of social mobility and a dynamic civil society, the transformation of class into status, and its inappropriateness for a modern industrial society. But in its most popular version it is the attitude of the elite that is seen as the main cause of the problem and also of the transformation of Britain from the dynamic and thrusting industrial powerhouse of the nineteenth century into the deindustrialising economy of the twentieth century.[17]

The key assumption made by such accounts is that cultural beliefs and values play the major role in determining economic behaviour. They also suggest that in Britain the upper class is both very dominant and highly sealed. The way in which it was formed has had a decisive effect upon the way in which the whole society has evolved. The implication for policy is either that the elite institutions need radical reform, or new elite institutions dedicated to instilling a different kind of culture need to be created. The main difficulty with the thesis is the quality of the evidence that is adduced in its support. Much of it is impressionistic and selective and ignores the prevalence of anti-industrial and anti-bourgeois cultures in countries which are supposed to have been much more successful at building industrial economies.[18] It also has to ignore or minimise the obvious fact that the anti-industrial culture did not prevent the appearance of numerous new entrepreneurs in the twentieth century and the founding of major new companies. If elite institutions were so inefficient at producing industrial managers and technologists, why did other institutions not spring up to supply them, as happened at earlier times in British history? The aristocratic ethos in Britain was surely stronger at the beginning of the nineteenth century than at any time since, yet it does not seem to have been able to prevent the explosive growth of industrial capital and the rise of a new class of industrialists.

The cultural thesis has been immensely popular because it suggests that the ultimate cause of decline is deeply embedded in culture rather than in policy or interests, and that until beliefs and attitudes are transformed, there is unlikely to be any significant change in economic performance. It was taken up by Keith Joseph and other leading Conservatives in the 1980s. They argued that creating an enterprise culture and changing popular attitudes towards risk-taking and economic modernisation were the key to economic recovery. Increasing the role of the state in the economy was thus a dead-end.

Finance

Britain has always been distinctive among other industrial economies for the size and role of its financial sector, and, in particular, the way in which the City has been allowed to regulate itself for long periods with minimal government intervention. The enormous success of the City is contrasted with the poor performance of so much of British industry and the argument advanced that the two are strongly linked. As Will Hutton expresses it: 'The story of British capitalism is at heart the peculiar history of the destructive relationship between

British finance and industry.'[19] The hegemony of the City over the British state has meant that, in comparison with other countries, relationships between finance and industry have been more strongly geared to the exploitation of global rather than domestic investment opportunities. Managers of companies in Britain have accordingly been forced to maximise short-term returns in order to satisfy the financial markets. The financial system has failed to nurture successful long-term relationships to support investment and development and the kind of culture and practices within firms which promote high productivity. The contrast is both with the United States and its strong system of local and regional banks which do provide financial support for local industry, and with Germany and Japan which have much higher levels of concentration in ownership of companies and close bank involvement in ownership and management.

The consequences of the relationship between British finance and industry have become increasingly serious as the economy has become exposed to international competition in the last thirty years. Large sectors of British industry have become uncompetitive because of their failure to invest, and the result has been a collapse of output and investment. This is the deindustrialisation thesis put forward by a number of economists in the 1970s.[20] They argued that the manufacturing sector in Britain had contracted to the point where it could no longer generate enough exports to sustain full employment.

The main assumption of the finance thesis is that a successful modern capitalist economy requires a close relationship between finance and industry, rather than the sharp divide which has been the British practice.[21] One rejoinder is that the most successful capitalist economy of all, the United States, enforces an even more distant relationship between finance and industry through legislation. But this is partly countered by the existence of different practices in the USA at local and regional level. Another critique is that British capitalism is a unique configuration and has always given priority to finance and commerce over industry. On this reading there never was a period when industry was supreme. Finance did not become dominant sometime towards the end of the nineteenth century; it always was dominant. Britain's particular niche in the global division of labour has always been the provision of financial and commercial services to the world economy.[22] Some versions of this view argue that Britain was never really suited to industry, so that deindustrialisation in the 1970s, far from being a disaster, was an adaptation which allowed the economy to reorient towards what it did best.[23] The issue depends not on how much employment the manufacturing sector provides (because this could be as low as the contemporary agricultural sector) but how productive it is, and whether any other sector can replace the manufacturing sector in generating sufficient foreign exchange to pay for basic imports.

Finance has always been a target, particularly for the social imperialist tradition (both Joseph Chamberlain and Oswald Mosley attacked the organisation of finance). But except for the period between 1931 and 1951 there has never been the political will or opportunity to subordinate finance to a national policy aimed at giving priority to the needs of industry, and even at that time no long-term restructuring of financial relationships or company legislation was undertaken. Defenders of finance argue that the financial sector was always efficient and competitive and would have provided long-term finance to industry had industry requested it and shown that the investment could pay. The failures of British industry are regarded as lying within industry rather than in the relationship between industry and finance.[24]

Empire

A third peculiarity is the contribution to decline which possession of the world's largest empire made. This thesis has been developed in terms of the opportunities during the closing decades of the nineteenth century for British industry to turn away from competing in world markets to the safer and protected markets of the Empire. The Empire therefore acted as a cushion which avoided the need for too much innovation and creative development. Britain could afford such a loss of competitiveness because of the enormous accumulated wealth from its investments and because of the size of its imperial markets.[25]

This argument has been further developed in the concept of imperial overstretch, the idea that in common with previous empires Britain reached a stage at which a conflict developed between the demands of military security and high consumption on one side, and productive investment on the other.[26] The relative neglect of the latter in favour of the former was facilitated by the formation of powerful military and bureaucratic elites keen to preserve their share of the budget. Such theories assume a cyclical view of history, a period of rise followed by decline. The conditions which were responsible for the initial success cannot be indefinitely sustained, and rivals arise to challenge the supremacy of the dominant power. The burdens of maintaining the leading position handicap the dominant power in resisting the challenge, and contribute to the onset of decadence. At a certain point this version of the imperial thesis merges with the cultural thesis.

Critics of the imperial thesis argue that British imperialism was closely tied to the interests of British finance and British commerce, rather than to industry, and that it continued to expand successfully through the first half of the twentieth century.[27] On this view the failure of Britain to develop the new technologies of the second industrial revolution at the end of the nineteenth century reflected the fact that industry had never been an important priority for British policy or for the structure of Britain's formal and informal Empire. This did not stop the continued expansion of that Empire (there was no long retreat), although ultimately it was one of the factors that brought its eventual collapse.

Other critics have challenged the whole notion of a split between British finance and industry, arguing that the leading companies in most sectors of British industry took full advantage of the financial and commercial opportunities which the Empire afforded them. There was therefore a close link between financial and industrial interests of a particular kind. Certain sectors lost out, but the support for the open seas and globally oriented financial and commercial policy came from a bloc of interests which spanned crucial sections of both industry and finance.[28] From this perspective the decline of the British national economy was not the same thing as the decline of British capitalism, which continued to flourish even while parts of the domestic economy languished.

State

A fourth peculiarity that has been singled out is the character of Britain's state. The key argument is that Britain has failed to develop the institutions and policy stance appropriate to a developmental state. It has developed a large public sector, and various kinds of interventionist and planning agencies, but not the kind of developmental role characteristic of other economies. The kind of economic success evident in Japan, for instance, is ascribed to the particular role which the state plays in the economy, creating a framework and infrastructure which promote long-term relationships of trust and close partnerships between finance and industry, and employers and employees, so making possible a dynamic private sector. A developmental state makes growth its chief priority rather than redistribution or welfare, but is also concerned to include rather than exclude its citizens, by providing all with the necessary skills and opportunities to participate in the economy. From this standpoint Britain's problem has been its persistent failure to ensure the creation of the institutions necessary to overcome weaknesses on the supply side of the economy, such as the training and skills of the workforce, and research and development of new products.

Arguments about the lack of a developmental state in Britain see the problem not in the particular circumstances of the policy failures and fiscal difficulties of the 1970s, which gave rise to arguments about government failure such as the overload thesis, but as an endemic feature in the particular form of state which has been established in Britain. The traditions of parliamentary sovereignty and preference for forms of indirect rule and 'club government' have rested uneasily with the development of modern forms of administration.[29]

These concerns are most vigorously expressed in the characterisation of Britain as an *ancien régime,* the last of the *anciens régimes* in Europe, possessed of a pre-modern constitution and form of state, which in important respects has survived intact to the present.[30] The issue is whether the notoriously peculiar features of the British constitution such as the absence of a single, codified constitutional document, the prerogative powers of the monarchy, the persistence of the hereditary principle in the House of Lords, the degree of centralisation, and the lack of a systematic code of administrative law, are merely outward, dignified forms or whether they do indicate that the British state is in important respects different from other states.

The developmental state thesis cuts across earlier debates about planning by assuming that the role of the state is to assist a free market economy to work better rather than to supplant it with a different system of production and allocation. It is about different models of capitalism rather than replacing capitalism with socialism. It assumes that the state is able to play a variety of roles in making an economy more efficient and dynamic, and it argues that in Britain the possibility of a developmental state requires radical constitutional reform to remove the obstacles to the state performing the kind of role which it performs in more successful industrial economies in western Europe and Japan, but also at a local and sectoral level in the United States.

Criticism of this view comes from neo-liberals who argue that the main cause of decline is not that the state has intervened too little or in the wrong way, but that it has consistently intervened too much. The public sector is too large and places significant burdens on the private sector through taxation, controls and interest rates. From this perspective it is the expansion of the state which has stifled enterprise and fostered inefficiency and is the main contributory factor to decline. The public sector is regarded as a parasite and a drain upon the private sector, because of the inefficiency of the nationalised industries and the cost of maintaining public services. The private sector has been forced to struggle under burdens that inevitably depressed enterprise, discouraged risk-taking and lowered profits. The remedy is to free the private sector from state control, to deregulate, to privatise, to reduce taxation and to limit the state to maintaining sound money and enforcing contracts, including labour contracts. Britain's economic decline is related directly to a set of policies which failed to give priority to the engine of wealth creation – the private sector. The remedy is to transform the state into an enterprise state. The idea of a developmental state is regarded as just another interventionist programme which will lead to the same government failures as before.

Industry

The final peculiarity which features heavily in explanations of decline has been industry. The problems of the British economy are traced to the poor quality of management and/or the poor state of industrial relations. While there are numerous studies berating either unions or management as the chief cause of decline, there is also an important institutionalist literature which argues that a number of institutional relationships have interacted in a particular way to create decline.[31] The patterns most often mentioned are the relationships between industry and finance, the fragmented unions, and the poor quality of training and education. Such theories draw on the idea of path dependency to suggest that societies can be locked into particular paths of development. Once the initial conditions had been established it proved very difficult to break away from them; the particular institutional configuration that was established was self-reinforcing. Studies of different sectors and industries confirm the destructive spiral of decline which became established in each of them.

One of the main criticisms of such institutional theories of decline is that they exaggerate the strength of path-dependency. Harmful and sub-optimal patterns can persist for a time but provided a society remains reasonably open and pluralist, older patterns will become outmoded and will eventually be displaced. Societies and industries that fall behind have a strong incentive to catch up, and before long forces enabling them to catch up make themselves felt. This backwardness thesis suggests that all societies are now interdependent, and that backwardness cannot persist indefinitely. Sooner or later the country or industry that is behind will catch up. Decline is therefore only a temporary phenomenon and to be expected in the normal pattern of development, which will always be uneven, but over time will tend to even up advantages.[32]

This thesis was originally part of classical Marxism, and has been much criticised for being too optimistic about the equalising factors which development sets in train. The hierarchy of wealth and power between groups of nations has barely altered in the last hundred years.[33] But it has also been applied to the analysis of the top group of industrial economies in the argument that the changes of relative position that can be observed among them have been caused primarily by particular events like world wars, and that there is no tendency for cumulative decline or advance. The great strides made, for example, by Germany and Japan in the 1950s and 1960s were a natural example of catch-up. Britain is a special case in this regard because it too, on this theory, should have benefited from the incentives for catch-up. Why Britain failed to respond is ascribed to other factors – one explanation is that institutional sclerosis afflicts countries with open democratic politics.[34] Britain avoided the shocks of invasion and revolution and suffered the price of pluralistic stagnation and a weak, overloaded government. But on a longer view it is argued the shock was only postponed. When it finally occurred in the 1980s it produced a sharp increase in British productivity.[35]

Conclusion

Over time the focus of concern in the political debates on decline has shifted. The concern in the first two debates before and after the First World War was about the British Empire and how Britain's power in the world might be best preserved or prolonged. From the late 1950s Britain's relative economic decline in comparison with similar economies in western Europe and Japan became central. The political debates on decline and what could be done to reverse it reached a peak of intensity in the 1970s. Now the ground has shifted again and the continuing relevance of decline is questioned.

There are several reasons for this. The first is whether discrete national economies any longer exist. During the era of national protectionism which lasted roughly from 1916 (the first suspension of the gold standard) to 1971 (the collapse of Bretton Woods), the concept of a national economy and policy instruments for controlling and steering it were well developed. But this has been put in question by the movement towards deeper European integration through the creation of a single market and the plans for a single currency, as well as the increasing importance of international financial markets and transnational companies in shaping government policies. The European Union is a new kind of state with a fragmented, multilevel authority and a common system of regulation. It undermines unitary states and unitary national economies like the British. Meanwhile the enormous growth of transnational exchanges through corporate, commercial and financial networks makes the statistical definition of the boundaries of national economic space and how its performance can be measured increasingly problematic.[36]

A second reason is that there has been a sharp fall in expectations that governments can change policy and deliver the outcomes they seek. During the era of national protectionism there was greater faith and trust in government. Although the size of the state has barely shrunk at all even in those countries like the USA and the UK where the ideological and political attack has been strongest, the ambition of government has been reduced, and all parties now seek to reduce expectations about what government can do, rather than raise them. The confident programmes of the national protectionist era on full employment, welfare, poverty and economic growth have been abandoned. Even if decline is still thought to exist, no one really thinks that a problem so complex and deep-rooted could be tackled by government.

The third reason is more prosaic. Many observers in Britain think that the decline is over because the economy has been turned around by the policies of the Conservative Governments since 1979.[37] The shock that was administered, partly by accident, at the beginning of the 1980s by the slump in output and the surge in unemployment led to conflicts and changes in behaviour which have altered the path of development of the British economy and broken the obstacles to higher productivity and greater enterprise. The acceptance by the Labour party of the new dispensation means, on this view, that the key peculiarities of British development which were preventing a more successful economic performance have been overcome. Some observers believe that the Thatcher years in Britain signalled the return to the traditional emphasis of British policy – commercial and financial, preserving the openness of the economy to the outside, and flexible institutions, particularly the labour market, within. In this way the particular, unique form of British capitalism can flourish again.[38]

A new period has certainly opened, and many of the old concerns and debates are no longer relevant. Some of the claims being made, however, are much too sweeping. The loss of power by national governments is much exaggerated, and though there has been a loss of confidence in many of the old ways in which governments acted, the size and importance of government have not diminished and new ways of exercising government influence and direction are sure to be developed.[39] The Conservative Governments were successful in improving the supply-side performance of the economy in some areas but by no means all. Investment, innovation, education and training all remain weak. There was an improvement in the 1980s but no miracle. Many economists still contend that the improvements in the supply side are not sufficient to ensure that the British economy has a large enough manufacturing sector to generate full employment or to prevent further decline in the future.[40]

The new language in which issues of decline are discussed is the language of national competitiveness. Some economists have rubbished the notion of competitiveness when it is applied to economies, arguing that at best it can only be applied to single industries or companies.[41] An emphasis on national competitiveness, they believe, leads to quite inappropriate policies which are protectionist because they treat international trade as a zero sum game. National governments can make supply-side improvements which help particular firms improve their productivity, but it makes no sense to talk of one nation competing against another. Thinking in such terms leads to policies which are harmful because they restrict trade and diminish cooperation and trust.

So long as there are national governments, however, the lure of thinking in terms of national economic spaces, how such territorially defined populations and economies perform against one another, and how policy might improve performance is bound to be strong. But on a longer view the discourse of decline seems likely to fade away. Many of the narratives underpinning it have collapsed. The era of national protectionism and developmental states is over, and Britain's Empire is becoming a distant memory. Within a single market and single-currency Europe, national economic decline would have no meaning. But even if Britain were to withdraw from the European Union or the European Union were to fall apart, decline will not be the dominant framework of interpretation in the twenty-first century in the way it has been in the twentieth. The reemergence of a unified global economy and the redistribution of state functions between different levels within the international state system profoundly changes the concerns of domestic politics and the way in which these are expressed.[42] Historians in the next century are likely to see decline, in part, as a specific episode in British history determined by the particular circumstances of Britain's loss of hegemony and the slow adjustment of the British political class to this change, and in part as a set of discourses which constructed decline as a problem and urged political action to remedy it.

3

The European Disunion[1]

In the spring of 2005 the EU constitutional treaty, which had been approved and signed by all states on 29 October 2004, was ratified by Spain and later by Luxembourg following successful referendums, and by nine other member states after votes in their Parliaments. But these successes were far outweighed by its rejection in referendums in two of the founder members of the Union, the Netherlands and France. Once France and the Netherlands had confirmed that they would not seek a further referendum to overturn the no-vote, several other countries, including Britain, then declared that they would not proceed with their own ratification process, despite some pressure to do so. Since ratification had to be unanimous, a decision against by just one state meant that the treaty could not come into force, even if the remaining states had all successfully ratified it. Of the twelve countries that suspended ratification, six were pledged to hold a referendum, and six a vote in Parliament.

The rejection of the constitutional treaty was an important moment in the debate on the EU in Britain. It confirmed the shift within British public opinion and the British political class, including the Labour Government, to a more Euro-sceptic position. A vote on Britain joining the euro had already been postponed indefinitely, and Tony Blair's decision to join the invasion of Iraq had split Britain from France and Germany and majority European opinion, by reaffirming the traditional British priority for the United States over Europe.[2] The 'no' campaign was disappointed that the British were not to be allowed to vote on the treaty, since polls were indicating that it would have been decisively rejected. The Government did not try to hide its relief. Attention shifted to the budget and the question of Britain's rebate in the light of the enlargement of the EU to twenty-five members. The Government declared that it would only accept a reduction in the British rebate in return for a substantial reform of the Common Agricultural Policy, which was immediately ruled out by France and Germany.

At the European Council held in June 2005 Britain's role as the awkward partner in the EU seemed to be accentuated once more.[3] Yet again a British government which had at first proclaimed its intention to be pro-European and to put Britain at the heart of the EU had become progressively more Euro-sceptic and antagonistic to further European cooperation.[4] Although Britain took over the EU presidency in July 2005, the impasse on the constitution and the budget made it unlikely that much progress could be made in resolving the EU's problems. Speaking at the European Parliament on 23 June 2005 Blair laid out the case for a wide-ranging reform of the EU. He argued for a strong, confident Europe which would continue to enlarge and to pool sovereignty, providing much more than just economic benefits to its citizens, but which would remain firmly grounded for its legitimacy on nation-states and would resist any moves to become a state itself. For some advocates of ever closer union, the kind of representative and democratic European polity and European civil society which Blair championed appeared to be precluded by his determination to maintain the EU primarily as an association of nation-states, while Euro-sceptics feared that powers would still slip away from nation-states to the federal centre.

Britain's uncertain and reluctant relationship with the EU derives from its sense of being apart from Europe, an attitude constantly reinforced by its distinctive constitutional identity both in its form of government and its political economy. Yet this constitutional identity has always been paradoxical. The way in which the modern British state was formed has made it difficult for the last five centuries for the British to join anyone else, to pool sovereignty or to accept a supranational jurisdiction which challenges parliamentary sovereignty.[5] But for the last three hundred years the British have also helped create and sustain an open world trading and financial order which has meant that in practice they have been prepared to pool sovereignty all the time, in the sense of accepting a set of rules necessary to maintain this world order in being.[6] British attitudes towards the EU have as a result often been ambiguous and rarely consistent.

Scenarios

The failure of the constitutional treaty prompted much questioning about the future of the EU – whether further integration would now be possible, whether enlargement would proceed, and even whether the EU could survive in the long term, or would lapse into a condition of increasing disunion. It was widely seen as a watershed moment in the development of the EU. There had always been tension between two different bases of EU legitimacy – one deriving from treaties between states and the other deriving from democracy and citizenship – but never before had the collision between them been so serious. The constitutional treaty was based on a fatal, and perhaps unavoidable ambiguity between the two and ended up pleasing almost no one. If it was simply a treaty between states confirming the essentially intergovernmental nature of the EU then there was no need for this to be ratified in a referendum, least of all in a country like Britain with its constitution founded on parliamentary not popular sovereignty. But if it really was a constitution for the European Union confirming the EU as a political entity with its own citizenship and its own capacities, then it required popular endorsement.

If its aim was to create a true modern constitution for the EU the European Convention should have adopted a Claim of Right,[7] 'We the people of Europe', at least as bold as the one which the Scottish Constitutional Convention had issued in 1989: 'We, gathered as the Scottish Constitutional Convention, do hereby acknowledge the sovereign right of the Scottish people to determine the form of Government best suited to their needs, and do hereby declare and pledge that in all our actions and deliberations their interests shall be paramount.' Such a Claim of Right was not adopted because it would have been unacceptable to many of the governments of the member states of the EU, Britain in particular, by elevating the people of Europe above the nation-states as the ultimate source of authority in the Union. But this political reality only underlined the flaw in describing the new treaty as a constitutional treaty. It suggested the treaty could be something which in reality it could never be. Instead of simply proposing a simplification and reorganisation of the existing treaties, the European Convention proposed a draft treaty establishing a constitution for the EU. The states all eventually signed up, but that was the easy part. In the aftermath of the failure there has been a great deal of discussion about what will now happen to the EU. Four particular scenarios have been canvassed.

Deadlock

This is a scenario beloved of Euro-sceptics, but it is also found among some despairing pro-Europeans. It depicts the EU as having reached its high point. The blocking of the constitutional treaty will lead to its slow atrophy. No further enlargement will be possible because no agreement will be reached on the admission of new members, particularly Turkey, even if accession talks do commence. At the same time machinery for coordinating the activities of the existing members will stay unreformed leading to inefficiency and inertia. Similarly, and for the same reasons, steps towards further integration will be blocked, and issues like agreement on the budget will become the source of long periods of deadlock. A new dynamic of *dis*integration will emerge, as states increasingly seek the repatriation of policies ceded to the European level, and to defend their national interests more tenaciously. With the decline in European cooperation and ethos, the budget far from expanding will remain capped at around 1 per cent, and this will stymie efforts to launch new EU initiatives. Extreme versions of this scenario see the disunion spreading to the euro, as the conditions of the Stability and Growth Pact become more onerous, and the political cost of remaining within the eurozone mounts. Without a momentum towards political and economic union some have always doubted that monetary union on its own makes sense or is sustainable.[8] In extreme circumstances it is conceivable that one or more states might seek to defect. Those states most vulnerable are the weak links of the eurozone, and when the possibility of defection was raised publicly in Italy by Liga Nord ministers in the ruling coalition, this did not go unremarked by British Euro-sceptics.

Business as usual

In this scenario the EU continues using the existing treaties and the de facto constitution which has gradually developed since the first treaties were signed. This is the scenario which requires least effort and least disturbance. The EU has acquired a substantial presence and a long reach through the various powers that have been ceded to it by national governments, and the development of its rules and the defining of its jurisdiction proceeds through the activity of the Commission and the European Court. The loss of the constitutional treaty makes it harder to make the Union more democratic and accountable, and the enlargement of the Union to twenty-five members poses particular coordination problems, and decisions may be harder, and certainly slower. But none of these difficulties need prove insuperable, and the powers and responsibilities of the EU would remain broadly the same. It gets back to doing what it does best, practical multilateral cooperation to solve particular problems.[9] The overall legitimacy of the EU remains low, which inhibits further moves towards integration or the launch of major new initiatives. The failure of the constitutional treaty ushers in a period of consolidation. Nevertheless as before, the existence of the EU as a legal, administrative and political entity beyond the nation-states that compose it means that there is some mission creep. The EU continues to extend its reach incrementally into the affairs of member states, causing periodic frictions, but no decisive rejection. Euro-sceptics continue to grumble and mutter about the need to renegotiate the treaties, but in a community of twenty-five states, such renegotiation looks unlikely to succeed unless a member state were prepared to leave altogether. The costs of doing that make it an unlikely prospect.

Core Europe

After the loss of the constitutional treaty the immediate options for the advocates of an ever closer Union have become limited. One possible scenario has been long discussed – the proposal for a core Europe, the acceptance of a two-speed or multi-speed EU, with the pace being set by an inner group of EU states who wish to integrate much further and faster.[10] Membership of this group fluctuates, but at present its most obvious members would be the twelve eurozone members, since they have taken the decisive step of abandoning their national currencies and submitting to the rules of the Stability and Growth Pact and the decisions of the European Central Bank (ECB) in the governance of their economies. For such a project to work certain additional measures to harmonise the fiscal policies and labour market policies of the eurozone economies would be necessary, and since it would be extremely difficult to get agreement from all twenty-five members of the EU to adopt these changes, that suggests that if it happens it will because the countries of the eurozone wish it. It will not be easy even for them to agree, but not impossible. If this project were successful it would make the gap between the core and the rest still greater. Variable speed Europe would have arrived. Britain has always said it would block such a development, but that was when Britain still intended to join the euro. In practice the British by seeking optouts in the past from the treaties have already conceded the principle of a variable speed Europe. Proposals to integrate the eurozone further would be very difficult to block, and Michael Howard, the former Conservative leader, said during the 2005 election campaign that he would welcome it. The attraction of a community within a community may grow, the longer the impasse over the constitution lasts. If the eurozone proves a success, and the conditions for making it work effectively as a single economy are met, then in due course that might attract other EU members to seek membership. But the bar on entry would now be higher than before, and the eurozone would develop its own *acquis communautaire* which would have to be accepted by any other state seeking entry.

Reform

A fourth scenario is favoured by those who remain optimistic about the EU and its future. Tony Blair gave voice to a version of it in his address to the European Parliament in 2005. It has as its starting point the new political geometry which a Union of twenty-five necessarily creates, and which the plans for further enlargement would intensify. It abandons the goal of ever closer union, concentrating instead on promoting enlargement, and recasting and celebrating the Union as a new kind of political association, which is more than a free trade area but less than a state, and which is not moving in the direction of turning itself into a sovereign state. For this to work the EU would seek to find new ways to assert common purposes and establish common policies, but these will be through investment in IT, human capital, mobility, research and languages rather than common agricultural and fisheries policies. In this way the EU would redefine itself as the enabler of European civil society and European networks. It would promote diversity and experimentation, and competing models of social Europe. It would seek to rebuild the European Union as a citizens' union, and one which commands much greater legitimacy than it has done in the past. There are different suggestions as to how to do this. Some argue that the only way forward is to supersede the nation-states and establish the EU as a true polity, based directly on the will of its citizens.[11] Others argue that it should be done through entrenching states' rights, reforming the budget, determining the exclusive competences of each level of jurisdiction in the Union, and developing the EU as a network of institutions.[12] The aim here is to create a citizens' Europe, but to do so through a political structure explicitly anchored in states' rights and in representative democracy.[13] In important respects this debate is a rerun of debates held in the early decades of the United States, although in very different circumstances, since from the start the United States as an entity claimed sovereignty which the EU does not.

Images of Europe

The current EU impasse and uncertainty about its future direction reflects the complex political space which Europe has become, imagined in so many different ways by its citizens, its elites, and its intellectuals.[14] Europe and the EU are not the same, although often treated interchangeably. Images of Europe exert a powerful normative pull in EU debates. The 'yes' and 'no' votes in the referendums that have been held were swayed by different and sometimes conflicting images of Europe. Although there are significant variations in attitudes towards the EU in different member states these images cut across national boundaries and are evidence of the first stirrings of a genuine European debate, and the construction of a European political space. From this perspective the eruption of Euro-scepticism in so many parts of the EU apart from Britain and Denmark is not necessarily a sign of weakness for the European project but a sign of maturity. It means that a genuine debate may be starting, one which accepts implicitly the existence of the EU, even while some of those taking part in it reject many existing EU policies and institutions.

From this perspective it was regrettable that the ratification process was interrupted, since it would have been good for more countries to have had the kind of debate that France and the Netherlands experienced. That wider debate was cut short by the decision to suspend the ratification process in twelve of the thirteen remaining states (only Luxembourg went ahead with its referendum, which returned a 'yes' vote). But it was also already undermined by the decision to consider the constitution as a treaty which had therefore to be ratified by the member states instead of a document which had to be approved by the citizens of the EU. If the latter had prevailed, then all member states would have been required to hold a referendum on the same day. Instead they were allowed to choose how and when they ratified it, whether through a referendum or through a vote in Parliament. Such a procedure markedly reduced the possibility of a trans-European debate, but it did not remove it altogether. A number of initiatives were made by both the 'no' and the 'yes' campaigns to make links across the European Union with groups and parties which shared their point of view. This was especially important for the Euro-sceptic campaign. By engaging with Euro-sceptics across the EU the 'no' campaign implicitly and at times explicitly recognised the existence of the EU as a political space, and put forward an image of Europe which required the rejection of the constitutional treaty and a block on further moves towards integration and to stop the EU ever becoming a state. Despite the predominantly negative tone of the Euro-sceptic campaign towards 'Europe', to win their case the Euro-sceptics also had to put forward their own positive image of how 'Europe' should be organised.

The heart of the Euro-sceptic image of the EU draws on the contrast between intergovernmental and supranational conceptions.[15] The tension between these two conceptions runs like a fault line down the middle of the constitutional treaty. The European Convention, for reasons that are readily understandable, was unable to produce the kind of proposal for a constitution which might have helped resolve the conflicting bases of legitimacy in the EU; instead it compounded the problem. The EU is a union formed by decision of its member states, but, as a result of the treaties and the institutions it has established, the EU has also become a self-referential legal entity, with its own uncodified constitution.[16] If the constitutional treaty had succeeded it would have given the EU greater legal clarity for its operation, and would have introduced important new provisions for democracy, accountability and subsidiarity, as well as providing a statement of its basic values and purposes.

Rejection of the constitutional treaty, however, does not mean that the EU has no constitution. It has long had one, just not a formal, codified one. Despite the failure to ratify the treaty, the whole of Part III remains in force, since it merely replicates what was already contained in earlier treaties. One of the ironies in the rejection of the constitutional treaty in France was that many of the people who voted 'no' did so in the belief that they were voting against the economic and social policies of the EU which they disliked. But those policies will continue under the authority of the earlier treaties. What has been lost are the new mechanisms for subjecting the institutions of the Commission to greater democracy and accountability, and to allow the EU to become subject to its citizens rather than to its political class. Euro-sceptics are pleased at this outcome because they do not want to see such a European polity established. The European polity which they want is an association of states, where all policies have to be agreed unanimously by states. There are no European citizens as such, only citizens of the individual states.

Sovereignty remains one of the central images through which the debate on the EU has been conducted and through which different ideas of Europe are reflected. But there are other powerful images as well — governance, political economy, and security among them. The existence of so many different ways to construct 'Europe' is what makes the EU so hard to define and such a complex and open political space. There are many different meanings and possibilities, which are constantly changing as the EU evolves, and which tend to make the language of the debates polarised and exaggerated. As rival attempts are made to imagine the character of the European political space — is it a polity, an association, a federation? – so fears and hopes are expressed as to what the EU is and what it might become.[17]

Sovereignty

Sovereignty remains central to the debate on the EU in Britain. It always has been. Persuading Europe's established nation-states and their political elites to cede powers to a new European centre was always difficult; so too was the task of reconciling national diversity with supranational sovereignty. It was perhaps especially hard for Britain, although some British leaders, like Churchill immediately after the war, were persuasive advocates of the new idea of Europe. As Churchill put it in a speech to the Congress of Europe about proposals for European union: 'It is said with truth that this involves some sacrifice or merger of national sovereignty. But it is also possible and not less agreeable to regard it as the gradual assumption by all the nations concerned of that larger sovereignty which can also protect their diverse and distinctive customs and characteristics and their national traditions all of which under totalitarian systems, whether Nazi, Fascist or Communist, would certainly be blotted out forever.'[18] Finding a way to harmonise that larger sovereignty with the protection of national diversity remains unfinished business, and not only in Britain, as the debate on the constitutional treaty in many member states makes plain. But the argument has been particularly acute in Britain, and Euro-sceptic opinion has been vocal in rejecting the larger sovereignty that the EU has come to represent.

There are parallels in the intensity and the inconclusiveness of this debate between Euro-believers and Euro-sceptics with the arguments between Federalists and Republicans in the early decades of the establishment of republican government in the United States. The division of powers between the federal government and the states was fiercely fought, since at stake was not just the question of whether the United States should be plural or singular, whether it should develop as a single polity or as a loose collection of states, but also how much diversity was acceptable. What was the minimum to which all states had to subscribe for there to be a union at all? The high ideals of the Declaration of Independence were sharply contradicted by the actual laws of many of the states. The diversity which the southern states sought to protect included their right to maintain slavery, and it was to protect that right that they eventually sought to secede from the Union.

The Federalist/Republican dispute in the United States focused on the primacy of the federal government as against the state governments;

the powers which should be given to the federal level, and those which should be retained at state level. Under what circumstances might the federal government legitimately increase its reach, and engage in new activities? Republican advocates of states' rights wanted the powers of the federal government to be kept to a minimum, and condemned every move by the Federalists to increase the power of the federal government as steps on the road to tyranny and a return to monarchy. With the exaggeration typical of partisan debate Federalists like Alexander Hamilton and John Adams were accused of actively plotting the return of monarchy, military despotism, and English rule, while the Republicans, under the leadership of Jefferson and Madison, were accused of being unwilling to make sacrifices to build a strong new nation and state, seeking instead to protect their landed estates and their slaves.[19]

During the building of the European Union this federalist/republican argument has been played out again between the supporters of a federal Europe and the supporters of a Europe of nation-states. It has been argued that the comparison is misleading because the US from the beginning was a sovereign state while the EU was not.[20] But although it is true that the EU is not a sovereign state and will not become one,[21] the experience of the US is still relevant to Europe, because much of the American debate was over whether the US was one state or many states. The issue that the Americans had to settle was how to reconcile federal authority with state authority. For the Europeans it is how to reconcile supranational authority with national authority.

The language used in these debate has often greatly exaggerated the differences at stake. Euro-believers in Britain have routinely been accused of wanting to destroy the nation-state altogether and hand over all powers to a federal European government. Similarly Euro-sceptics have often been accused of wanting to strip the 'federal' centre of all its powers, effectively abolishing it. But almost no one in the British political class holds such views. The argument is a narrower one, not about whether there should be a federal centre at all or whether nation-states should continue to exist, but what the division of powers should be between them. The core of the Euro-sceptic argument is the desire to resist the encroachment of the federal centre on the powers and jurisdiction of the member states.[22] Euro-sceptics characterise the federal centre in terms every bit as extravagant as the Jeffersonian Republicans characterised the federal government in the United States. In both cases the number of employees of the federal centre and the size of its budget was minuscule, in relation to total employment and to GDP. In the case of the EU it was also minuscule in relation to employment and taxation at the level of the individual states. Both the EU and the US embarked on a career of expansion in their first fifty years, but in the case of the United States this expansion was within the vast and lightly populated continental space of North America, whereas that of the EU took place in a densely populated continent with highly developed states and societies. Nevertheless, the principle of allowing the federal centre to personify and symbolise the United States and to act in the name of the United States was necessary for the United States to develop political will and political identity and to become a strategic actor in world politics. France, England and Spain in the early decades of the American Republic doubted that the Americans were capable of developing such a political will and identity, and many expected the strong pull of the states to lead to the fragmentation and dissolution of the Union, which almost occurred at the time of the civil war.

The Federalist/Republican argument pinpoints the different constitutional arguments for legitimacy, which reverberate today in the European Union. Do citizens benefit from the construction of a federal centre with powers to act strategically for the whole union, and to come to personify that union? Or is it better to keep any union strictly limited, no more than an association of states, who retain all the most important levers for self-government. However terms like subsidiarity are employed, the question of who in any polity has the right to formulate new binding rules remains crucial. The Americans were fortunate in that they possessed a founding myth for their new nation, and a sense of starting out anew.[23] None of that has been possible in Europe; the separate national traditions and cultures are highly differentiated. But even with their advantages the Americans had huge difficulties constructing a strong nation-state whose legitimacy was broadly accepted. In Europe the legitimacy of the existing nation-states, and the unwillingness of their political elites to surrender control of their national systems, makes arguments for the federal centre, the supranational part of the Union, always start on the back foot. It is a tribute to the persistence of the advocates of the European Union that the project has advanced as far as it has. But that is in part because the argument has been an unbalanced one, and the European political class has excluded or marginalised the 'Republican' or Euro-sceptic position, while assuming much greater popular support for the 'federalist' position than was warranted. The Dutch and French referendums showed that this support, while still substantial, was much less than had been supposed, even in two of the original founders of the EU project. In member states like Britain where the Euro-sceptic tone of debate has become so pronounced, the starting point for any recasting of the EU has to start from a Euro-sceptic/Republican position. Only then might progress be made.

Governance

The different images of the proper locus of sovereignty in Europe are closely connected (at times confusingly) to contrasting images of the EU as a system of governance. The main polarity is between network and territorial governance. Network governance emphasises steering mechanisms that involve networks, markets and other decentralised forms of coordination across legal jurisdictions and administrative boundaries. Such governance is inherently multilevel governance.[24] The conception of Network Europe[25] imagines Europe as a civil society rather than a state, in which citizens interact freely within a framework of common rules and institutions. Such networks include sport, culture, professions, universities, and business, as well as the policy, financial and legal communities. By increasing interaction between citizens and generating a common consciousness of things European, they help define European political, social and economic spaces at the same time as they protect and promote diversity. The rationale of network governance is to promote the spread of networks and decentralised forms of coordination.

Central to network governance is also the idea of Europe as a single economic space, involving the breaking down of all obstacles to the free movement of labour, goods and capital. It defined the single market programme of the 1980s and then the plans for the euro in the 1990s. The single market programme and the euro have been regarded by many as the heart of the neo-liberal programme for Europe, and indeed many neo-liberals have been prominent in advocating them. But here the idea of Network Europe conflicts with Nation-State Europe, so that many neo-liberals who think retaining full national sovereignty more important than the creation of a single market in Europe have baulked at the implications of the latter, particularly in terms of the euro. The split in the ranks of the Thatcherites in Britain over this issue has been well documented.[26]

Governance is not only about networks, however. There are other steering mechanisms, and part of the resistance of British Euro-sceptics to the institutional requirements of the single market, particularly the euro, was that it seemed to involve the creation of state capacity at the European level which threatened national sovereignty. Such state capacity allows the EU to be seen in more traditional terms as a form of territorial governance, seeking to centralise power and authority in order to create the capacity at the centre to achieve particular goals. Its critics see it as statist, bureaucratic, inflexible, while its advocates regard it as the indispensable foundation for successful and powerful states, for the promotion of successful networks across and beyond the EU, as well as for accountable, representative and therefore democratic politics. Many British pro-Europeans have sought to legitimate the EU as a means of delivering on a European level certain things, for example a capacity for strategic industrial intervention, which can no longer be delivered at the national level.[27] They used the image of a Developmental State Europe, seeing the EU as a means of developing and protecting capacity in certain key industries, and resisting the challenge from the US, Japan, or more recently China and India. Such arguments have always had a certain resonance on the interventionist right. But on the left too arguments about industrial protection, industrial capacity, and industrial innovation have also been powerful, as well as arguments about the ability of a powerful EU to establish and protect common standards on employment and welfare.[28]

Euro-sceptics like to identify the EU as a particular malign form of territorial governance, imagining the EU Commission in particular as a bureaucratic behemoth strangling the life out of the vigorous and diverse civil societies of the member states.[29] This has created a discourse which treats the EU as seeking to impose uniformity and control from the centre, and condemning the EU to creeping economic paralysis.[30] But since most of these critics are vigorous proponents of network governance in the form of global markets, this sets up a number of contradictions, since support for national sovereignty frequently involves the imposition of obstacles, such as immigration controls, to a free and unified economic space, while support for global markets implies a state capacity at regional level to break down local impediments to free markets. Many neo-liberals have always supported the EU as a vehicle for breaking down national particularisms, and creating the kind of strong, minimal state at the European level necessary to create the right conditions for a free market order, which is precisely why so many on the left have been critics of the EU. The difficulty for neo-liberals is where to draw the line. A strong European Commission is necessary to promote the kind of free market order in Europe they think desirable, yet such a Commission clashes for some of them with their desire to keep the powers of the EU as limited as possible, and to maintain the nation-state as the prime source of legitimacy.[31] Neo-liberals in many member states of the EU remain sharply divided on this issue.

Political economy

Governance issues merge naturally into those of political economy. Here the two dominant images have been those of Social Europe against Laissez-Faire or Neo-Liberal Europe. There is not one European social model, but many different ones, as well as many hybrids. There are several different worlds of welfare capitalism in Europe, and all of them involve some kind of *welfare*, even if there are significant variations between them. The argument is over what kind of social model is appropriate for Europe, and here the battlelines have been drawn between on one side the German and Scandinavian models, and on the other the British and Irish models. This divide is also reflected in the distinction that has long been made between different forms of political economy in Europe.[32] A recent version of this is the distinction between liberal market economies and coordinated market economies.[33]

This contrast is often rhetorically given the form of an Anglo–American model versus a European model, as in a recent speech by the former leader of the British Conservatives, Michael Howard, addressing News International executives at Cancun in 2004. Howard argued that the most successful form of capitalism in the free world had been created in the United States, but that instead of simply copying this model many European governments had rejected liberal economic policies in favour of a more regulatory, and in some cases corporatist, approach. This social model, developed in Germany and other countries, had as its aim the protection of the weak, but in Howard's view, the outcome had been the opposite, because it had made European economies less flexible and less competitive, resulting in a real cost in terms of jobs and growth. In particular Howard claimed that if the American and European models were compared, then it was clear that labour costs and taxes were much higher in Europe than in the US, and that growth and job creation were much lower. With growing competition from India and China, Europe faced a difficult future, since its average tax burden at 41 per cent of GDP was much higher than the tax burden in the Pacific region or the United States. According to Howard, 'the EU was designed to free up our markets so that we could compete globally. But the weight of tax and regulation it has introduced has had almost exactly the opposite effect – damming the flood of enterprise that should be sweeping across Europe.'[34]

As so often in political debate such a sharp delineation of two radically opposed models hardly matches the reality. All of the European economies are hybrids; they have distinctive institutional features, and all are subject to the competitive pressures from American, Japanese and now Chinese companies. A composite European model does not exist, and there are many difficulties in interpreting the figures on relative performance. Nevertheless, the perception that the European social model which at one time appeared so strong has entered a period of difficulty and retrenchment is widely shared, and has produced within Europe much agitation to introduce reforms, to deregulate, and to introduce greater flexibility in order to reduce high levels of unemployment and achieve faster rates of economic growth. Much of this thinking was brought together in the 2000 Lisbon agenda, which proposed transforming the EU into a variety of competition or market state,[35] adjusting the European economy to the challenges, opportunities and threats of the global capitalist economy. In his speech to the European Parliament in 2005 Blair argued that there was no contradiction between linking social justice with economic efficiency. Only if the European economy was liberalised could EU member states continue to afford the social state.

Against these pressures to liberalise, the idea of a European model to chart a European *Sonderweg* in industrial relations, welfare spending, and social investment remains a seductive one, particularly for the left, since it provides a means to give the EU both legitimacy and identity. Standing for a different kind of capitalism and welfare system than the American or the Japanese, the European social model would maintain European values and provide an example for others. A difficulty for the European social model is, however, that in several countries of the Union, notably Germany, it is under attack, while in many of the new member states in Eastern Europe the social model is not attractive. The enthusiasm in Eastern Europe for experiments with the flat tax highlights this gulf very well. Britain is actually much closer to the European social model than are some of the East European countries, and is likely to remain so, Michael Howard's rhetoric notwithstanding. Sweden and the other Scandinavian countries offer a version of the European social model which currently enjoys a great deal of prestige, combining high welfare spending and taxation with a liberalised economy, but there are considerable difficulties in extending this model to the rest of the EU, particularly to the new entrants. The European social model cannot be imposed on member states; national electorates would have to vote for it, and progress towards it is therefore likely to be slow. But it does provide a standard to which members can aspire. The part it has played in the debate on left and right in recent years about the standard of welfare and public services at which Britain should be aiming is an interesting example of this.

In the debate on the constitutional treaty in several member states it became clear that much opposition to the treaty was founded on the belief that if the treaty were accepted it would hasten the dismantling of the European social model, and the turn to neo-liberal policies throughout Europe. Social Europe would be replaced by Neo-Liberal Europe. Voting down the constitutional treaty became a way of preserving the option of Social Europe. However, since many of the neo-liberal elements to which the objections were strongest were already contained in the existing treaties, they were unaffected by the rejection of the constitutional treaty. If Neo-Liberal Europe really is a danger, then rejecting the treaty has done nothing to dispel it. It may even have made it more likely, by decreasing the capacity of the EU as a whole to determine common policies.

Security

A fourth contrasting pair of images relates to security. Here the contrast is between Security or Fortress Europe on the one hand and Multilateral Europe on the other. The term Fortress Europe is a negative image, adopted by critics, but it has always been a powerful legitimating idea for the European Union, because it taps into the sense that in an insecure world there is safety in numbers, and that it is better for the European nations to have a formal association to promote their common interests in defence and the economy than to stay divided and apart. In particular the idea of Fortress Europe appeals to many European citizens as a means of controlling borders and fighting crime, as well as protecting European agriculture and industry against imports from low cost countries, and projecting European power in the world. Some of these objectives clash with the objective of promoting the EU as a single economic space with free movement of goods and people, and it is perhaps the fear that Fortress Europe will never be a reality which encourages many European citizens to fall back on the nation-state as a more effective guarantor of their security.

Fortress Europe as its name suggests is inherently defensive and inward-looking. Multilateral Europe is the reverse of this – it is the image of an EU that promotes the security of its citizens by being proactive and presenting a positive model of democracy, human rights, and welfare to the rest of the world. Such an EU still sees a leadership role for itself, although not a military one. It projects itself as a partner in the management of the international system which has been constructed since 1945, and as both a partner and a counterweight to the United States. This image of the EU is not of the EU as a great power, but as a support for multilateral solutions, demonstrating by its own example the way in which national interests can be pooled for broader public goods. This image is a very positive one, and favoured by many in the political class. The problem with it is that it often requires capacities which the EU does not possess, because the provision of these capacities requires a pooling of sovereignty beyond what has been agreed or is politically feasible. The EU is an unfinished work, so it frequently exhibits potential which has not yet been realised, and may never be realised, since whenever the potential is glimpsed, this sparks off fierce opposition from those with a different image of what Europe should be.

Conclusion

The legitimacy of the EU is continually shifting as the arguments about what it is and what it is capable of being go back and forth. What the rejection of the constitutional treaty has shown is that the arguments of those who wish to limit further expansion and further integration of the EU are currently in the ascendancy, and that the more positive images of the EU entertained by its political class are not shared to the same degree by the electorates. It seems clear that if further progress is to be made the EU may need to be built again, this time from the bottom. The new openness in the debate that the constitutional treaty introduced was a positive feature in this respect, even though it meant the expression of a great deal of negative sentiment about the EU. Only if the EU becomes a polity founded on the legitimacy either of the entrenched rights of states or the legitimacy of the European demos, is there likely to be further development of the European project. Without it the present stalemate could last indefinitely. 'Europe' would remain as a factor in the domestic politics of all the member states, always available as the external other to be blamed for the manifold ills that afflict citizens. 'Business as usual' is in this sense the most likely of the scenarios to be realised. All the political elites could live with it, and the EU would continue undisturbed. If the EU abandons projects for further integration then it will remain an irritant to Euro-sceptic opinion but not an immediate threat. The EU is unlikely to unravel because too many common interests are at stake. But the fate of the constitutional treaty seems to have demonstrated that the EU can no longer advance in the old way, through understandings between the political elites of the European states, with the consent of the citizens assumed. To find a new legitimacy for building the union, the lessons of the US experience remain pertinent. The creation of a larger sovereignty that is legitimate must either rest on the foundation of states' rights or on the consent of the whole European citizen body. If the legitimacy of the centre were refounded on the basis of the former, Euro-sceptic opinion might become reconciled to the existence of the EU, and in time a European demos might emerge. But without such a refounding the possibilities for progress appear slim.

4

The Anglo–American World View[1]

America is becoming not English merely, but world embracing ... and as the English element has given language and history to that land, America offers the English race the moral directorship of the globe, by ruling mankind through Saxon institutions and the English tongue. Through America England is speaking to the world.

Charles Dilke[2]

Britain's unruly North American colonists broke away from the British Crown and established the United States of America almost two hundred and fifty years ago. The subsequent relationship between Britain and its former colonies, whose new state developed over time into the most powerful state in the world, has always been complex, at times a source of conflict, at others of cooperation. A variety of terms have been used to describe this relationship. They include the Anglo-world, the English-speaking world, Anglo-America and most recently the Anglosphere.[3]

Anglo-America is the broadest term, denoting for example that part of America that feels a particular empathy to things British, a relationship between particular states, a transnational political space, a political myth, and a political project. The Anglosphere is a very good instance of the last of these. Anglo-America is, however, more than a political project, it is an 'imagined community',[4] encompassing both ideals and interests, which is constructed and sustained through various narratives and embodied in particular institutions. Such transnational political spaces are a key feature of our world, although less studied than either nation-states or the global economy. Such spaces arise particularly around the great powers of each era, but they exist to some extent for all states, since no state is entirely self-contained. Some states because of their history are involved in many such transnational spaces, some of them overlapping. For Britain the three most important have been the Empire, Europe, and Anglo-America. Such spaces and the communities of interest and ideals to which they give rise can be a potent source of political identity and political projects.

This notion of Anglo-America as a transnational political space embracing the English-speaking world is particularly important for understanding the relationship between Britain and the United States, and in particular for understanding the Anglo–American world view and the project for Anglo–American hegemony which arose in the final decades of the nineteenth century and the early decades of the twentieth, and has assumed many forms – Greater Britain, the Grand Area, the Atlantic Partnership, and most recently, the Anglosphere.[5] The vote in the 2016 UK Referendum to leave the EU has breathed new life into it, since the idea of Global Britain advocated by the Leave campaign is yet another iteration of the belief in the manifest destiny of the Anglo-Saxon race.

The claim that there is an Anglo–American world view is not about whether presidents and prime ministers happen to agree with one another and form a strong bond. It is about whether the UK and US, despite at times having conflicting interests, have nevertheless collaborated in the creation and sustaining of a particular form of world order. Viewed from outside, the UK and US are seen as having successfully established an Anglo–American hegemony in which first Britain and later the US took the leading role. It has endured for most of the last two hundred years since the defeat of Napoleon at Waterloo, and which has promoted a particular kind of world order, and even in recent times a particular form of globalisation, *Anglobalisation*.

The question of world order

The political economy of the modern world has been founded on two contradictory principles – a capitalist market economy which seeks to expand without limit, and a state system which remains fragmented in many separate jurisdictions. The tension between the two has been both creative and destructive. It has helped produce the extraordinary growth in wealth, productivity and population over the last two hundred years, but it has been responsible for many conflicts, both commercial and military. Every state has sought to maximise its advantages within the expanding division of labour and the commercial opportunities of the global world economy, but states have also come to recognise the extent of global interdependence and therefore the advantage of securing cooperative and peaceful solutions for mutual benefit. A stable world order is in everyone's interest. The problem is how to achieve it.

World order is a contested concept. There has always been disagreement on how it is best established and maintained. For some the priority has always been regional and national order imposed by sovereign nation-states. From this territorial perspective, world order arises when there is a balance of power between sovereign nation-states, but such a balance can only ever be temporary, and so too is world order. International politics is anarchic and there is no global Leviathan to impose order. The rival view, from which has developed the cosmopolitan and the hegemonic perspective, is that world order is possible and increasingly necessary because as global interdependence deepens the global economy requires governance, not on normative grounds but as a matter of fact.[6]

Three conceptions of world order – territorial, cosmopolitan and hegemonic – have shaped the Anglo–American world view. The territorial conception of world order treats sovereign states as the basic building block of the international state system. The world economy is not a global economy but an international economy, mediated through the separate and independent jurisdictions of nation-states. The order that becomes established depends on the calculations made by nation-states of the advantages to themselves to be derived from cooperation rather than conflict. A balance of power may result which ensures reasonable stability, although it is a stability which is always fragile and capable of being undermined, because states can at any time review their interests and decide they are not being well served by current arrangements. So long as they see their interests being protected, however, states will cooperate, and quite extensive forms of interdependence may arise. But their foundation remains the interest of states in preserving their territorial security. From this perspective national control can always be reasserted and powers that have been pooled or shared can be restored. The state may choose to permit free movement of goods and capital and even people, but this is always conditional, and in extreme circumstances the powers can be revoked.

The cosmopolitan conception of world order emphasises not state sovereignty but market sovereignty. Its basic claim, which is both empirical and normative, is that the state and politics are subordinate to the way in which the economy is organised. The market supplies the ordering principles for both economy and society. The rise of the global market is regarded as the key development in the construction of modernity, because it allowed the development of an interdependent system of global production and exchange which escaped the control of states and national jurisdictions and became an overarching reality to which states found they had to adjust. Their autonomy was undermined and circumscribed by the global market. States and the separate jurisdictions associated with them have not disappeared or been destroyed, but the global market has created powers, resources, networks and institutions which constantly reach beyond them and tower over them. States find they cannot reject the constraints which markets place upon them without destroying the conditions for the economic growth and prosperity of the territories they control, and with it the fiscal basis for their own existence.

The hegemonic perspective on world order which is at the heart of the Anglo–American world view combines aspects of both the territorial and the cosmopolitan conceptions. It is primarily concerned with the political conditions of world order.[7] It accepts the reality of the global economy which the neo-liberals so eloquently describe, but at the same time notes the persistence of the international state system, and the necessity for the global market to be embedded in non-market institutions and practices. It focuses on the institutions and the functions which the global market requires to sustain it.

This conception of order is hegemonic, because it examines the forms of governance which, however imperfectly and unevenly, provide a set of ordering principles to tackle the problems thrown up by the tensions between an increasingly interdependent global economy and global civil society, and the continuing fragmentation of political rule.[8] Hegemony has in the past been associated with the existence of a hegemon, a sovereign state which by virtue of its economic, financial, and military predominance exercises rule-making functions for the global economy and society. But such periods of dominance have tended to be short, because rivals arise to challenge the hegemon, and because the hegemon is caught in a perpetual tension between pursuit of its own interests and acting in the interests of the system as a whole. The existence of a hegemonic state has been a key factor in providing the conditions which enable expansion, prosperity and profitability in the global economy, the peaceful movement of peoples and transfer of technologies.

The term hegemony has a number of meanings associated with it, and there are both strong and weak senses. In the weak sense the hegemon is simply the dominant power able to impose its leadership on others. In the strong sense the power of the hegemon becomes authority, and is exercised through consent. This latter kind of hegemony is always likely to be more durable because its roots lie both in ideological legitimation of what the hegemon does, and also in the accommodation of the interests of those over whom rule is exercised. A successful project for world order has to find means of ideological legitimation which justify its purposes and its methods, and it has to be flexible enough to make concessions to accommodate the vital interests of the ruled.[9]

The political conditions for order in a world system characterised by increasing global economic interdependence and fragmented political rule have common features that stretch back to the beginnings of the modern period. Globalisation is associated with the tendency for global economic interdependence and interconnectedness to increase.[10] As such globalisation is not new. Since the sixteenth century the capitalist world economy inaugurated trends towards cultural, political, ideological, economic and racial homogenisation – the creation of One World. Progress towards this has been very uneven, and is unlikely ever to be complete. From the beginning globalisation has been constituted and propelled by politics, in particular by nation-states which have been economically and political dominant.[11]

The establishment of world order has been highly dependent first on Britain and then on the United States. The degree of continuity and overlap between these two hegemonies makes it possible to speak of 'Anglo-America' and the Anglo–American world view as the most powerful determinant of the way the system of global governance has evolved, because these two states have actively encouraged the development of a liberal, cosmopolitan order, and have done so partly by establishing rules and norms for such an order, and partly by holding in check territorial claims of other states. Britain's period of hegemony was marked by the simultaneous pursuit of an informal cosmopolitan empire alongside a formal territorial empire. British policy was always pulled in two directions, but the more important legacy of British hegemony was the cosmopolitan empire, the empire of trade. The opportunity for this to develop to the extent it did in the nineteenth century owed much to the successful breakaway of the American colonies from Britain's territorial empire.

US hegemony has been on a quite different scale to the British. After 1945 the United States rebuilt the institutions of the liberal world order which Britain had established, only this time the claims have been more universal, less compromised by the direct possession of a territorial empire, or the harbouring of specific territorial claims. What this liberal order has permitted is the creation of conditions for the flourishing of a large number of small and relatively autonomous states;

respect for the territorial principle and national self-determination (where this did not conflict with US security or economic interests) conferred sovereignty and territorial jurisdiction upon a wide range of states, while the maintenance of a (relatively) open system of trade and finance offered opportunities for states to adjust their domestic policies to take full advantage of them.[12] The spur which economic openness provided to these states was the result of the conditions which US hegemony established. But territorial sovereignty was also key.

Globalisation in the 1990s became the latest project of Anglo-America for maintaining its two hundred year old hegemony and ensuring that the world economy continued to be governed by liberal rules and objectives. Globalisation was only the latest doctrine used to promote the virtues and advantages of a liberal world order. The international Keynesianism of Bretton Woods, or the free trade doctrines of the nineteenth century were earlier examples.[13] The new policy doctrines in the discourse of globalisation emerged in the 1970s, mainly in the United States and Britain, and quickly became established in the main agencies of global governance, the financial markets, and the networks of transnational capital. By the 1980s aided by two like-minded ideological regimes in the US and Britain, led by Reagan and Thatcher they became crystallised into what became known as the Washington consensus.[14]

The globalisation discourse was in part an attempt to reestablish control of how states responded to the financial crises and economic recessions of the new era. In particular the governing institutions of the post-war order wanted to discourage protectionism and any retreat to closed blocs or autarchy. At the same time the purpose of globalisation was also to take the attack to those countries, particularly Japan, who were seen as free-riding on the liberal world order by not opening their domestic markets sufficiently to goods from the rest of the world. By proposing new trade rules the aim was to recast the basis of the liberal world order in a way which served the interests of the United States rather better than it had in the past, when the United States had been prepared to make more sacrifices in the interests of rebuilding the liberal world order and containing communism. Japan had indeed benefited greatly from the post-war liberal trading order, and had emerged as the second most important industrial power and a major financial power. But the Japanese were very reluctant to accede to the demands of the United States to open their markets, fearing that this could lead to the destruction of key features of the Japanese model which had served them so well in the post-war era.[15] Yet at the same time Japan, although a full member of the G8, appeared reluctant to take on wider responsibilities for managing the global system, or to reshape the institutional pattern of US hegemony, for fear of disrupting the international order which had served it so well.[16]

Important features of what became the Anglo–American world view in the twentieth century were developed by Britain when it was the hegemonic power in the nineteenth century. British practices and beliefs were projected on to the world economy and became the model which other countries sought to emulate. It universalised particular rules about property, finance and trade. It was both a doctrine, centred on the ideals of liberal political economy – free trade, sound finance, and laissez-faire – and a reflection of the institutional means by which the British economy and the global economy were coordinated and governed. The celebration of the power, productivity and efficiency of markets as the main instrument of economic governance was the backbone of the laissez-faire vision. The state had an important role, but it was a minimal one; it had to remove the obstacles to the working of the free market, and ensure that they were not reestablished. The state had specific functions to discharge – enforcement of law, maintenance of social order, safeguarding of the currency – and was much more active than the popular image of laissez-faire suggests, since there were a great number of obstacles to the efficient working of markets. But there was no requirement for the state at the national level to be responsible for the level of employment or for economic prosperity. Its responsibilities for human capital and for infrastructure were also small. What the liberal economic constitution assumed was that once the basic laws and institutions had been established the economy was in principle self-governing. The market itself provided the steering and corrective mechanisms, in particular the price system, which were required for successful economic governance. Interventions by the state risked disturbing the delicate mechanism which coordinated economic activity across the globe and ensured such high and rising levels of prosperity.

The policy rules for national governments emphasised that governments should pursue sound finance, by maintaining balanced budgets and keeping expenditure and therefore taxation to a minimum; they should adhere to the gold standard, thus imposing on themselves a severe external financial discipline which would ensure that money would be stable in value; they should support open markets and free trade, and resist the lobbying of special interests whatever the implications for particular sectors of the economy, in order to maximise wealth for the whole community; and they should confine their internal interventions to making sure that markets were as competitive as possible, and that all restraints on trade, from whatever source they came, were outlawed. The division between the public and the private was relatively clear-cut. There was an important if limited public sphere and an important role for the public interest in defining and enforcing the conditions for a thriving market economy. But the dynamism emanated from the private sphere itself. Economic agency was located in private individuals, and the main role of the state was restricted to maintaining the conditions for the market to function.

The development of Anglo–American collaboration

The Anglosphere is not just about Britain and the United States, it also includes Australia, New Zealand, Canada, and Ireland. But the relationship between Britain and the United States has been pivotal to its development, ever since the thirteen colonies successfully threw off British rule. The Declaration of Independence in 1776 plunged Britain into a second civil war, which rehearsed many of the arguments of the first civil war, one hundred and forty years earlier. The ideological debate was about the rights of free born Englishmen against the authority of the Crown, and the struggle over these principles was as fierce within England as it was in the American colonies. The programme of the rebel colonists was much influenced by John Locke and Tom Paine and drew on the main themes of English radicalism.[17] The inability of the British state to accommodate those demands made compromise impossible, and following the intervention of the French on the side of the rebels led to the loss of a large part of Britain's empire in North America.

During the nineteenth century relationships between the two states gradually improved, particularly as there were for a time common economic interests. British capital poured into the United States to fund the development of its agriculture and its infrastructure, especially its railways. The cultural ties between the two states remained very close, but the growing power of the United States alarmed British governments. During the American civil war the British political class predominantly favoured the Confederacy, partly because it was landowning and aristocratic, and partly because a breakup of the Union was considered in Britain's strategic interest.[18] The consolidation of a more centralised federal union across the whole of the North American landmass was opposed, and this partly explains why the British government maintained a policy of neutrality in the conflict, and was prepared to supply arms to the Confederacy, while British radicals, notably Cobden and sections of the working class, gave strong support to the Federal Government because of its stance against slavery.

In the nineteenth century no one would have spoken of a special relationship between Britain and the United States or of an Anglo–American world view. That was only to develop after 1880 and particularly in the twentieth century with the emergence of the United States as the world's leading economic, financial and subsequently military power. Britain's position in the nineteenth-century global order was challenged by the rise of Germany and the United States, which forced a major strategic readjustment.[19] The story of the special relationship in the twentieth century is about how that readjustment was made and its consequences. Britain concluded that it could not fight both Germany and America, and also that it could not defeat Germany without the help of the United States. In the course of defeating Germany, however, it became apparent that the British Empire was no longer sustainable on the old basis and also that Britain's position of hegemony over the liberal world order had been fatally undermined.[20]

Harold Macmillan remarked during the Second World War that Britain was increasingly compelled to play Greece to America's Rome, but as Christopher Hitchens pointed out, the real relationship was between two Romes – a declining Rome, and a rising Rome.[21] The accommodation that was reached between them and which the special relationship expressed was that Britain would acquiesce in the rise to world power of the United States and would seek to transfer its hegemonic role to the United States in order to preserve the liberal global order which remained a fundamental British interest. This peaceful replacement of one hegemonic power by another was unprecedented, and was not accomplished without considerable friction and misunderstandings, but there was no war. Instead Britain became the foremost ally of the United States.[22]

This idea of succession between Britain and the United States was widely discussed among politicians and commentators on both sides of the Atlantic in the early part of the twentieth century. On the British side, Halford Mackinder, Winston Churchill, Leo Amery, John Buchan, James Garvin, Lord Milner and Arthur Balfour were prominent advocates of the need for a new understanding; this view was shared by many Americans, among them Alfred Mahan, Theodore Roosevelt, Henry Cabot Lodge, John Hay, Henry Adams and Brooks Adams. The same idea was later applied retrospectively in the 1970s and 1980s by theorists of hegemonic stability which became for a time a popular narrative for some in the US and British political class. It treated the global order as an embryonic global polity, which required the provision of public goods by a global hegemon, to deal with the collective action problems created by the increasing interdependence of the global economy.[23] Britain had been that global hegemon in the nineteenth century, presiding over the rise of liberal economic order, formulating and enforcing many of its rules, while also acting as a model of economic and political development to which others aspired. The breakdown of that liberal world order in the First World War also saw the displacement of Britain as the world's hegemon. An interregnum ensured, because Britain although it had the political will no longer had the capacity, while the United States, although it had the capacity did not have the political will.

The process by which Britain surrendered hegemony and the United States gained it was far from smooth, and was enormously aided by the circumstances of the two world wars, which forced Britain to become financially dependent upon the United States. From the beginning of the twentieth century important sections of the British political class came to recognise that maintaining the liberal world order against the challenges it faced could only be done by involving the United States in the leadership of it, with all the implications for Britain's position which that entailed. Following the Venezuela incident in 1898, when the United States invoked the Monroe doctrine to claim that Venezuela lay within its sphere of influence, the British chiefs of staff concluded that Britain did not have the capacity to wage a war simultaneously on the eastern seaboard of the United States and in Europe. The inevitable conclusion was that American power had to be appeased, and if possible coopted.[24] Although both nations drew up contingency plans for war with the other, these were never tested, and when the United States finally became involved in world affairs as a great power it was in alliance with Britain rather than in opposition to it.

One important factor in this outcome was that it had long been the settled purpose of influential sections of the political elite in both Britain and the United States to ensure that it came about. The idea of a Greater Britain, of uniting all the disparate sections of English-speaking peoples into a grand confederation, had become popular in the late nineteenth century.[25] Anglo-America was an imagined community with both cultural and racial roots, and cooperation between its leading states was promoted as a matter of prudence in an increasingly threatening and hostile world. There were many dissenters to this vision of Anglo-America. Many British Conservatives wanted above all to sustain the British Empire and feared that alliance with the United States would require the dismantling of that Empire;[26] while many Americans were totally opposed to the maintenance of the British Empire and resolutely opposed their government becoming a support for it.[27] The strength of feeling in the United States against being drawn into the quarrels and wars of the old world was responsible for the hesitation of US administrations to become involved in both world wars.[28]

The eventual entry of the United States proved decisive to the outcome of both wars, but after the First World War the United States was not yet ready to undertake world leadership by organising its own hegemony. In the intervening period Britain, the former hegemon, attempted to reassemble the elements of its former economic, financial and naval supremacy. It failed. Naval supremacy was given up following American insistence at the 1921 Washington Naval Conference that Britain should accept parity of its fleet with that of the United States. Financial supremacy was lost following the restoration then final collapse of the gold standard in 1931. Industrial supremacy had been severely eroded before 1914, and vanished completely after 1918. Britain retained control of its Empire, but by 1939 it was ill-prepared for another major military struggle, and in the early years of the Second World War was close to being overwhelmed.

The entry of the United States into the war in 1941 transformed the prospects for the survival not just of Britain but of the British Empire. But it was clear from the outset that this survival was to be on American terms. The close alliance that was forged after 1941 between Britain and the United States saw close collaboration particularly between the military and intelligence establishments of both states, and this continued into the post-war period, and is still in important respects intact today. But the United States fiercely resisted any moves by Britain which it judged were aimed mainly at restoring its imperial power, and it also exerted severe financial pressure on Britain, which limited the capacity of Britain to preserve its imperial position after 1945 even had it had the political will to do so. The withdrawal from empire might have been even speedier than it was had it not been for the advent of the cold war, which persuaded the Americans, now ready and eager to exercise a global hegemonic role, that there should not be a too precipitate withdrawal by Britain from areas which were vulnerable to communist insurgencies.

Nevertheless it was clear that after 1945 Britain could no longer claim to be the equal of the United States, although it remained the most important military power in the western alliance, and until the 1950s the most important economic power as well. The new relationship was symbolically illustrated by the ill-fated Suez invasion of 1956, when the Anglo-French invasion force was first halted, and then withdrawn, having achieved its military objectives, by the use of American financial pressure. Britain never acted independently in such a major military enterprise again. The Falklands War in 1982 was heavily dependent on American logistical support, and it was highly exceptional. Everywhere else British forces were withdrawn and colonies given their independence. By the time of the return of Hong Kong to China in 1997 the British Empire had been reduced to a few isolated far-flung islands like the Falklands and old fortress colonies like Gibraltar.

Through this period from 1945 to 1990 the special relationship waned, especially after 1956, but it still possessed a reality through the extensive defence and intelligence collaboration between the two states. These were two extremely well-developed Anglo–American communities, which contributed a great deal to the Anglo–American world view. The special relationship also at times burst into fresh life, as in the 1980s when Britain under Margaret Thatcher proved the most reliable of all the NATO allies for the United States during the new cold war. But Britain's overall importance as a global power was much less in 1980 than it had been in 1950. It was only one of many allies of the United States, and ties of culture and race were not sufficient to outweigh hard-headed calculations of national interest. Many concluded as a result that the special relationship was now a fiction, perhaps had always been a fiction, a rhetorical device invented by Churchill and used by his successors to disguise the fact of Britain's displacement as a great power.[29]

The hegemonic stability theory has been widely criticised, and along with it the idea there was a coherent Anglo–American world view, or that Britain was ever a hegemon. In the 1880s Constantin Frantz had suggested there was something insubstantial about Britain, it was at best *eine künstliche Weltmacht*, an artificial world power.[30] Patrick O'Brien has argued that comparisons between Britain and the United States are misplaced. Britain was at best an underdeveloped hegemon, and always an unconscious and unaspiring one. Britain only became interested in hegemony when the possibilities for exercising it were fast disappearing. He sees a huge gulf between Britain and the United States as 'hegemons' in relation to their respective intentions, capacities, and the instruments at their disposal. Their institutional, military, economic and political capacities were so different that it puts the United States into a different class. The kind of hegemony Britain was able to exercise in the nineteenth century is radically different from that exercised by the US from the middle of the twentieth century.

What O'Brien overlooks is that the world economy that emerged after 1815 was in certain respects qualitatively new. It took time to recognise how new, and that it required governing and stabilising in new ways that went beyond the old ways of territory and empire, and the balancing of great powers. Britain had a foot in both worlds – accumulator of the largest territorial empire, but simultaneously the architect, however unplanned, of the new liberal world order. Britain was therefore increasingly torn between a hegemonic and an imperial logic. The modern meaning of hegemony refers not to territory and empire, but to the rules and regimes based order created by a leading state.[31] The hegemon comes to identify its own interest with the openness and stability of the larger political system, and Britain is the first major example of this.

There is also an important distinction between passive and active hegemony, between a structural position of leadership in the global economy, which Britain undoubtedly enjoyed in the middle of the nineteenth century,[32] and active management of the international state system and the global economy, which the United States practised in the second half of the twentieth century. There is indeed a gulf in capacity and intention between nineteenth-century Britain and the twentieth-century United States. But this is partly a matter of perspective. United States' capacities do look huge in relation to the state system and the global economy of the nineteenth century, but in relation to the state system and global economy of the twenty-first century they look rather inadequate.[33]

It is easy also to underestimate the influence and reach of the British model in the nineteenth century. Britain was for a time a model to the rest of the world in terms of many of the institutions it pioneered – political, financial, commercial, industrial, and legal, as well as in civil society and in ideas.[34] The British political class became convinced that the British were exceptional, and many of them also came to believe that because the Americans had so much in common with the British, they might one day become collaborators in the same enterprise.

The Anglosphere, Brexit and Trump

The Anglosphere is the latest narrative of Anglo–American hegemony,[35] developed primarily by neo-conservative circles in the US in the period since the end of the cold war, although with some British contributions. The idea behind the Anglosphere is that the United States should recognise the special contribution which the English-speaking nation, and the countries associated with them, make to US hegemony. They provide an inner ring, a line of first defence, a coalition of the willing.

They are states which are closest to the United States because they share its values, its language, and its world view.

The claims go further than this. For some time now there has been a current of writing which has celebrated the contribution of the Anglosphere to the modern world, providing the institutions which made the breakthrough to modernity possible.[36] The countries of the Anglosphere are regarded as pathfinder societies, the shock troops of modernity, which gave the world the first modern nation-state, the first liberal democratic state, the first large secular republic, and first industrial society and most recently the first information economy.[37] The Anglosphere has been more successful, it is argued, than other industrial societies in the past and will continue to be so in the future because English-speaking societies are high trust civil societies, naturally enterprising and innovative, and open and receptive to other cultures. This is what makes them economically dynamic.[38]

Proponents of the Anglosphere do not share the older ideas of some form of federal union to link the English-speaking states. They favour instead the creation of a network commonwealth, or association of English-speaking states,[39] which could foster a range of coalitions of the willing on security, on trade, and on science. What would be needed would be for the countries of the Anglosphere to recognise that their primary loyalty and identity was to their fellow members in the Anglosphere, rather than to any other grouping, such as the EU. They would identify themselves as Anglosphere countries with a special relationship to Europe, rather than European countries with a special relationship to the United States. The thinking shared much in common with Samuel Huntington who, although he showed no interest in the idea of the Anglosphere, emphasised the English roots of American identity, and the importance of affirming it.[40]

Looked at from the point of view of the United States, the Anglosphere appears as one of many strategies by which the United States seeks to maintain its hegemony over its allies,[41] and prevent any serious rival emerging. From Britain's standpoint, the Anglosphere shows how the dream of a 'Greater Britain' remains potent despite everything. The British political class is still attracted to the idea of playing a role in a larger space than a national territory can afford, and, with empire gone and hegemony lost, the link to the United States and to some share, however small, in the hegemony which the Americans have established is the favoured option for an important section of the political class. It may be a delusion, but if so it is a delusion that goes back a very long way, and still exerts considerable power. It was an important factor in the Brexit vote and the idea of 'Global Britain' which supported close ties with the US and the wider Anglosphere rather than with Europe.

The pull of Anglo-America remains strong for a section of the British political class. Every US President from Kennedy to Obama encouraged Britain to be a full member of the EU, seeing advantages in having a country as closely in step with the US as Britain was, and sharing the same perspective on world order and the need for US leadership, at the heart of the EU. which from the US perspective was a key pillar of that order and the wider western alliance. The election of Donald Trump in 2016 threatened all that. Trump openly supported Brexit, declared the EU a 'foe', identified himself with the forces of populist nationalism around the world, and sought to divide and weaken the western alliance by dismantling multilateral institutions and pursuing an aggressive America First strategy.

It is not yet clear whether Donald Trump's presidency is a passing aberration in US foreign policy, or whether it represents a more lasting shift. If it is the latter there are profound implications for the UK. Signing up to a regional bloc dominated by a protectionist US is very different from the post-war commitment to a liberal rules-based international world order and a western alliance led by the United States. It would spell the end of the Anglo–American world view which came to dominate the twentieth century.

The Free Economy and
the Strong State[1]

During the last ten years the long post-war period of expansion and stability has come to an end. We are living through a crisis that should never have happened, the crisis that Keynesian techniques and social democratic policies and institutions were supposed to have banished for ever, because they had overcome the tendency of the capitalist economy towards deficient demand and underconsumption. No slump on anything approaching the scale of the 1930s has occurred, and the pattern of economic performance has been varied, but the overall slowdown in rates of economic growth has still been marked. There has been a deep-seated crisis of profitability reflected both in declining short-run rates of return and a fall in long-term opportunities for investment. Barriers to further rapid accumulation have multiplied and determined the ground on which major conflicts have erupted: struggles over pay, new technology and employment; struggles over the size and composition of public expenditure; and struggles over trade and financial imbalances between surplus and deficit states.

The most striking feature of the new recession which divides it so sharply from the last great crisis in the world economy is the behaviour of the price level. Unemployment has been rising steadily, but it has been inflation that has repeatedly threatened to get out of control, and in the face of which economic policy-makers have appeared most powerless. Inflation is in turn a contributor to the instabilities in the financial markets, the imbalances in trade, and to the fiscal crisis of the state and has also done much to undermine the political cohesion of the major states. With the spread of uncertainty and instability it is hardly surprising that the reputation of governments for successful economic management has rapidly waned and that politicians, having benefited during the long years of boom from the identification of economic prosperity with government economic policies, now suffer from the identification of those same policies with the dismal succession of crises and failures over which they have to preside. In Britain where the problem of relative economic decline has been aggravated by the impact of the recession, no government has won reelection after serving a full term since 1959, and there has been a significant decline in support for both major parties (most notably in 1974 but still marked in 1979).

The slowdown in the pace of accumulation has provided the opportunity for a widespread rejection of Keynesian political economy and an onslaught on the policies, values and organisations of social democracy. There has always been an element among British intellectuals which has never required much inducement to join a collective stampede to the right. We are constantly being told that 'intellectuals' are finally losing faith in socialism (this follows their previous final rejection of it in the early 1950s). They have been converted, even at this late hour, to the need to resist totalitarianism and the British Labour party, and to reject the beliefs in collectivism and equality that were enshrined in the policies and institutions established in the 1940s.[2] There has also been in recent years a real intellectual change, a remarkable revival of liberal political economy through the elaboration of the doctrine of the social market economy, a doctrine which, under different labels, has made increasing headway within the Conservative party in the last ten years. The Conservative Government elected in 1979 had a group of ministers in the crucial economic ministries (Treasury, Industry, Trade, Energy), who were all adherents of the doctrine and prepared to govern in accordance with its prescriptions.[3]

The term social market economy originated in Germany from the neo-liberal ideas that were current there after 1945.[4] In Britain and America similar ideas have been put forward by a number of theorists including F.A. Hayek and Milton Friedman, and popularised in Britain by organisations like the Institute for Economic Affairs (IEA) and the Centre for Policy Studies,[5] by leader writers in *The Times* and *Daily Telegraph*, by economic commentators such as Peter Jay, Samuel Brittan, and Patrick Hutber,[6] and by Conservative politicians (Enoch Powell at first; more recently, Keith Joseph).

Although many of the intellectuals prominent in this broad tendency (often labelled, rather inaccurately, monetarist) like to imagine themselves as romantic outsiders breaking lances against the formidable walls of the Keynesian economic and political establishment, the ease with which they have penetrated the citadel and the speed with which the Keynesian defences have crumbled in the past few years suggest otherwise. At any other time the jousting between monetarists and Keynesians would probably have remained a technical debate about the best instruments for economic management. But the monetarists have not been content to carve a place for themselves within Keynesianism, but have launched a broad assault on the political forces that underpin Keynesianism, the forces and organisations of social democracy. Monetarism and economic liberalism have become linked with other ideas and movements, the most significant of which is the populist right in the Conservative party, most vigorously represented by groups such as the Monday Club and the National Association for Freedom, which are strongly critical of trends in British society since the war and are closely identified with the beliefs and attitudes of the present Conservative leader, Margaret Thatcher. The populist assault on social democracy has concentrated upon the burden of taxation, the abuse of welfare, the inefficiencies of public provision and public enterprise, and the threat to public order and well-being posed by immigrants, unions, students, and other minority groups.[7] A big attempt has been made to appeal to that section of the working-class electorate for whom the policies and organisations of social democracy have become increasingly unpopular.

The political vision of these new ideologues of the right is that Britain, having just passed through its 'watershed' election, is about to experience a renaissance of liberty and the liberal society, the creation of a new national consensus by means of which the chains of collectivism will be thrown off, the trends of the past thirty years reversed, and Britain's national and economic fortunes revived. On the left two main views of Thatcherism and the new liberal political economy are evident. On the one hand there is the strongly held belief that the underlying trend in modern capitalism is towards some form of 'corporatism' with the state constantly tending to increase its powers of direction over the economy. This treats Thatcherism simply as an ideology, a veil drawn over the real development of capitalism, and a poor guide as to how governments are obliged to behave in reality. Liberal political economy is seen as appropriate to the era of competitive capitalism but no longer relevant to the problems of monopoly or corporate capitalism. If any attempt were made to apply its principles chaos would result; the experience of the Heath Government in its first two years is often cited. Many on the left go on to argue that so poorly adapted is the ideology of the right to the problems of managing modern capitalist economies that often social democratic parties like the Labour party are better suited for it, and secretly preferred by capitalists themselves to the explicitly capitalist parties.

A second response to Thatcherism and the revival of liberal political economy is to see them not simply as ideology but as a means for reorganising the state sector in a period of recession, increasing spending on maintaining order and reducing it on certain kinds of welfare. The rolling back of the state in some areas is seen to involve rolling it forward in others. The crisis has to be policed as well as managed, and this implies a more active role for some state agencies. While there is much more to be said for this point of view than for the first it can lead to a neglect of the scope of the right-wing revival and the sources of its strength, because it focuses on the state sector and the mobilisation of populist attitudes towards welfare, immigrants and strikes. But Thatcherism and liberal political economy should not be treated as one, however important is the fact of their present linking in practice. Liberal political economy has far deeper roots and permanence within capitalist social formations and contributes ideas and programmes to the conservative 'left' as well as the 'right'. Even many of the intellectuals who currently advocate a 'social market economy' do not by any means share the populist positions of Thatcherism and are extremely unhappy that monetarism and the social market economy should appear as 'right-wing' doctrines.[8]

The role of government

One of the main reasons why the social market economy has acquired right-wing associations is because it is often regarded as a euphemism for laissez-faire economy, and because so many political issues are now defined as left or right depending on whether they involve the extension or the retreat of central government powers and responsibilities. The problem with the term laissez-faire is that it suggests a quiescent or inattentive state. Capitalist states have never been that. The crucial question is the dividing line between those areas where the state feels obliged to intervene and those where it does not. There have always been issues like the protection of property and the enforceability of contracts on which the state has never followed a laissez-faire policy. Where the dividing line comes has often been determined by political and social struggles. The importance of the social market doctrine is not that it is against all state intervention but that it wants the state to intervene less in some areas and more in others. 'Free economy – strong state' is no idle slogan, and marks the continuity of the doctrine with the tradition of liberal political economy, not a departure from it. Nobody in this tradition has seriously suggested that capitalism could do without a strong and active state,[9] although this has sometimes been obscured by laissez-faire ideologies of self-help and business enterprise. The key problem for economic liberals has always been how limits to the sphere and tasks of government should be fixed, and where the strength of the state should be concentrated. This means that there is nothing in social market doctrine that rules out collective provision of welfare or public enterprise, provided that these are justified in terms economic liberals can accept.

During the boom the theoretical differences between the social welfare or 'mixed' economy in Britain, supported by the Labour party, and the social market economy in Germany supported by the SPD were not very obvious (although the contrast in economic performance was sharp enough). There has always been a debate within social democracy about whether certain agreed ends can best be achieved through the market or through planning. The real significance of the social market doctrine has only appeared during the recession. In the vacuum caused by the discrediting of Keynesianism and the evident disarray of social democracy, the social market doctrine has provided the intellectual bedrock for the rallying of the right around a programme aimed at breaking theoretically with the universe of social democratic thought in order to establish the principles that will enable governments to break from social democracy in practice also. For the first time since the war the right has acquired a set of distinctive principles on which to base the conduct of economic policy and attempt to reverse some of the political advances made by organised labour. Social democrats, whatever their party affiliation,[10] accurately perceive the fundamental hostility of social market doctrine to their beliefs and policies, but have found themselves on the defensive because of the translation of the theoretical principles and distinctions of social market doctrine into the language and demands of the authoritarian populism of Margaret Thatcher.

At its most elementary level the break that social market doctrine seeks is with the basic standpoint of Keynesianism and social democracy. The standpoint of the Keynesian school in approaching problems of managing capitalism is that of the national economy. Social democrats have come increasingly to share that standpoint, particularly when they are in government, although they operate as well with an older frame of reference, usually when they are in opposition – the interests of the working class. Taking the national economy as the starting point for the development of a political economy, a set of principles for guiding economic policy, means adopting the standpoint of the nation-state and its agencies. This does not preclude reliance on free market methods, but it means they are evaluated in terms of their contribution to the success and progress of the national economy.

The true mark of a social market theorist is the rejection of this intellectual construction and the return to the concerns of liberal political economy – the standpoint of the market, the sphere of commodity relations regulated by law. This sphere is composed of a multitude of different markets, some of which reach well beyond national political structures, and their proper functioning is considered to be an important end in itself, as well as the best means to the achievement of certain national ends. This does not entail that adherents of social market doctrine are all internationalists and cosmopolitans, although some are. Others are passionate nationalists and British race patriots. But all accord an importance to markets and the voluntary relationships of exchange they establish, which they regard as setting definite limits to what national economic policy can and ought to accomplish.

The principles of liberal political economy on which the concept of the social market economy rests have been restated most fully and most influentially in Britain and America by Friedrich Hayek, whose writings repay careful study.[11] There is very little written by the popularisers of social market doctrine that is not already contained (somewhere) in Hayek. His thought revolves around three crucial distinctions – those between liberty and democracy, law and bureaucracy, and the market and planning. From these oppositions flow most of the practical conclusions of the social market theorists. Hayek makes it very clear that while he is by no means hostile to democracy, it is liberty that is more important. A democratic state may protect liberty, if it is properly organised, but it is not the only kind of state that can do so. Liberty is defined as 'that condition of men in which coercion of some by others is reduced as much as possible in society'.[12] Coercion by individuals can be greatly reduced if one social agency, the state, is able to punish individuals who infringe laws governing individual exchange. The problem then becomes how to reduce coercion by the state itself; the answer is the construction of a private sphere free from public interference. Such a private sphere can only come into existence if there are certain activities and rights which are protected and cannot be infringed by the government. This requires that the state as well as individuals be bound by laws (the idea of a *Rechtstaat,* or constitutional state), and that decisions of government agents be subject to legal appeal and reversal in the courts. Such a notion of liberty naturally clashes with the notion of popular sovereignty because it implies that there are many laws which should be beyond the power of a government to alter, whereas the doctrine of popular sovereignty suggests that a government elected by the people has the right to overturn and refashion all laws.

It is not surprising therefore that in the era of mass democracy and popular sovereignty, liberal political economy should frequently inspire dreams of an apolitical state – a state whose agencies are so constituted that they supply the least possible scope for interference by the temporary democratic majorities that inhabit legislatures. Montagu Norman's[13] search, as Governor of the Bank of England, for a system of central bank co-operation which would take the important questions of monetary policy out of the hands of politicians has found a recent echo in the advocacy of a Currency Commission which would remove control of the money supply from the Treasury and the Cabinet. The thinking behind such proposals is simple. A sound currency is one of the conditions for markets to function, hence for liberty to exist. 'Politicians and bureaucrats' are prone to interfere with the money supply in pursuit of other objectives, so its regulation should cease to be a matter of discretion and become a constraint within which all governments are obliged to operate.

What gives such notions credibility is that the modern state is organised in precisely this manner with many agencies, for example the judiciary, but also the military, and parts of the bureaucracy, enjoying varying degrees of autonomy from the government and constituting an orchestra which governments cannot command but must persuade to play. The great bulk of state agencies are not subject to democratic election and control and the liberal proposal is to strip away a few more functions of government and hand them to agencies who can be more readily trusted with the public interest than can politicians swayed by short-term political pressures.

An alternative approach to removing certain areas of state activity from political scrutiny and democratic pressure is the attempt to limit government activity by identifying individual rights which are presumed so fundamental that no government can infringe them and still be called free. This approach leads to Bills of Rights and written constitutions, which have enjoyed a considerable revival in recent years.[14] Robert Moss, a former director of the National Association for Freedom and speech writer to Margaret Thatcher, puts forward a list of measures which he argues should be beyond the powers of any elected government: the abolition of democracy, the banning of religious beliefs, the destruction of the family, the withdrawal of the right to own or bequeath property, and the prevention of the exercise of individual choice in health and education.[15]

The idea behind both approaches is that the preservation of liberty requires that there be very precise limits to legislation, however democratically constituted the legislative authority may be. Democracy is seen as the least harmful form of government, but still suffers from major flaws – there is for instance no 'budget constraint' to limit what the voter can vote for in the same way that there is limiting what the consumer can buy. Since voters are not obliged to consider costs, competitive bidding between the parties develops, and democratic governments come to offer more than they can deliver with serious consequences for their handling of economic policy. As Milton Friedman has put it:[16]

> The fundamental defect of the political mechanism (is that) it is a system of highly weighted voting under which the special interests have great incentive to promote their own interests at the expense of the general public. The benefits are concentrated; the costs are diffused; and you have therefore a bias in the market place which leads to ever greater expansion in the scope of government and ultimately to control over the individual ... In the economic market ... each person gets what he pays for. There is a dollar-for-dollar relationship. Therefore, you have an incentive proportionate to the cost to examine what you are getting.

Democracy therefore encourages ever greater bureaucratic interference with the privileged private sphere – the sphere of market relationships between individuals. As bureaucracy rises, so the law declines – the second of Hayek's basic distinctions. He does not suggest that bureaucracy can be dispensed with (his thought is never utopian in that sense), but he does argue that for liberty to flourish the realm of law must dominate the realm of bureaucracy. General laws, known rules that are applicable to all, must regulate social behaviour over as wide an area as possible and discretionary administrative decisions be minimised as much as possible. The essence of collectivism (what makes it, for Hayek, the prelude to totalitarianism and allows him to range welfare state and New Deal policies along the same continuum as socialism, fascism and communism) is the disregarding of the distinction between law and administration, so that law becomes not a means for checking the growth of administration but a means of facilitating it, by providing new unspecified discretionary powers for government agencies. From this flows the opposition between planning and the market. The market is potentially the sphere of free, voluntary individual behaviour regulated by law, and protected from the coercion practised either by other individuals or by the state. Planning signifies the intrusion of the unregulated discretionary power of politicians and bureaucrats,[17] supposedly acting in the national interest, in accordance with the wishes of the electorate, but in practice interfering with and reducing the only kind of liberty that is possible.

The message that bubbles from the fermenting pot of social market writings is that democracy is dangerous and can threaten liberty, so needs to be rigorously controlled and limited. The attachment of these thinkers to democracy is precarious, because during times of economic difficulty the workings of democracy are one more burden that the liberal society must carry. It becomes very hard to pursue the right economic policies because the immediate consequences in terms of unemployment and living standards, and the active opposition of many parties, organisations, and groups, soon lead to the collapse of both electoral support and the political confidence and determination of the government.

How much easier the restoration of the liberal society would be, muse these theorists, if the need to secure a renewed popular mandate and to maintain civil liberties were removed or at least suspended for a time. Great play is made in this literature of the distinction between authoritarianism and totalitarianism. Authoritarian regimes, like Chile, are regarded as far preferable to totalitarian regimes like Russia and Nazi Germany, because while they interfere with political freedoms, they do not interfere with economic freedom; trade unions are of course disbanded or repressed, but foreign investment is not interfered with and citizens are still free to own and bequeath property, and to buy and sell their products and their labour power. Nazi Germany is regarded as totalitarian rather than authoritarian, despite the evidence that, like Franco's Spain and Pinochet's Chile and Papadopoulos's Greece, the regime did not interfere with the economic freedom of private capital, but considerably increased it, by suppressing trade unions and providing stable financial and commercial conditions and a climate of expansion. The destruction of political freedom is always regrettable, according to Friedman, but clearly it is not to be compared to the far more serious loss of economic freedom.

Monetarism and inflation

Defining freedom as they do, and distrusting democracy and bureaucracy as a result, certain definite consequences follow for economic policy – a set of principles which rooted in the notion of the individual are extremely durable, capable of wide application, and form the backbone of the current intellectual revival on the right. The state has to be both strong and active – maintaining the conditions which guarantee 'individual liberty'. Three main ones are identified – the security of property and contract; free competition; and stable money. Or as Keith Joseph has put it more discursively:[18]

> Governments can help hold the ring, provide infrastructure, maintain a stable currency, a framework of laws, implementation of law and order, provision of a safety net, defence of property rights and all other rights involved in the economic process.

The contrast with Keynesian political economy is very marked. Post-war Keynesian thinking proposed four targets for economic policy – full employment, economic growth, stable prices, and a surplus on the balance of payments – and conceived managing the economy as a matter of fine tuning, of steering, of adjusting the economic aggregates through a constant process of intervention to keep the national economy in balance. The social market doctrine would still set targets, but only for those things like money supply and public expenditure that were specifically under government control. On all other detailed questions of economic policy – particularly employment, the rate of economic growth, and the exchange rate for the currency – the government would adopt a 'neutral policy stance', so disclaiming responsibility for economic outcomes.[19] Responsibility for employment would be passed to the trade unions, and responsibility for growth to the individual preferences of savers, investors, consumers, as well as external circumstances and divine providence. This means that no one need be unemployed so long as they are prepared to accept a wage low enough to make someone want to employ them, and so long as trade unions do not try to 'prevent' people taking or being forced into employment at such wages.

The centrepiece of this strategy is money, so it is no accident that monetarism has received such wide attention as the spearhead of the economic liberal assault on Keynesianism. Monetarism, however, as its advocates point out, is not a new doctrine and for most of the past two hundred years has been the orthodox approach of economists to monetary questions.[20] The ideals of sound money and a balanced budget and exchange rates fixed in terms of an incorruptible standard, gold, dominated the early development and spread of industrial capitalism.

The idea of inflation as a 'monetary phenomenon' that can be traced to an over-expansion of the money supply by governments, has long been a central tenet of liberal political economy and conservative statesmanship. The significance of the restatement of this doctrine now, lies not in its efficiency as a technical device but in its implications for policy in other fields, particularly the management of demand and the public sector. As a technical device monetarism is merely one further instrument that can and has been added to the armoury of governments seeking to keep the confidence of the financial markets and external creditors. As the 1974–79 Labour Government showed, monetarism, in the sense of firm monetary guidelines and control of public expenditure through cash limits, is quite compatible with incomes policies, price controls, industrial strategies, and all the other interventionist paraphernalia. The conversion of all governments to monetarist ideas is a concession that was forced on them in order to maintain the confidence of the international financial markets. The price of continuing to fund the public sector borrowing requirement and maintain external confidence in the currency was that governments had to reduce the domestic rate of inflation by restricting the money supply and announcing monetary targets.

For economic liberals, however, monetarism is not simply a means for easing the management problems of interventionist governments, but the key obligation laid upon government in economic policy. The link between an expanding public sector and inflation is constantly stressed – inflation being regarded as a tax that is constantly redistributing income to the advantage of the state, and therefore one of the chief sources of finance for the government, while at the same time it destroys savings, enterprise and investment (although it greatly boosts speculation). At the root of this position is the notion that only in exceptional and highly temporary circumstances (some economic liberals think the 1930s was one) can unemployment be reduced by an expansion of demand that is initiated by central government and does not make the prospects for unemployment worse in the long run. If governments cannot reduce unemployment by tolerating a slightly higher rate of inflation, then commitment to expansionary demand policies undermines prosperity both by distorting the pattern of demand (stopping firms going bankrupt that otherwise would), and facilitating a constant transfer of resources and employment into the public sector.

Keynes's benevolent tolerance of inflation as a lesser evil than unemployment is what economic liberals so bitterly attack now, because they regard any acceptance of inflationary policies as undermining the basis of the market order. When Keynes argues that 'Inflation is unjust and Deflation is expedient. Of the two perhaps Deflation is the worse; because it is worse in an impoverished world to provoke unemployment rather than to disappoint the rentier', or again that 'the right remedy for the trade cycle is not to be found in abolishing booms and thus keeping us permanently in a semi-slump; but in abolishing slumps and thus keeping us permanently in a quasi-boom',[21] he was making practical suggestions as to how governments could mitigate the impact of the Depression by using their control of the already vast state sector to manipulate the level of demand in the economy. Governments in many capitalist economies had long been interventionist, particularly in industrial and trade policy. Keynes, however, provided one of the first persuasive theoretical justifications for suspending the principles of orthodox finance, and so unwittingly provided a set of principles that underwrote the great inflationary boom of the 1950s and 1960s, which was certainly assisted, though not caused, by the relaxation of controls on private credit and the remarkable expansion of public sectors everywhere.

If the government's monetary policies are sound, then one major check to the encroachment of the public sector onto the private and to the undermining of thrift, industry and enterprise has been established. It relieves government of its responsibility for expansion and prosperity, but it does not relieve it of its obligation to make markets function as they should, nor does it rule out specific government expenditures or interventions in the private sector. The whole tradition of liberal political economy has insisted that governments have a duty to undertake the provision of 'public goods', defence being the case that is always cited. Aside from these, the presumption is that the market will normally supply goods at much lower cost than the state, and should be preferred. This argument turns on the notion of competition and the contrast between the 'imperfect' market and the 'imperfect' state – the imperfections of the state being so much greater because it has monopoly powers. John Jewkes expresses this standard liberal idea:[22]

> the efforts ... of governments to manipulate or 'restructure' a system as subtle and complex as competitive private industry are as likely to fail as would the efforts of a group of curious and playful children to repair a modern chronometer.

The industrial policy that would accompany sound money would therefore require drastic restrictions on all state economic activities, whether investment and regional subsidies, or help for mergers. It is typical of this approach that most economic liberals would think it more important to introduce competition into the nationalised industries by decentralising them and ending their legal monopoly and accountability to ministers, than by handing them back to private owners.[23] It also follows that the government's chief role in preserving competition is to ensure freedom of entry into all industries and this necessarily involves a basic commitment to free trade, particularly in view of the growth of world trade and the increased interpenetration of capital and national economies over the last thirty years.

An emphasis on free competition and freedom from state interference is often regarded as a cardinal belief of shopkeepers and small manufacturers, and generates demands for the control and dispersal of private monopolies. Social market literature, however, at least in Britain and America, sees no need to present its proposals in this way. Large-scale corporate capital is explicitly vindicated. ICI is as respectable an economic individual as a small shopkeeper and entitled to the same consideration, freedom and rights. As Hayek says with his usual clarity:[24]

> The most conspicuous gap in the following survey is probably the omission of any systematic discussion of enterprise monopoly. The subject was excluded after careful consideration mainly because it seemed not to possess the importance commonly attached to it. For liberals anti-monopoly policy has usually been the main object of their reformatory zeal. I believe I have myself in the past used the tactical argument that we cannot hope to curb the coercive powers of labour unions unless we at the same time attack enterprise monopoly. I have, however, become convinced that it would be disingenuous to represent the existing monopolies in the field of labour and those in the field of enterprise as being of the same kind ... I have become increasingly sceptical ... about the beneficial character of any discretionary action of government against particular monopolies, and I am seriously alarmed at the arbitrary nature of all policy aimed at limiting the size of individual enterprises.

After inflation and anarchy the main threat to the foundations of the market order is seen as the privileges and organisations of trade unions. The legitimacy which is accorded to corporate capital is not extended to the unions. This might seem odd since most theories that justify corporate capitalism also regard trade unions as a necessary adjunct for the efficient planning and integration of the labour force. British and American social market theorists do not take this view because they regard monopoly powers of unions in the labour markets as the principal reason for growing government regulation of the economy and lax monetary policy. This is because trade unions 'distort' relative prices in the labour market, making many activities unprofitable that would otherwise be profitable, so creating unemployment; and they impede the introduction of new technology, so reducing mobility and freezing the pattern of employment while the pattern of demand is shifting. The economy performs less well than it should, and governments under pressure to retain and win votes intervene in private industry to try to make it more efficient, and expand demand to reduce unemployment. This creates inflation, which keeps the economy prosperous for a while but at the expense of making the final crash and the scale of reorganisation more extensive.[25] What is particularly irksome for economic liberals about the existence of trade unions is that they cannot discover any economic role for them at all. Hayek grants that unions have social functions and assist in simplifying the bargaining process in large organisations, and thinks they perform a most valuable service as friendly societies, when they insure their members against illness and unemployment. But the idea that the unions have had anything to do with the permanent raising of absolute wages is vigorously resisted. They can only introduce artificial rigidities into the setting of relative wages, so pricing some non-unionists out of work and preventing the most rapid adjustment of the economy to new technology.

The basis of union power is seen as private coercion, the interference with the individual liberty of workers and employers. Enoch Powell argued in 1968[26] that union power rested on three legal privileges; the freedom to intimidate (ie, picketing); the freedom to impose costs with impunity; and the immunity of trade unions from actions of tort. Withdrawal of these three privileges would certainly revolutionise the workings of the labour market; it would certainly keep the courts busy and, if successful, it would change decisively the balance of forces between the classes in production itself. In Marxist terms it would restore the full operation of the industrial reserve army of labour. The perennial problem of labour supply in capitalist social formations – the right labour, in the right quantity, at the right price – would be alleviated.

In its attitude towards trade unions the political character of social market doctrine becomes clear. This is corporate liberalism, but a corporate liberalism which in a period of recession chafes under the extra burdens which trade unions and interventionist bureaucracies impose on their operations. Social democracy could be afforded in times of expansion; in a period of recession it suddenly becomes costly. If the economy is to remain free the state has to become strong, and nowhere stronger than in its dealings with organised labour. The unions are excused direct responsibility for inflation (since wage rises can only cause inflation if the government allows the money supply to increase to finance higher prices). But they are made directly responsible for all other ills of the market economy – unemployment, stagnation, and disruption, and so the strongest measures can be justified against them as being in the 'public interest'. Social market doctrine offers intellectual reasons to fortify the political onslaught on social democracy and its main organisational support, the trade unions.

The discipline of the market

The doctrine of the social market economy as it has been presented here can be seen to be a restatement and revival of some of the key themes of liberal political economy, which have tended to be buried with the ascendancy of Keynesianism and the increasing specialisation of economics as a branch of mathematics. What the social market economy is not, is any simple reversion to the ideal of a competitive laissez-faire economy which acts as an ideological veil for the present problems of capital accumulation. The continuing strength and new relevance of liberal political economy has to be sought in the basic structure of capitalist social formations. It is not just a question of ideological beliefs but of the social practices on which they arise.[27]

From this standpoint liberal political economy is the theory which treats capitalism primarily as a system of simple commodity production, what Marx termed the sphere of circulation or commodity exchange, 'a very Eden of the innate rights of man'. The problem of maintaining capitalism and improving its functioning is viewed almost entirely from the standpoint of how markets work. The market is viewed as the most efficient way of finding solutions to the problem of satisfying material needs because it searches out those methods of social cooperation that ensure maximum individual choice and minimum (measurable) costs. The key concerns of the social market doctrine are therefore with the basic conditions that make markets work – sound money, security of property, competition – and such is the commitment to the idea of individual exchange as a supreme value that all the problems of capitalism are ascribed to rigidities and inflexibilities in institutions and practices which prevent the market economy from working. One of the most notorious examples was the doctrine of the 1920s and 1930s that unemployment only existed because wage rates would not fall far enough. It is an idea that has been reborn today with Milton Friedman's doctrine of the natural rate of unemployment[28] – a rate which is determined primarily by the degree of 'imperfection' in the labour market, which includes such incidentals as trade union organisation, subsidised council housing, and social security benefits. Liberal economists recently calculated that the real wage necessary for full employment was now some way below the social security minimum.

The social market doctrine seeks to dispose of unemployment as a matter for political concern or government intervention, by putting the blame for unemployment on the failure of individuals and institutions to adapt themselves to the requirements of the market, whatever the cost in low wages and poverty, demoralisation and uprooted communities, lost skills and lost purposes. As Keith Joseph recently told workers on Clydeside faced with redundancy – '100,000 workers change jobs in Britain every week, and you may have to do the same'. With more than fifteen million unemployed in the major capitalist states this doctrine serves to reconcile governments and electorates to permanent high levels of unemployment.

The power of the social market economy, therefore, is not that it revives an ancient ideology, but that it restores a way of looking at capitalism and its problems which has been pushed aside by other conceptions and by the political intervention of the working-class movement, but which has revived because of the continuing importance of the sphere of commodity exchange in the actual workings of capitalist economies. Indeed this sphere has not shrunk but expanded since the heyday of the so-called laissez-faire economy, as more and more areas of social life have been commercialised, and brought within the sphere of exchange. In a fully developed exchange economy, a catallaxy as Hayek prefers to call it,[29] everything has its price, and everyone is forced to become a merchant and live by buying and selling. A nation of self-acting commodities experiences the truths of liberal political economy daily.

The grave defect, however, of liberal political economy lies in its handling of capital, in its failure to perceive how radically the structure of the market economy is transformed by first the emergence and then the development of capital within it. To the logic of individual exchange is added the logic of capital accumulation. If simple commodity production were undisturbed and everyone was a merchant or an independent producer the theory of the social market economy would accurately describe the economy that existed. But it is because it is possible for some of those independent producers and merchants to become capitalists, buying labour power, organising production, and selling commodities to realise a surplus value, that imparts a quite different dynamic to the development of the market economy. Accumulation has to work through exchange, but it gives rise to a different order of problems and a different direction to social development.

The first of these problems is class conflict between the two classes of agents that, having bought and sold labour power in the market, now confront one another in production. This conflict of interest brings the creation of defensive organisations which break with individual choice and exchange in favour of the benefits from collective action and solidarity. In acting in this way they seriously impair the free working of labour markets. Such organisations have at times been suppressed but more often allowed to become legal institutions as trade unions and political parties. Since for social market theorists labour power is a commodity just like any other ('the worker has only his productivity to sell' is a favourite aphorism) they need to recommend either repression of trade unions in order to recreate an atomised labour market or a programme of measures which will strip away the harmful effects of the concessions that have been made to working-class organisations in order to reduce and control class conflict. The problem is that the benefits of collective action and defence normally outweigh the benefits from greater individual market freedom and choice. As many of its warmest admirers have noted regretfully, the legitimacy of market institutions is difficult to secure, because the market is essentially amoral, directionless, and to some extent arbitrary in the way in which it distributes income and wealth, rewarding luck and status as much as skill and effort. An older moral justification for capitalism, which Thatcher regularly mentions, is that reward is related to effort and skill. But such a crude notion has long been discarded by Hayek and the other advanced thinkers of liberal political economy.[30] They argue that it is fruitless to seek either merit or fairness in the pattern of market outcomes. Attempts to establish either lead to grave distortions of the market order. The way in which society develops means that unfair and unmerited opportunities and rewards are constantly being created. The sophisticated message of these theorists is that the amoral outcomes of the market should be accepted by everyone as legitimate because of the general benefits everyone receives from the maximising of opportunities for individual exchange and choice. This notion has not proved a great popular success as yet, and has certainly either been misunderstood or ignored by those who write speeches for the Conservative leader.

It points to a permanent weakness in the populist ideology of self-help, because only a minority can ever help themselves to the abundance the ideology promises. If the best hopes of Hayek were realised, and the legitimacy of capitalism were to be founded no longer on the traditional authority of Church and State or on populist ideologies of Race, Religion, or Empire, but squarely on the market order, then at the very least a capitalism of some abundance would be required, so that the vast majority of the population without property, without inheritance, and without luck, would at least derive some tangible benefit, and give thanks to the great international capitalist catallaxy which rules their lives. Such abundance is hard to guarantee due to the second set of problems which capital accumulation poses for the market order – the profitability of its enterprises. Since the driving purpose of production is no longer consumption but accumulation, profits assume great importance and at the same time appear highly precarious, a quality which increases as the scale of capitalist production expands. As a result capitalist development has been punctuated by severe crises, instabilities and depressions. The relentless search for new sources of profit has brought constant reorganisation of its productive base, leading to increasing concentration and centralisation of capital, rapid technological innovation, the gradual expulsion of living labour from the production process, and the establishment of a world division of labour.

So massive has been this development of social production and so radical its transformation of social institutions that it required the growth of public responsibilities and new state agencies in many fields. The social market theorists are mostly blind to this rather obvious fact. Milton Friedman ascribes the steady growth of public spending from 1906 onwards to a misplaced charitable intent.[31] Politicians and intellectuals wanted to do good to improve society, but they chose a method which was ultimately destructive of their intentions. According to Friedman the eleventh commandment should read 'everyone shall be free to do good at his own expense'. This would solve the problem of the growth of the state. Such extreme political naivety arises from a theoretical system in which the problems of capital accumulation for the organisation of industrial societies do not appear, so the material basis for state intervention is generally not glimpsed. It is ascribed simply to political 'will' and mistaken ideas. This imposes severe limitation on the theory, because it means it contains no means for thinking through some of the most important problems confronting capitalist societies and their governments.[32]

One implication of the analysis in this essay is that the real test of the seriousness of a social market strategy in Britain does not lie in policies it prescribes for money supply, taxation and public expenditure, which only amount to an orthodox deflationary policy, but in the readiness to tackle the main obstacle to the realisation of a social market economy – the organised working class.[33] Without measures to radically reduce trade union 'monopoly' powers, the success of a monetarist policy might be seriously hampered through the creation of a level of unemployment and rate of growth that would be hard to tolerate politically or electorally. One of the structural features of the political market, which social market theorists often overlook, is that the great majority of electors are not capitalists and savers but workers and consumers. The achievement of prosperity has become something that is expected from government policies, not something that is the responsibility of each individual. Deflation if pursued for long enough may make money sound again and halt the encroachments of the state, but it will not bring prosperity unless the free functioning of the labour market is restored. The only alternative would be to introduce the kind of import controls urged by the Cambridge Economic Policy Group, the one technical policy for managing the British economy which might rescue it from heavy and continuing deflation and stagnation to protect the balance of payments and keep control of the money supply.

Social market doctrine encourages passivity and resignation by policy-makers faced with stagnation and recession. Talk is already being heard of the 'libertarian' advantages of cuts in taxes and public expenditure, regardless of whether they succeed in stimulating expansion. Whether such policies can be maintained depends on whether the populist scapegoating of trade unionists, immigrants and welfare claimants can retain sufficient political and electoral support, and further intimidate and demoralise the labour movement, so weakening its political opposition.

Political implications

The argument presented here is that the social market economy must be distinguished from the populist presentation of some of its key themes in order to understand the driving force it has imparted to the intellectual revival on the right. It now dominates much of the intellectual assessment of the modern state and prescribes policies for the recession that are rapidly becoming orthodoxy.

On the left the same clarity and fundamental rethinking has not occurred. The alliance between the state and the labour movement during the war created the political basis for the social democratic Keynesian consensus and the belief in the efficiency, desirability and justice of state action. This consensus maintained a remarkable social peace through the long boom, but now that the problems of managing capitalism loom so large it is visibly failing. The revival of the perspective of liberal political economy is one response, and is proving extremely powerful, reinforced as it is by its easy translation into populist arguments where all economic ills are seen both as the result of an overbearing and inefficient state, *and* as the work of ill-intentioned, subversive minorities who disturb order and threaten security.

The major response to this within the British labour movement has been the alternative economic strategy, a reaffirmation of the old collectivist faith of social democracy – the preference for solutions that involve greater centralisation, more public ownership and more public expenditure, all of which entail the strengthening of parts of the existing state. The fight is for a socialist incomes policy, a socialist National Enterprise Board, and socialist import controls. The extension and strengthening of the state that was achieved by social democracy and Keynesianism are regarded as part of the conquests of the labour movement, to be defended against attack and to be used as the base from which to make the next advance.

Another response starts from the ideological and political weakness of the left and seeks to recreate the oppositional and independent role of socialists and the labour movement within capitalist society. It asks why the best efforts of socialists should go towards strengthening the existing agencies of the state or to extending their powers. This response is often criticised because it appears to accept much of the case for the social market economy, at least where the attitude to collectivism and state interference is concerned. It includes both the defensive celebration of the pluralism of the free market, on the grounds that free collective bargaining best preserves the ability of working-class organisations to defend working-class interests, and the currently strong revival of interest in guild socialism, industrial democracy, and cooperatives in housing, industry and education – attempts to create new socialist communities and experiments, using the freedoms a market order provides.

These two principal responses on the left to the current recession and the political challenge from the right both attempt to mark out an independent socialist line based on a class standpoint, one in terms of policies, the other in terms of institutions, but they are often too easily contained within the universe of thought and practice they seek to challenge. One reason why the social market doctrine is proving such a successful catalyst for populist ideologies on the right is that it goes back to fundamentals. Since exchange and the market do provide a basis upon which all social relations in capitalist society can be grasped and evaluated, social market doctrine has a universal reach, constantly suggesting ways of approaching and solving practical problems. If the right currently enjoys the advantage in arguments about how to cope with the recession, it is partly because of the skilful populist translation of its key themes into grievances about taxes, strikes and bureaucracies, but it is also because the social market doctrine goes deeper than the instrumental and managerial approach of Keynesianism, and restates the case for capitalism in its most fundamental and strongest form – as a market order which maximises individual freedom and choice.

It is the case which Marx set out and analysed at length in the *Grundrisse* and in *Capital,* because he believed it was necessary to base socialist politics and socialist strategy upon a critique of it. He wanted to go beyond either a 'socialist political economy' or a socialist market economy' by providing instead a socialist critique of the assumptions on which liberal political economy was based, in order to assist the practical efforts of the working-class movement in transforming the social relations of a class society. It is this critique which needs reviving again today, now that fundamentals are once again at stake. It emphasises the sphere of production relations and the labour process as the starting point for criticising the idealised conception of the market – the individual calculation and pursuit of self-interest, and the accommodation and adjustment of interests through competition – as the model of all social relations.

Fundamentalism, in the sense of a dogmatic adherence to the writings and precepts of past thinkers, is always sterile, but fundamentalism, in the sense of a rediscovery and rethinking of the essential positions of a political movement, is a necessity if its independence and vigour are to continue. In the present period technical and managerial doctrines will not by themselves provide the basis upon which socialists can win back the initiative in arguments and struggles, and develop a coherent strategy for socialist transformation. To do this it is not sufficient to know which institutions and policies have to be defended, but also which features of capitalist social relations have to be changed for a socialist society to come into existence. How, for example, does socialist theory cope with the three oppositions which lie at the heart of the social market doctrine: democracy/liberty; bureaucracy/law; planning/freedom? Can any set of social relations other than the market limit bureaucracy and state power? Must the basic forms of exchange relations, such as money, law, and the commodity be eventually superseded if a stage of social development is to be realised which does not reproduce the social relations and individual experience of a market order? Social market doctrine urges the furthest possible extension of alienated relations of commodity exchange and, through them, the rule of capital. Socialists can regain their intellectual conviction and confidence if they confront the arguments for the social market economy by restating and rethinking the basic premises on which the intellectual and practical case for socialism has been and must continue to be based.[34]

6

Thatcherism and
Conservative Politics[1]

In April 1979 the willingness of the minor parties to sustain the Labour administration finally fell away, bringing to a close another period of dispiriting and ineffectual Labour government. Labour had returned to office in 1974 in the midst of an industrial and political crisis and at the beginning of a major downturn in the world economy. It was ejected once more following the collapse of its pay policy and its devolution policy. A Labour administration had presided over a further episode in Britain's economic decline. It had attempted to mitigate the worst effects of the recession, but increasingly without any clear policy or strategy other than day-to-day survival. The control of inflation had become its chief priority, and unemployment had risen to 1.5 million. At the general election in May 1979 the Conservatives won a decisive parliamentary majority. It would have been surprising had they not done so. Since 1959 no government after serving a full term had been reelected, chiefly because no government had succeeded in interrupting the record of deepening economic failure. The Callaghan administration was certainly no exception.

In terms of votes the Conservative victory in 1979 was less impressive. The parliamentary majority of the new government was 43, but it enjoyed the support of less than half of those actually voting (44.9 per cent) and only a third of those entitled to vote. But this was a significant advance over October 1974 when only one in three voters and only one in four electors had supported the Conservatives – the lowest level of support the party had recorded at any general election this century. The revival of electoral support for the Conservatives was most marked in England, particularly in the South and in the Midlands.[2] But the movement was not uniform. The swing of support to the Tories in Scotland and the North of England was significantly lower, and this increased still further the already marked regional bias of Conservative support. In 1955 the Conservatives had won 111 seats in Scotland and the North of England, but they only managed 78 in 1979; in the South, by contrast, the Conservatives captured 261 seats (as against 223 in 1955).

The revival of Conservative electoral fortunes therefore did not mark any great popular landslide towards them, nor did it assure them an impregnable electoral position, but it did allow the Conservative leaders to claim a mandate, and in marked contrast to the behaviour of Labour administrations, to set about the implementation of a highly partisan programme with great vigour, enthusiasm, and confidence. As a result the significance of May 1979 for many of the architects and advocates of the Government's new strategy, and for many of its opponents on the left, went beyond electoral arithmetic. It signalled the crossing of a major political watershed, the decisive break with the social democratic consensus, the marking out of a new terrain for British politics. The Thatcher Government was soon being described as the most radical government in Britain since the war, and as the most reactionary government in Europe.

This reputation rested on the programme which became known as Thatcherism.[3] Thatcherism constitutes a major new perspective and strategy for the Conservatives, although it also reactivates and continues certain traditions of the party. Its rise within the party is a response to the party's gradual long-term decline. But the Conservatives are not alone in their plight – in the last twenty years the strength of the support for both major parties had been noticeably undermined and along with it the legitimacy and stability of parliamentary government.

Thatcherism and the politics of support

The reasons for the deepening crisis of the British party system lie in the wider political and economic decline of the British state. The inability of either party to come to terms with this decline, or to reverse it, has caused a long-drawn-out crisis of identity and purpose for both of them. For the Conservatives the loss of British world power and the continuing relative failure of British industry to become internationally competitive has threatened the ability of the party to identify itself and win support either as the party of nation, or as the party of competent government and prosperity.

The dilemma for the Conservatives is acute. Ever since the rise of mass democracy it has had to rely on working-class votes, and since the 1920s it has had to maintain its working-class support against the competition of a party claiming to be the exclusive representative of the interests of that class. Since 1918 occupational class identity has been the most important factor in determining the way in which the majority of people cast their votes in Britain, yet the party which has won most general elections and which has been most frequently in government has been the Conservatives. This means that the party has always had to draw at least half its support from across that occupational class divide. Conservative leaders have generally been acutely aware of the precariousness of their position, and of the need constantly to win over working-class opinion by articulating national interests and concerns, maintaining a popular bloc, and presenting themselves as governing for the people rather than for any one section of it. But Conservatives have never been primarily a party of the nation but a party of the state. Their objective in organising and maintaining a broad national coalition has not been to force demands on government but to ensure popular support for whatever policies the Conservative leadership judge are necessary.

The party's electoral fortunes after 1880 were built upon projecting itself as the party of the Union, the Empire, and the constitution, and identifying the party with the established institutions and the symbols of national legitimacy. National issues and national causes were used to great effect to rally a substantial section of working-class and trade unionist support behind Conservatism, and the Falklands War shows that they still can. The Empire, however, has gone, the constitution is in disarray, and even the Union has recently proved unsteady. The identity of the Conservatives as the national party is no longer so automatic or so easy, especially after Macmillan and Heath had identified the party so strongly with the Common Market, and Labour had developed its own national rather than class appeal. The Falklands War tells us more about Britain's past than its future.

The end of British expansion and world power was always certain to damage the Conservatives more than their electoral rivals. As the themes of patriotism and national greatness dimmed, so the Conservatives came to rely more on their appeal and standing as the party of prosperity, the party which knew how to manage the national economy – 'Life's better under the Conservatives: don't let Labour ruin it', as the famous 1959 election poster proclaimed. This approach appeared to pay handsomely in the 1950s, when the Conservatives presided over an economy comfortably afloat in the backwash created by the boom in the world economy. In the last twenty years, however, the problem of the relative decline of the British economy and the steady worsening of Britain's economic problems, particularly since the deepening world recession after 1974, have made all British governments appear powerless. Support as measured by opinion polls, by-elections and general elections has fluctuated violently, in marked contrast with the period from 1945 to 1959, during which no government lost a single by-election until 1957.

The Conservatives particularly suffered from their spell in office from 1970–74, which saw four states of emergency, an unprecedented post-war level of industrial conflict, high unemployment, high inflation, and the spectacular shipwreck of the Government's attempt to expand the economy on the rocks of the oil crisis, the miners' strike, and the three-day week. After that experience and the earlier one between 1960 and 1964, the Conservatives could no longer very plausibly claim to be the party of prosperity and successful economic management. They were further handicapped by having moved from being the party of Empire and protection to becoming the party of free trade and Europe. The Conservatives were finding it increasingly difficult to project themselves as the defenders of the national economy, since so much of domestic capital had made their operations international and powerfully reinforced the traditional pressure from the City for free movement of goods and capital.

It is against this background that the rise of Thatcherism must be seen. The last twenty years have produced major debates and rifts within the party and at times the Conservatives have seemed on the way to becoming a party of ideology and doctrine, the very things they derided in their political opponents. Conservatives have normally prided themselves on their unity and the absence of factions and splits, which used to make the party very different from many mass parties of the right elsewhere, such as the Italian Christian Democrats. The new preoccupation of the party with ideological debate has originated from a ferment among party supporters which precedes the current recession but has been enormously amplified by it.

When the Conservatives were in opposition between 1964 and 1970, a New Right took shape in the party which was distinct from the traditional right (although membership often overlapped) in so far as it drew its strength from a rejection of the consensus around social democratic values and objectives that had been established ever since the war-time coalition. The New Right is the seedbed from which Thatcherism has grown, and is composed of two rather different strands. There is the revival of liberal political economy, which seeks the abandonment of Keynesianism and certain kinds of government intervention; and there is a new populism – the focusing on issues like immigration, crime and punishment, strikes, social security abuse, taxation and bureaucracy.[4]

Central to the gospel of the new economic liberalism is the doctrine of the social market economy and the concept of a market order.[5] These notions can be traced back a long way in liberal thought, and they have been restated with great clarity by Friedrich Hayek, the most important theorist of the new liberal political economy. He makes three crucial theoretical distinctions – between liberty and democracy, between law and bureaucracy, and between the market and planning. The ideal society is a market order in which all actions and choices and exchanges between individuals are regulated by general rules which are known in advance and apply to all indiscriminately. The existence of such general rules permits a sphere of economic liberty to arise, but only if a strong public power is organised to enforce them. Such a power must exist if all individuals are to enjoy liberty, but what safeguards can be created to prevent the public power itself from taking away the liberty of individuals? If liberty is to be preserved then this public power must refrain from trying to influence the choices and outcomes of the market, and limit itself to guaranteeing the framework (in particular property and contract, free competition, and sound money) and removing all obstacles to the unimpeded development of free choice.

The doctrine reconsecrates the divide between the public and the private. All collective measures to regulate industry or to provide welfare benefits or services are infringements of individual liberty and substitute the arbitrariness of bureaucracy for the impersonality and even-handedness of the rule of law. The results are both morally wrong and economically inefficient. The doctrine does not suggest that there should be no state welfare services and no collective provision. A *social* market economy is intended to guarantee certain minimum standards. But beyond those the freest possible scope is to be given to private initiative, individual responsibility, and free choice. Such an economy is expected to generate high and rising levels of welfare spending, but only because an increasing proportion is provided through the market itself. Market outcomes are preferred to planning outcomes and have to be accepted, whatever they are. There is no justification for any collective redistribution of resources, except for the provision of certain minimum standards, and this is because there is no sense in which market outcomes can be regarded in ethical terms at all. Social justice resides not in what individuals get, but in the rules governing how they get it. In return for economic liberty, individuals must reconcile themselves to great and often arbitrary inequalities.

The doctrine supplies a most powerful set of ideological weapons against social democracy. For social democracy involves constant interference with market outcomes in the name of popular sovereignty and the claims of the community over the individual. The new liberal political economy attacks this at its root. The economic demands of the New Right are not primarily tactical or opportunistic but are grounded in ideological principles which are fundamentally hostile to the principles of social democracy. This can be seen by looking at the main economic doctrines proclaimed by Thatcherism. There are three key propositions:

1 The public sector is an unproductive burden on the wealth-creating sector in general and on taxpayers in particular. From this follows the need to drastically reduce public expenditure and to return as many services in the public sector as possible to the market and to the family. The aim is first to prevent the real cost of public services rising at a time when output and productivity are stagnant or falling. But it is also to permit the kind of tax cuts that are intended both to secure electoral support and to encourage the revival of private enterprise, the regeneration of the capitalist class, and to restore family and individual responsibility.

2 The chief aim of government economic policy should be maintaining price stability by firm control of the money supply. This is because control of the money supply is believed (though many economists doubt it and events in 1980 belied it) to be the one thing that governments actually can control in a capitalist economy. The money supply can be controlled if governments steadily reduce their borrowing, so removing any temptation to resort to the printing press to increase revenue, and if government sets monetary targets and controls the volume of private credit in line with them.

To believe that governments can and should control the money supply means believing that governments are directly responsible for whatever rate of inflation exists. Wage demands by trade unions, according to monetarist doctrine, do not by themselves raise or lower the rate of inflation, so income policies and the involvement of unions in discussions about general economic policy are entirely unnecessary. But trade unions are directly responsible for the level of unemployment if they insist on a level of real wages which firms cannot pay. Trade unions are also responsible for stagnation and a slow rate of growth to the extent that they are capable of resisting rationalisation and reorganisation of the labour process aimed at raising productivity. The effects of high unemployment and stagnant or falling living standards can create political pressures for an expansion of money supply which governments find hard to resist. If they give in to them, higher rates of inflation will result, which will indirectly be the consequence of trade-union action. But it is a key doctrine of monetarism that government efforts to realise a higher level of employment or a faster rate of growth by expanding demand (the mainstream Keynesian prescription) are doomed to failure because of the existence of a 'natural' rate of unemployment and a 'natural' rate of growth. These are determined not by the level of demand but by the institutional organisation of markets. Expanding demand can only raise the rate of inflation.

3 The role of government in the economy should accordingly be confined to maintaining the conditions for markets to function properly. Stable money is one such condition, security of property and enforceability of contracts are others. In addition governments have the duty to intervene to remove any obstacles which prevent markets functioning properly. Taken together these tasks do not imply a small role for government or a non-interventionist role. On the contrary it signifies not a withdrawal but a redirection of state energies and goals, and constant vigilance to maintain and extend the market order. The free economy requires a strong state.

Thatcher and Heath

How far do these doctrines and the strategy which is based upon them represent a break with the strategies employed by Conservative governments in the past, and in particular by the Heath Government? There are certain undeniable resemblances between the two. Both the Heath and Thatcher administrations presented programmes which ostensibly broke with central priorities of the social democratic consensus. Both followed periods of ineffectual Labour government and intense internal ideological ferment directed against social democracy. Both began with aggression and confidence. The Heath Government proclaimed a withdrawal from intervention, it ended assistance to lame ducks, it conducted a selective massacre of the quangos, it committed itself to reducing public expenditure and proposed a series of new charges on public services, and it put forward a wide-ranging programme of trade-union reform.

But these similarities should not blind us to the essential differences. Although Heath's policy appeared at the time to mark a break with social democracy, in retrospect it can be seen as a last attempt to operate within its confines. The Heath Government sought to put

British capitalism on a new course, to arrest national economic decline, and make British companies competitive within the EEC. Heath's competition policy was an attempt to overcome the specific competitive weaknesses of British capital. The means tried at first were certainly influenced by the new current of social market thinking, but once these failed to produce faster growth because of the scale of unemployment and working-class resistance they created, the Government made significant changes in its policies (the so-called U-turns), and opted instead for statutory wage controls, increased public expenditure and much greater intervention in industry. The basic aim remained the same – achieving a higher rate of growth in the British economy. Faster growth was seen as indispensable to enable British capital to succeed in the EEC, to ease the problems of funding the public sector, and to restore the Conservatives' reputation for successful economic management to which their electoral fortunes since the war had become so closely linked.

The Thatcher Government began operating in very different circumstances. The world recession had changed the framework of political calculation. Since growth in the world economy can no longer be assumed, the whole basis of social democratic politics – increasing public provision and a measure of redistribution financed out of steadily expanding output – has been undermined. The recession has at the same time made the relative decline of the British economy potentially catastrophic. British capitalism is now the weakest national capitalism among the developed capitalist states. In the last world recession in the 1930s it was one of the strongest, and did not suffer the worst effects. The loss of empire is only partly offset by the good fortune of North Sea oil.

One consequence of Britain's deteriorating economic position has been that a significant section of the Conservative leadership has now broken with social democratic politics. It does not believe social democracy can be resuscitated nor does it wish it to be, although it disagrees on how fast and how far the party should proceed in dismantling it. This is the reason for a remarkable paradox. The Heath Government, committed to making social democracy work, was prepared to take greater political risks and pursue more radical policies in its first two years than the Thatcher Government attempted.

The Thatcher Government in its first two years proceeded cautiously, particularly as regards trade union reform. But although it is more cautious there is also much less chance that it will indulge in the kind of U-turns the Heath Government performed. This is because those kinds of U-turns could only be performed by a government still committed to the social democratic goals of full employment and growth. The Heath leadership flirted with the doctrines of the social market economy as techniques for improving efficiency and raising growth. Since they were only seen as techniques they could always be changed. For Thatcher and her supporters they were not techniques but principles. The resolve of the Thatcher Government was much more solid because clear alternatives were so much less evident.

A majority of Thatcher's Cabinet believed from the outset that a Thatcherite economic strategy would fail. But they were also convinced that the strategy would have to be seen to fail comprehensively before a major change was possible. The confidence of Tory leaders in their traditional governing style of pragmatism, compromise and flexibility has temporarily left them, as a result of the seriousness of the plight of the national economy and the precariousness of their own party's electoral fortunes. If Thatcherism succeeds in restabilising the economy, shifting the political balance permanently and creating a new and broader working-class constituency for the Conservatives, the bulk of the present leadership, reared amid the constraints and procedures of social democratic politics, will speedily adapt to ruling in the new set of circumstances. On this basis Thatcherism was seen as worth exploring and supporting for a while. But some of Thatcher's Conservative critics still fear that a resort by the Conservatives to doctrinal and partisan politics and an explicit reopening of long-settled class questions risks a similar response from the left, and a dangerous polarisation between the two main parties. This could endanger a political system which, though outwardly characterised by the elaborate rituals of adversary politics, inwardly relies upon a fundamental consensus derived from the institutional continuity of the state and the acceptance of both party leaderships when in government of the need to govern within the constraints which the permanent agencies of the state do not hesitate to point out to them.

Thatcherism and Conservatism

In one sense at least Thatcherism is very alien to Conservative traditions – because of its acceptance of certain of the doctrines of liberal political economy as a guide and criterion for its policies. This supreme old bourgeois party once took pride in distancing itself from the most characteristic expression of bourgeois ideology. The Conservatives presented themselves as the party of the national economy and the state, the party of the community rather than the market, the party of protection, imperialism, paternalism, and intervention, not the party of free trade, cosmopolitanism, self-help, and laissez-faire. Before 1914 Tory hostility to liberal political economy was pronounced, particularly because it promoted individualism and questioned the authority of established institutions, and encouraged selfishness and competition between individuals and classes. The Conservatives believed that there were some things worth dying in the last ditch for – the Union of the United Kingdom and the rights of property being two – but the preservation of an egalitarian and competitive market order was not among them. The Conservatives were always renowned for their hostility to doctrine and their lack of principle. Churchill, after he had left the Conservatives and joined the Liberals over the issue of free trade in 1904, described his former party as: 'a party of great vested interests, banded together in a formidable confederation … corruption at home, aggression to cover it up abroad; the trickery of tariff juggles, the tyranny of a party machine; sentiment by the bucketful; patriotism by the imperial pint; the open hand at the public exchequer, the open door at the public house; dear food for the million, cheap labour for the millionaire.'

The hostility of Conservatism to liberalism and individualism was modified in the 1920s with the breakup of the old Liberal party and the entry of large numbers of former Liberals, including Churchill himself, into the Conservative party. But although these new elements created a new ideological bloc – Liberal Conservatism – and helped tip the balance of party opinion towards orthodoxy in economic policy, it did not mean the implanting of a doctrinal liberal political economy in the party. The Conservatives became the dominant governing party and increasingly the umbrella party for the defence of all the interests of property against the threat posed by the rise of Labour at home and world revolution abroad. This meant that in the 1920s the party accepted the main lines of the foreign economic policy of the British state – the commitment to free trade and the international role of sterling, the recreation of a world liberal economic order, rather than a protectionist and self-sufficient imperial federation. This was accompanied by domestic policies emphasising financial retrenchment. Neither policy involved, however, a crusading commitment to restore and develop the principles of a market order, rather an acceptance of policies that had become orthodoxies and which expressed the enduring facts of Britain's external position and the influence the doctrines of liberal political economy had exercised over economic policy-making for seventy years.[6] The imperial and protectionist wing of the party regained its ascendancy after the collapse of the gold standard in 1931, and finally imposed tariffs, but its dream of an imperial federation proved unachievable, and the Empire itself was fatally undermined by the Second World War.

The revival of liberal political economy which began in the 1960s and which has become steadily more influential in the Conservative party, is different from the liberal Conservatism of the 1920s in that it does not reflect an established policy consensus, but on the contrary seeks to break with established policies and challenges the essential assumptions and priorities of economic management which social democracy and Keynesian economics established. One of the most striking features of present British politics is the absence of protectionism in the Conservative party. This favourite refuge of right-wing parties in the face of world depression and external economic challenge holds only the National Front at present in Britain. Some of the most nationalistic British politicians are also those most committed to the social market doctrine. This reflects in part the far-reaching accommodation and subordination of British strategic and economic interests to those of the United States since 1941, and also the degree to which British capital has been internationalised. A viable protectionist strategy would necessarily attack the interests of the dominant multinational and financial sectors of the British economy. Like many other states Britain no longer has a unified national bourgeoisie and its governments must balance the needs and pressures of the national economy and national electorate on one side with the needs and pressures of international capital on the other.

A liberal foreign economic policy has been maintained by all governments in Britain since the war. The new social market doctrine is aimed not at the external policy but the internal policy of economic management. It criticises, first, the techniques of demand management whose purpose is to achieve full employment by smoothing out cycles and raising the rate of growth; second, the considerable increase in the volume and range of public expenditure and public involvement at all levels in the economy.

Liberal political economy is not a single doctrine, and Thatcherism represents a specific combination of its key elements – the family, economy and state. The emphasis of Thatcherism upon a free economy, an unfettered market order, is what has attracted most comment and which appears most at variance with traditional Conservative ideology. But the other terms of the trinity are interpreted in ways which are much more closely linked to traditional Conservative ideological concerns. All versions of liberal political economy prescribe a strong state, able to establish the highly artificial conditions of a market order, but whereas a strong state can also be a minimal state, Thatcherism seeks a greater not a smaller role for the agencies charged with internal security and external defence. The state is to be rolled back in some areas and rolled forward in others. Similarly Thatcherism does not seek to reduce but to enlarge the scope of the family. Its emphasis upon family responsibility is accompanied by an emphasis upon family morality and the need for greater discipline and higher moral standards. The real innovation of Thatcherism is the way it has linked traditional Conservative concern with the basis of authority in social institutions and the importance of internal order and external security, with a new emphasis upon reestablishing free markets and extending market criteria into new fields.

Through its revival of several of the key doctrines of liberal political economy and the restating of them in terms of populist causes, Thatcherism created a much closer identity than has been usual in the Conservative party between the ideologies that mobilise support and the principles that guide the formulation of government policy. Thatcherism reactivated what has been for the last fifty years one of the central features of the Conservative party's appeal to the electorate – its hostility to the state sector and to the trade unions. The party has long won the support of significant numbers of workers in the private sector and in non-unionised occupations. In its policies in government, however, between 1951 and 1964, the Conservatives proved far from hostile either to the trade unions or to the state sector, and showed themselves quite content to negotiate with the former and to administer the latter. In electoral terms Thatcherism repaired the ravages wrought by the highly interventionist policies of the Heath administration, and reestablished the identity of the party as the 'anti-state' party on economic policy. This was the same strategy the Conservatives pursued in opposition in 1964–70 or indeed between 1945 and 1951. What proved different after 1979 was that once the Conservatives were back in government this electoral ideology, far from being discarded having served its purpose, formed the basis for the economic programme the Government attempted to implement.

What nobody foresaw was the opportunity created by the Falklands War for Thatcher to combine the populist anti-state programme with the traditional One Nation theme of strong leadership and national greatness. By this means the criteria for judging the Conservatives' economic policy were changed. Fitness for national leadership, resoluteness and determination came to count for more in 1982 than the actual consequences of the policies themselves. Strong leadership appeared for a time to be compensation enough.

Thatcherism and the politics of power

Thatcherism has so far been examined as a bid to establish a new electoral coalition and as an ideological break with post-war consensus politics and with post-war Conservatism. But when we pass from the glitter and media dazzle of electoral politics to the prosaic realities of government, a different question arises. What is the relationship of Thatcherism as an ideological doctrine to Thatcherism as a programme for government? In the realm of government, questions of strategy become not ideological but technical questions. Policies are expected to work and to produce results. Is Thatcherism simply a response to popular discontent with social democracy and discontent within the party to post-war Conservatism? Is it mainly a means by which the legitimacy of the state is refurbished, or does it also represent a shift in the kind of policies that can be implemented? Is it in fact a response to certain objective interests of the British ruling class?

The general interests of the ruling class are the preservation of capital and the conditions for its reproduction and accumulation. But the practical political task of defining these general interests and identifying these specific conditions gives rise at any one time to several different strategies for securing them. Such strategies have to embody not merely economic realism but political realism; they must take account of the complex field of pressures within which governments move. The sources of such pressures include the state bureaucracy, organised interests, and foreign governments. Governments must also keep the confidence of the agents in the main markets which sustain the conditions for the economic and political reproduction of capital; these include the financial, commercial, labour and political markets. The task of knitting together policies that are practicable at the level of government with a programme and an electoral image that can win popular endorsement for the government falls on the political parties.

British capitalism as a whole is weaker than at any time this century, but there is a clear division between those sectors of business, including much of the financial sector and the multinational sector of big business which operate internationally and remain internationally competitive, and those sectors which are confined entirely to the national economy and have found it increasingly difficult to compete. The international and financial sectors of British capital have long reinforced the policy of maintaining the openness of the British economy. But the consequence of that policy, particularly in the post-war era, has been to accelerate the decline of the national economy. At the root of this relative decline have been the persistent lower levels of productivity and the associated higher rates of inflation and falling share of world trade. After the failure of the different attempts in the 1960s and early 1970s to pursue a modernisation strategy and following the onset of the world recession after 1974, the comfortable economic decline of the years of the long boom has threatened to become something much more serious. Political positions and technical prescriptions have polarised, and three broad strategic options have emerged.

1 *Deindustrialisation.* This is the line of least resistance. It is the necessary consequence of pursuing the kind of disinflationary policies which have been in force since 1976. They entail high and rising unemployment, and stagnant or falling output, and the progressive run-down of all those industries unable to compete internationally. A slow demoralisation sets in as factories close and public expenditure is subjected to round after round of cuts. The political effects of high unemployment are contained because it is confined to certain areas, and because some of its effects can be offset by using North Sea oil revenues to maintain unemployment benefit at a sufficient level, and by strengthening the police. At the same time the service sector and the high-technology sector of the economy expand, and these together with the multinational and financial sectors earn enough export and rentier incomes to keep a sizeable part of the economy afloat. The industrial decline is inexorable and no determined attempt is made to reverse it. Trade union membership begins to fall and the unions are outflanked rather than confronted, their rank-and-file demoralised and divided by the disinflationary policy. The problem of the strength of the British working class is dealt with by shifting the economy away from those sectors where union strength is greatest. This is at the expense of Britain remaining a major industrial power, but the policy carries least political risk and least challenge to established interests. In particular the openness of the British economy to world trade and world capital is not questioned. What is incalculable is the effect of the world recession and the possibility that deindustrialisation is turned from a slow retreat into a headlong rout.

2 *Industrial Regeneration I.* The second option is much bolder. It is to use the political opportunity of the present recession to restructure the industrial base of the economy and to confront and materially weaken the power of organised labour. Trade-union power is not outflanked but confronted and destroyed. The internal barriers to accumulation are removed, particularly the ability and willingness of

workers to resist changes in work practices and the introduction of new machinery, and the tax burden of the state is reduced through major cutbacks in the collective provision of welfare, health and education. Such policies would mean an open and bitter onslaught on trade unions as independent organisations on a much bigger scale than was attempted by the Heath Government. The major risk involved is the likely scale of resistance to direct attacks upon the unions as organisations. The Conservatives have unhappy memories of the last such attempt. A second drawback is that removing the internal obstacles to internal accumulation is no guarantee of success so long as the external obstacles remain.

3 *Industrial Regeneration II.* The third option, associated with the Labour Left, seeks to achieve industrial regeneration through a large increase in state involvement in the economy – state investment, planning agreements, and wage controls. They would have to be accompanied by import and foreign exchange controls, as well as a continuation and extension of egalitarian welfare measures, particularly to assist in redeployment of the labour force. This kind of strategy has never been resorted to in Britain except during war, in 1916 and 1940. It involves the suspension of the market in many areas and an attempt to manage the economy through direct collaboration between the classes. Such strategies, when implemented, are often seen in retrospect as being in the long-term interests of capital, are rarely in the short-term interests of individual capitals, and so are employed only in conditions of extreme crisis. This is partly because such strategies provide openings to the left as well as the right and can precipitate more radical challenges to the social order.

There is scarcely any need to remark on how distant Thatcherism is from this last option. For many reasons such a programme is anathema to almost all sections of British business and would only be accepted in dire circumstances. Big and small capital alike are willing and often anxious for specific and limited state interventions to reduce their costs, but a wholesale programme of national reconstruction is very different. Ideological suspicion of the state is still very strong. In these circumstances only the second option – the social market strategy – is a plausible alternative to accepting further deindustrialisation. A rollback of the state, a reduction of taxes, a restoration of incentives, an end to bureaucratic meddling in industry's affairs – all these are measures strongly supported by all sectors of business. The priority given to the control of inflation is also welcomed.

But while all sectors of British business deploy the language of economic realism, endorsing the social market strategy in practice has not been so easy. The ambition of the social market strategy is breathtaking. It seeks decisively to reverse all the gains and encroachments which the labour movement has made both politically and industrially in the last fifty years. It was always inevitable that if it were to be seriously implemented it would hurt not only organised labour but would squeeze large sections of British capital and eliminate some of them. This is the strength of the strategy – that it recognises that if state intervention and class collaboration are ruled out, the only way for a thoroughgoing revival of British capitalism is for a decisive defeat of shop-floor power.

Yet political support for it from business remains relatively limited. The low-risk first option is preferred, particularly by those firms which already operate internationally and do not welcome any policy that might threaten their British operations. The Conservatives found the deindustrialisation option already well established when they entered office in May 1979. The Labour Government had pioneered monetarism in Britain, and was the first administration to set monetary targets, introduce cash limits, and attempt the containment of public expenditure, at the same time that it emasculated its own industrial strategy and resisted pressure for import controls. This disinflationary policy, which necessarily meant the abandonment of the goal of full employment was carried through on the basis of formal cooperation between the trade unions and the government, an agreement not threatened until the Callaghan Government's last winter.

The first two years of the Thatcher Government were a remarkable period in British politics. The Cabinet was uneasily balanced from the start between a small group of committed monetarists, whom Thatcher appointed, to the main economic ministries and the bulk of the leadership, many of whom had held office under Heath and whose instincts inclined them to traditional Conservative policy. Their attitude may be summed up as governing according to circumstances rather than principles, making careful assessment of the political balance between classes and interests, being prepared to make concessions where necessary, and only pursuing those lines of action for which support can be won and which do not threaten the security of the state. Since 1940 this had meant governing within the limits imposed by social democracy, using government powers to promote full employment and prosperity, accepting a considerable public sector alongside the private, financing high government spending on welfare out of high taxation, and conciliating trade-union power.

The bulk of the leadership in 1979 would have been quite content to continue the main line of the Labour Government's policy. But Thatcher herself and her closest supporters were determined that the social market strategy should have a trial. From the start, however, they were confronted by an extremely difficult tactical problem. They had to choose between fighting a war of manoeuvre, aimed at storming all the important positions of social democracy simultaneously, or settling for a much more drawn-out war of position, gradually transforming the context within which government operated. Hayek himself urged the first tactic, the *Blitzkrieg,* on the grounds that the Government would run out of time if it did not act quickly and decisively. He suggested a referendum on the issue of abolishing all trade union legal immunities granted since 1906. He also favoured policies to precipitate a short but very severe slump by the sudden withdrawal of all subsidies to industry, by drastic reductions in public expenditure, and by an immediate return to 'sound finance'. The rewards would be considerable; trade-union power would be broken, the market order would be repaired, and major cuts in personal and business taxation would be possible.

Some of the advocates of the social market strategy were undoubtedly tempted by the idea of a *Blitzkrieg* on social democracy. But the divisions in the Conservative party and the Cabinet, and the scale of the political risk involved in openly confronting the labour movement, persuaded Thatcher to settle for the less dramatic war of position, a series of engagements on many separate fronts. The Government aimed to press forward whenever conditions were favourable. But because the struggle as a result became so diffuse it became difficult to maintain any overall strategic control, and numerous reverses began to accumulate. This was made worse because, although the Government had in practice chosen to conduct a war of position, much of its rhetoric suggested that it was actually engaged on a war of manoeuvre. It kept taking credit for the recession by describing it as a necessary medicine which the British economy had to take if it was to recover, while constantly intervening to stop the recession developing into a slump.

The attempt to implement the social market strategy was also gravely weakened because of the Government's adherence to inconsistent objectives. The manifesto commitments to lower direct taxation, higher defence spending, and higher pay for the armed forces and the police were implemented immediately, although they were obviously inconsistent with the overriding priority to bring inflation down by establishing firm control over public spending and the money supply. So, too, was the surprising decision to honour the Clegg Commission pay settlements for other public sector workers.[7] The consequence was that the Government lost control of public spending and was forced onto the defensive right at the beginning of its term of office. In order to maintain its financial objectives it found itself obliged to allow first interest rates and then taxation to rise.

By the time of the third Conservative budget in 1981 Britain was suffering a more severe recession than any other major capitalist economy. Unemployment was close to 2½ million while manufacturing output had fallen by 15½ per cent during 1980. The recession had outflanked and significantly weakened the organised labour movement and strengthened the hand of management. A major shakeout of labour was in progress throughout British industry, and the number of industrial disputes had fallen sharply. Inflation was moving towards single figures and interest rates were beginning to come down. But on most other fronts the Government's strategy was in disarray. It had proposed only relatively minor new curbs on trade-union powers, and had publicly backed away from a confrontation with the miners in February 1981. So trade-union power had not been broken, only contained. The Government had also failed to control either public spending or the money supply. The borrowing requirement in 1980–81 was £4 billion more than planned, and the money supply (sterling M3) was twice as high as the target announced in the 1980 budget. This failure to control public spending reflected the earlier decision over the Clegg awards and tax cuts, but also the extra cost of dole for the unemployed and the successful resistance to public spending cuts mounted by Cabinet ministers in the Autumn of 1980, and by the series of decisions to continue supporting major industries such as British Leyland and the British Steel Corporation.

A pragmatic Tory government at this stage might well have abandoned its monetarist doctrines and launched a new industrial strategy. But this was not the path Thatcher chose. She decided instead to stick to the financial targets announced in the first two budgets and to seek to realise them by making whatever short-term increases in taxation were necessary. This decision created a storm of protest from business, the unions and the media, and widespread unease in the Conservative party. It meant that the burden of taxation two years after the Conservatives took office was significantly higher than it had been under Labour. Even the proportion of direct taxation was higher. After a period which had seen such steep falls in industrial output and such large rises in unemployment the Government introduced a budget which, combined with falling pay settlements, was sure to severely reduce living standards over the next two years.

The 1981 budget was a notable expression of the internal contradictions of Thatcherism. As one of the Treasury ministers admitted, the retreat which had been forced on the Government meant that if the Conservatives were to realise their 1979 manifesto pledge to cut income tax, they would need to achieve new additional cuts in public expenditure of £6,000 million. Most commentators concluded that the budget was the last chance for maintaining even the financial part of the strategy. The defeats on so many fronts and the numerous predictions that unemployment was set to climb above three million, and that the living standards of those in work which hitherto had been protected were about to fall sharply, faced the party with the possibility of an electoral collapse. Only a major economic recovery could rescue the Government, but the Government had hardly begun to do the things which in terms of its own strategy it had to do in order to bring such a recovery about.

By the spring of 1981 the fate of the Thatcher Government was closely tied to the question of when the slump would bottom out, and how broad-based the recovery would prove to be. The electoral and political bases for Thatcherism were visibly declining and other electoral alternatives, particularly the possibility of an alliance between the Liberal party and the Social Democratic party (SDP), a breakaway from Labour, looked formidable.[8]

The arrival of the Thatcher Government marked the moment that the break with social democratic politics was explicitly acknowledged. The disinflationary strategy which had led to a shrinking industrial base was no longer justified as an expedient and temporary tactic, but as the only possible course of action for restoring prosperity. The political and economic pressures in 1981 made the failure of this strategy highly likely, yet like so many of its predecessors the Government hesitated to take more radical measures which seemed certain to be needed if the British economy was to be successfully reconstructed.

What transformed the political prospects of the Government and for the Thatcher experiment was not its economic policies but the Falklands War in 1982. The economic record on which to fight an election remained extremely weak through 1982. Inflation had come down but at the expense of the deepest slump since the war from which there were still no sure signs of recovery. Nevertheless there was some evidence that the Government was not widely blamed for the recession, while at the same time it received enormous credit for its handling of the Falklands War. Despite the bleak economic prospect the Conservatives had become favourites to win the next election. Victory would give the Thatcher experiment the second term its adherents had always thought would be necessary to carry through the full programme. A second term would give the opportunity to consolidate the new directions for British politics which had emerged in the 1970s and marked the ending of the post-war consensus on the right balance between the public and private sectors, on the priority to be given to full employment, on universal welfare provision, on free state education, and on trade union rights. But in 1982 the decline had not yet been reversed and the question remained open as to whether the Government would succeed in achieving the radical transformation of Britain which some of its members desired.

Economic Growth and
Political Dilemmas[1]

It is now a possibility that the market oriented polyarchies
cannot much longer reconcile the necessary privileged
demands of business with the demands of strong unions
and the welfare state ... Britain has already succumbed to
a fundamental problem in irreconcilable demands.

Charles Lindblom[2]

In writings completed shortly before he died, in particular *Social Limits
to Growth*, Fred Hirsch developed a rich and suggestive analysis of the
political dilemmas confronting the affluent consumer societies of the
advanced capitalist world.[3] His work was part of a broad and pessimistic
reassessment of the economic and political prospects of western
capitalism following upon the onset of new economic difficulties in
the 1970s.

This mood contrasted sharply with the considerable optimism
and complacency about the future of the capitalist economy and the
legitimacy of its political institutions that existed in the 1950s and early
1960s. The principal threat faced by western capitalism at that time was
generally perceived as an external one – the militancy and economic
challenge of the Soviet bloc. The internal problems appeared to have
been overcome. No one expressed this mood better than Seymour
Martin Lipset in a famous passage in *Political Man*:[4]

The fundamental political problems of the industrial
revolution have been solved: the workers have achieved
industrial and political citizenship; the conservatives have
accepted the welfare state; and the democratic Left has

recognised that an increase in overall state power carries with it more dangers to freedom than solutions for economic problems.

These lines were written in the middle of the longest and most rapid period of expansion that the capitalist world economy had ever experienced. In the 1930s neither the friends nor the enemies of capitalism could envisage a new period of sustained expansion. The ideologies of left and right were starkly opposed. Even those, like Keynes, who believed there were better ways to manage capitalism to avoid under-employment of resources did not foresee an early return to economic growth. The key economic and political question was mass unemployment and whether it should be blamed on workers' resistance to wage cuts, on the capitalist organisation of production, or on the mistaken policies of financial orthodoxy pursued by governments.[5]

The issue was never resolved in Britain in the 1930s. There was economic recovery but little decline in the numbers unemployed. Keynesian remedies were proposed by Lloyd George and the Liberals, by Oswald Mosley, and by Harold Macmillan, but none were adopted.[6] Yet, following the transformation wrought by war, a new world economic order and domestic political order emerged; with the sudden quickening of growth in the 1950s, Keynesianism became formalised as a set of ideas justifying the increased economic role for the state that was visible everywhere. It was recognised as an integral part of the new social democratic consensus. For a time the achievement of this consensus appeared to ensure economic growth and political legitimacy, an easing of the problem of how the national income should be shared out, and a weakening of political ideologies and social conflict.

The reasons for the undermining of this consensus is one of Hirsch's central themes. He wrote in a post-Keynesian era at a time when the easy optimism of the 1950s had already been dispelled, when ideology and social conflict had burst out with new vigour, and when many of the problems that were thought to have been banished forever had begun to reemerge. The clearest sign that the Keynesian era was at an end was shown by the return of mass unemployment to every western capitalist economy after 1974, and the inability of governments to prevent it.

The discrediting of Keynesianism was already well under way, however, before it was clear that the long boom was over and that a new major slump had commenced. The challenge to Keynesian techniques of economic management, and the undermining of the social democratic consensus on such issues as the level of welfare spending and the need to protect trade union rights, arose because of the earlier failure to halt inflation. The gradual acceleration of inflation prompted many new analyses of the conditions which favoured economic progress and social stability. One major new perspective that grew in prominence was the revival of liberal political economy by Hayek and Friedman and its application to the problems of the public sector by the new school of public choice theorists.

Hirsch's theory of capitalism

Hirsch's work is especially interesting because while it shares the assumptions of an 'economic approach' with these theorists it is more aware than many of them are of its limitations. Hirsch has criticised much orthodox economic analysis of public policy for confining itself to a model of rationality appropriate only to private economic goods. This makes all the interesting questions 'residual categories', outside the scope of the analysis. What Hirsch is chiefly concerned with is precisely the relationship between economic and non-economic factors. In particular he seeks to develop the idea that the very manner in which economic behaviour is organised in a capitalist economy produces results which undermine the non-economic conditions which must be sustained if capitalism as a mode of economic organisation is to persist. His analysis and conclusions are of general application and universal interest but they have a special relevance to British experience, since Britain has displayed in an acute form the contradictions and dilemmas which Hirsch describes.

He identifies three features of modern capitalism that are central to the way it works. The economic dynamism of the system arises from the organisation of economic activity through a system of free markets. This enthrones the needs and wants of individuals as the spur for production and enlists the self-interest of each individual in producing the goods and services which are demanded or for which a demand can be created. Demand and supply are balanced through the adjustment of prices which signal changing wants and changing costs. This system of decentralised markets, which rests upon free exchange between independent, equal and sovereign individuals, has its counterpart in a political system whose legitimacy is founded upon 'universal participation'. All individuals are citizens, equal members of the political community, with rights to join voluntary associations, to speak freely, and to vote. The sovereign power of the state derives from the people and, once properly constituted, its claims to authority over its citizens and their social arrangements are potentially unlimited.

The third crucial aspect is that for all its affluence capitalism has not yet abolished scarcity. So the distribution of what is produced to different classes and groups remains highly contentious.

The problem as Hirsch sees it is that the organisation of the economic system and the organisation of the political system supply conflicting criteria for distributing the goods and services produced by the capitalist *economy* which may undermine its legitimacy. If distribution is organised through the market individuals will be rewarded according to the value of what they have to sell or, as Hirsch prefers to put it, according to their market power – derived from chance, heredity, talent, skill, and ownership of specific resources. This will create a highly unequal distribution of income. The heights of consumption and civilised living are in practice available only to a few, although formally open to all. Only abstinence from consumption and a dedication to accumulation by capitalists may make this inequality tolerable. Hirsch refers to the celebrated passage in *The Economic Consequences of the Peace* where Keynes reflects on the success of nineteenth-century capitalism:[7]

> Europe was so organised socially and economically as to secure the maximum accumulation of capital. While there was some continuous improvement in the daily conditions of life of the mass of the population, society was so framed as to throw a great part of the increased income into the control of the class least likely to consume it. The new rich of the nineteenth century were not brought up to large expenditures, and preferred the power which investment gave them to the pleasures of immediate consumption. In fact it was precisely the inequality of the distribution of wealth which made possible those vast accumulations of fixed wealth and of capital improvements which distinguished that age from all others.

The second criterion for distribution is political and derives from the egalitarian basis of the modern democratic state. Equal citizenship leads to demands for equal treatment and equal access to the necessities, the luxuries and the opportunities of life. Markets too require equality, for if markets are to function successfully then exchange must be equal and fair and the rights of buyer and seller must be respected and enforced. But the political criterion of distribution goes far beyond legal equality at the point of exchange and introduces notions of equality of opportunity and equality of outcomes. The first means ensuring that all possible handicaps are removed in the competition for wealth and status; the second suggests that beyond this there should be rough equality between the goods, the wealth and the status individuals actually attain.

The results of the two principles of distribution are clearly very different in the amount of inequality that is aimed at and Hirsch is right to argue that each tends to subvert the other. This is because of the third aspect he identifies – scarcity. If goods and services are scarce their distribution according to market power will create such inequalities that it undermines the legitimacy of the political order which is based on the equality of all citizens. This may create political hostility to the principle of free markets. On the other hand if the political criterion is allowed to dominate, political legitimacy will be secured but economic efficiency may be lost, because material incentives may not be sufficient to encourage the performance of many essential economic functions. In time this will in turn undermine the basis of political legitimacy since the people will be denied the steady flow of goods and services which they have come to expect governments to guarantee.

In political terms Hirsch is describing the political options as many saw them in the 1920s and 1930s for the future development of capitalism. On the left there were those like Tawney who argued that the conflict between the two criteria should be resolved in favour of the political by relating the distribution of income to service and function rather than to market power.[8] This would make the economy collectivist rather than individualistic and would mean the supersession of the acquisitive society. On the right there were those like Hayek and Schumpeter who argued that since the political criterion threatened economic efficiency and economic liberty the overriding need was to restrain universal participation and lessen the scope for democratic policy-making, and in particular its interference in the workings of the market economy.[9] Marxists tended to agree with Hayek on the grounds that the distribution of the national product and the nature of state action were inseparable from the way in which the economy was organised. The state was a capitalist state and redistribution, they argued, would not be allowed to threaten the inequality in ownership of wealth that sustained private accumulation of capital.[10]

The post-war settlement

The actual compromise that emerged in the 1940s was different from any of the options as they were perceived in the 1930s. Post-war reconstruction was initiated by the war-time Coalition Government which was presiding over the highly centralised and controlled war economy. The political price of a national war effort was a commitment to post-war reconstruction, the main aspects of which, as popularly perceived, were that there should be no return to mass unemployment and there should be much more generous and comprehensive social security provision. The two characteristic products of the reconstruction programme were, first, the Beveridge reports and, second, the 1944 White Paper on full employment. The experience of a war economy in which resources and labour were fully employed made it seem intolerable there should ever be a return to the conditions of the 1930s. As many of the leaders of the 'new Conservatism' acknowledged, government must henceforward be conducted on new principles. Quintin Hogg exaggerated when he told the House of Commons in 1943 that 'if you do not give the people social reform they will give you social revolution' but there was a wide appreciation that the emergence of a new consensus between the political parties on domestic political issues would have to concede many of the long-standing demands of the Labour movement.[11]

The real nature of the consensus between the parties did not emerge until the 1950s when the Conservatives returned to office and found themselves presiding over the British economy during the world economic boom. The period of reconstruction in the 1940s was a time of austerity and financial discipline, and only gradually were the controls on the economy relaxed. Labour implemented the plans of the Coalition Government and the Conservatives offered only mild criticism. There was much fiercer resistance, however, over Labour's plans to extend public ownership beyond the public utilities. The nationalisation of iron and steel, followed by the proposals to nationalise sugar, chemicals and cement, was taken as a clear sign that the thinking of the Labour leadership was still directed to the goal of a gradual socialisation of the main centres of private capital and the replacement of private profit by public service throughout the economy. The general expectation was still that after the reconstruction boom the old problems of stagnation and unemployment would reappear. Tawney's views that redistribution was necessary to create equality and that public ownership was the best way to end unemployment had been reinforced by the experience in the 1930s of an economy that had apparently ceased to grow.

The social democratic consensus that blossomed in the 1950s was not initially because of a genuine consensus of view between the Labour and Conservative parties. Labour had not renounced its commitment to clause IV or the desirability of a progressive socialisation of the economy; it had significantly enlarged the public sector both in terms of public enterprise and public spending on welfare, and it had brought the trade unions into the policy-making processes of the state. But it had failed to reduce very much the economic and financial power of private capital (the compensation for nationalised assets had been particularly generous), and through its support for NATO and acceptance of American leadership, the traditional international orientation of British economic policy and British business was consolidated, not challenged.

There was an important change for policy, however, which has been well summarised by Hirsch: '[since 1945] organised labour has … exerted a counterforce to the extra-parliamentary influence traditionally commanded by business and financial interests through both their market responses and their informal contacts with government ministers and officials.'[12]

Rethinking on left and right

This idea that there was a stalemate between labour and capital in post-war Britain rather than an active consensus is widely shared on right and left. But the stalemate, by defining the constraints on policy so tightly, contributed to rather than hindered the continuity of policy between different governments while the ideological argument about capitalism and socialism was bypassed by the new ideology of growth. For many social democrats a steady increase in the wealth of the community offered a means to effect redistribution without attempting to transfer ownership or risking massive social conflict. Many Conservatives, forced to relinquish the conception of Britain as the centre of an empire and a leading world power, found some compensation in their new role as successful managers of welfare capitalism. If inequalities of wealth and power could no longer be outweighed in popular consciousness by the more potent experience of belonging to the imperial nation and participating in the story of Britain's expansion overseas, the constant and increasing flow of goods and services backed by universal welfare benefits might achieve the same. Conservatives were not disposed to be defensive in the 1950s or to 'appease' socialism. They believed they had won. The 'Middle Way' that Macmillan had written about in the 1930s was being substantially achieved. Macmillan had wanted to see an industrial society, the strategic control of which would rest with the state while the tactical management remained in private hands; public and private industry would work together in a mixed economy. Laissez-faire, Macmillan had argued:[13]

leads inevitably to socialism. The only anti-socialist programme that has any chance of success is the organisation of a social and industrial structure which shall be neither capitalist nor socialist but democratic; where the wage earner shall be neither slave nor tyrant but truly and in the widest sense partner.

Three general election victories in the 1950s convinced many Conservatives that capitalism could become popular again because of its evident success in creating wealth and distributing it.[14] The role of the state was to maintain a high level of demand in the economy, ironing out fluctuations, and ensuring that everyone was provided with a minimum standard of living. The government should be committed to managing the economy so that unemployment remained low, prices stable, expansion brisk, and the balance of payments in surplus. The main engine of wealth creation was to be the private sector but the public sector had an important supporting role and, after ritual denationalising of steel and road haulage, the Conservative Governments between 1951 and 1964 made no moves to contract the public sector. They made no serious attack on welfare spending nor did they try to cut the taxes necessary to sustain it. They brought forward no proposals for changing trade union law. They were content to preside over the status quo they inherited. Growth made other choices for a time unnecessary.

The counterpart of this new Conservatism was the rethinking of the traditional socialist positions by leading Labour party intellectuals such as Anthony Crosland and John Strachey. Strachey's argument was rooted in the preoccupations of the 1930s when he had been a prominent Marxist intellectual. In the 1950s he argued that capitalism might not have changed but its prospects had been transformed by democracy. If the people were sufficiently well organised politically then the power of the modern state could be deployed to counter the inherent tendency of capitalism to stagnation, mass unemployment, and growing inequality. Keynesian techniques of economic management could ensure prosperity, full employment, and growth, while public expenditure programmes could both assist in sustaining a high level of demand and in redistributing the wealth that the economy was creating. If democracy weakened, capitalism would again become a malign destructive system, but if the democracy remained strong and the popular forces vigilant, then the prospect opened of a successful capitalism purged of many of its former failings and serving the public welfare.[15]

Crosland's position went beyond this in several respects.[16] He argued, first, that the modern economy was no longer capitalist. Major institutional changes, such as the divorce of ownership from control, the changing class structure, the growth of the public sector, and the elimination of poverty, made the old socialist analysis based on class conflict and exploitation redundant. Second, he argued that socialists were often confused between means and ends. Equality was the ultimate end which all socialists were seeking. Nationalisation was at best a means of realising equality, sometimes an important one, but not to be mistaken for the goal of socialist activity itself. In modern circumstances, Crosland argued, equality could be secured better by other means. If economic growth could be maintained the transformation of society which socialists sought could be achieved far more painlessly than had previously been imagined. An expanding public spending programme, funded by progressive taxation, could ensure a gradual redistribution of wealth and power and a gradual approach to equality of opportunity.

What was central to Crosland's new political agenda for the Labour party was growth. The engine of this growth, as for the new Conservatism, was to be the private sector. This sector had to be organised through markets, it had to be competitive, and it had to be profitable. It was to be supported by a state using Keynesian regulatory techniques as well as fiscal and monetary policies to sustain growth and maintain high levels of employment.

Despite an underlying stalemate between the two leading political forces it did appear in the 1950s that the legitimacy of the modern capitalist order would not be challenged so long as growth was sustained. A greater and greater priority came to be attached to growth, reaching its climax in the 'growth mania' of the 1960s. This was the period when Britain's relatively slow rate of growth was pinpointed and became the focus for major political concern. Few politicians were prepared to question that governments could and should raise the rate of economic growth. Competition between the parties ensured that the 1964 election was fought on rival programmes to modernise British institutions and to raise economic efficiency and productivity by means of major new government initiatives and spending programmes – in fields such as planning, prices and incomes, technology, education, roads and health.

The modernisation strategy of the 1964 Labour Government built on measures already introduced by the Conservatives. At stake between the parties was not ideology, but which party could prove more competent managers of the national economy and which could raise the British economic performance at least to that of its European competitors. The parties were responding to the growing gap that was emerging between the expectations of the people for higher living standards and the sluggish economic performance. Perhaps that was understandable. With unemployment at such low levels and inflation a minor irritant, it was natural that the focus should have been on increasing wealth.

The British disease

What is so striking about recent British politics and economic policy is how quickly the consensus on the need for growth collapsed and how complete was the failure to solve the problems of the economy within the constraints of post-war social democracy. Both parties competed to provide better economic management. But to the electorate each new attempt seemed worse than the one which preceded it, each new government more incompetent than its predecessor, and each in turn was rejected. Government changed hands in 1964, 1970, 1974 and 1979. The problems mounted and the political resources for dealing with them dwindled. Not surprisingly the result, especially after such a long period of technocratic rather than ideological politics, was to detach a growing part of the electorate from loyalty to either party, amid signs of new political and ideological polarisation of opinion among party activists.

The reason for Britain's turmoil in the 1960s and 1970s has sometimes been ascribed to a malignant tumour – the British disease – which has been eating away at the nation's vital parts. Observers, journalists, and politicians have recognised this illness in different symptoms. At times it has been the British balance of payments, at times pay, recently it has been public expenditure which, slipping its leash, has allegedly been dragging the whole nation towards a totalitarian future. This atmosphere of disquiet in the British political class contrasts with the much greater calm and confidence that has been observed among the people.[17] Yet there is a good reason for the anxiety. The failure of the modernisation strategies of Macmillan, Wilson and Heath has exposed the fragility of the consensus which has governed post-war policy and has reopened many of the unsettled questions concerning the special institutional character of British capitalism, the antique British state, and the manner of its integration in the world economy, as well as the institutions and goals of the British Labour movement.[18] In Britain, growth came to be regarded as the solvent for the tensions that Britain's earlier political and industrial history had created. By the end of the 1970s it had become clear that there was little life left in the old political formulas of Macmillan and Crosland, though Crosland himself protested against this conclusion. In *Socialism Now*, published in 1974, he wrote:[19]

> Extreme class inequalities remain, poverty is far from eliminated, the economy is in a state of semi-permanent crisis and inflation is rampant. All this undoubtedly belies the relative optimism of *The Future of Socialism* ... Do these setbacks to our hopes demonstrate that the revisionist analysis of means and ends was wrong, and the Marxist analysis which it sought to rebut was right?

He thought not. The onset of economic problems was peculiarly British and the revival of Marxism was limited to Britain. 'If one examines the western world as a whole there are no clear signs of a new and fundamental crisis. ... No long-term crisis comparable to that of the 1930s seems imminent.'[20] Many commentators said the same.

The difficulty for Crosland in admitting that a new slump had begun was that it undercut the assumptions on which his politics had been based. It would have indicated that in certain fundamental respects capitalism had not changed and that all the questions about redistribution in a period of zero growth and the transfer of ownership that he had declared irrelevant might have to be reopened. Both liberal political economy and socialist political economy reemerged as radical perspectives in the 1970s, while the social democrats of all parties looked temporarily disillusioned and bereft of ideas. But new ideas and new analyses have begun to flow again. One major concern has been to identify why the priorities of post-war policy have been abandoned and what needs to be done to restore a coherent social democratic programme, which in the spirit of New Liberal and social democratic writings of the past seeks to sustain a capitalist organisation of the economy, not by the subordination of the people to the disciplines of the market or by the coercion of the state, but by the fullest possible extension of democratic citizenship and participation that is compatible with an efficient and productive economy.[21]

Hirsch has played an important part in this reorientation by showing how the process of growth in a modern capitalist economy is not the simple smooth process it is often taken to be. Instead it generates conflicts and instabilities which threaten its survival. One expression of these tensions is inflation. What Hirsch offers is a non-monetary account of the causes of inflation and how it can be traced back to the competitive struggle for individual and group advancement. World recession makes the consequences of the growth failure devastating, because it heightens the struggle over distribution and potentially threatens the legitimacy of the entire social order for large parts of the population. But the importance of Hirsch's analysis is that he argues that growth has not halted because of some unfortunate external shock such as the quadrupling of oil prices in 1973. The process of growth itself created the tensions which destroyed it. This might seem to align Hirsch with Hayek who has also argued that the long boom was increasingly artificial, maintained by methods which seriously distorted the pattern of demand and the distribution of labour and made a slump inevitable.[22] The methods, according to Hayek, were Keynesian monetary policy, which tolerated deficit financing and excessive credit creation, public expenditure programmes which restricted the scope of economic activities, and the political and legal tolerance afforded trade unions, which prevented many markets from functioning properly. The conclusions for policy which Hayek and New Right opinion in the Conservative party have drawn are that Keynesianism must be abandoned and the market order restored. This means severely curtailing the range of intervention which public agencies currently undertake, obliging governments to adopt a neutral policy stance renouncing responsibility for either full employment or economic growth.[23]

The social market critique of British economic policy in the 1960s and 1970s focuses on the role played by the state in the economy. On this view the commitment to maintain high levels of employment and faster rates of growth meant that when these did not materialise the immediate response by government was to intervene still more in the market – by pumping in extra demand, by giving new incentives and subsidies, by setting up new public agencies to supplement and often supplant market forces.[24] The social market critique of Keynesianism was never better stated than by James Callaghan at the Labour party conference in 1976:

> We used to think that you could just spend your way out of a recession and increase employment by cutting taxes and boosting government spending. I tell you in all candour that that option no longer exists, and that in so far as it ever did exist, it worked by injecting inflation into the economy. And each time that happened the average level of unemployment has risen. Higher inflation, followed by higher unemployment. That is the history of the last twenty years.
>
> (Blackpool, 28 September 1976)

It is ironic that the only clear examples of such reflations are the 'Maudling boom' of 1963–64 and the 'Barber boom' of 1972–73. Both were in part prompted by an increase in unemployment (although in neither case had unemployment reached even one million). Both were also deliberate attempts to use the machinery of demand creation to stimulate a faster rate of growth in the economy, to break out of the depressing cycle of slow growth, low investment, and low productivity. In monetarist terms both made possible a sharp acceleration of inflation.[25] These governments and their advisers were not blind to the inflationary risks of their policy. Their 'crime' was that they gave a lower priority to maintaining sound money than to full employment and economic growth. This meant that they were always inclined to deal with inflation not by introducing sound money policies but by attempting to suppress it by intervening still more in the market economy. The favourite device of the 1960s and 1970s was incomes policy.

Incomes policies have always been anathema to monetarists and New Right opinion. The reason is simple. As Hirsch explains, 'there is no doubt that the internal logic of a continuing incomes policy involves progressive departures from market principles in regulation of the economy'.[26] This is because incomes policies invite political negotiation about many aspects of economic policy and the establishment of political criteria for determining relativities and rates of pay. For social market theorists the resort to incomes policy to suppress the inflation which the excessive creation of money has unleashed is a fateful step which can progressively lead to the destruction of the market order and to the establishment of a command economy. For they note that every incomes policy has eventually been sabotaged by both employers and unions. Accepted with varying degrees of reluctance at first, every incomes policy in Britain was more and more resisted as time went on, until finally it collapsed.[27] Each succeeding incomes policy tended therefore to be wider in scope and more draconian in its proposed penalties. The logical outcome was plainly suspension of the market altogether in the determination of prices and wages.

The failure to control inflation was accompanied by mounting unemployment and a declining rate of growth. They naturally appeared to be linked together. Certainly the failure to evolve a permanent framework for the regulation of prices and incomes was one of the most important aspects of the failure of the modernisation programme. The pay explosions in 1969–70, 1974–75, and 1978–79, which followed periods of severe restraint, undermined faith in social democracy and in political methods of resolving economic problems, and raised fears that the country was becoming 'ungovernable'.[28] The new wage militancy which inflation and the frustration of hopes for higher living standards generated was directed as much at the social democratic order as at the capitalist order and this aroused forebodings not just on the centre but on the left of British politics also. For the industrial militancy was often aggressively sectional, it was focused primarily on questions of pay and there was little wider sense of class solidarity or a general working-class political interest beyond the competitive struggle for higher pay. In retrospect it has been argued this made such militancy extremely fragile and transient.[29] It played its part in undermining the credibility of social democracy and opened the way to deflation and the rigours of monetarism.

As inflation accelerated and the modernisation strategy in all its different forms fell apart, so the polarisation of political opinion proceeded apace and so new ideologies and doctrines emerged to shape the debate. The stark contrast between capitalism and socialism was once more openly posed, the social market strategy of the Conservative New Right confronted the alternative economic strategy of the Labour left. Since 1975 the New Right has been in the ascendancy and a prolonged assault on the institutions and policies of social democracy has begun. But social democracy, precisely because it was embedded in specific institutions and did arise on the basis of a particular balance of political forces, is not proving as easy to dislodge as if it had been simply a set of policies, ideas, and ideals. The social democrats of all parties have been regrouping not just politically (the most dramatic instance being the formation of the SDP in 1981 and the establishment of an alliance with the Liberals),[30] but also intellectually, searching for an analysis of what went wrong with British economic policy which does not lead to monetarist and social market conclusions.

Reforming capitalism

Hirsch offers important signposts in this search since he draws quite different lessons from Britain's recent experience of inflation, rising unemployment, and stuttering growth than does Hayek. This is because he rejects the naive faith in markets which is widespread, although not universal, among monetarists. The failure of capitalism to maintain high employment and a high rate of growth is blamed by New Right opinion on social democracy – on external interference with the workings of markets. Hence their programme: establish sound money by squeezing inflation out of the economy, no matter what the short-term consequences are for employment and output; at the same time improve the long-term prospects for employment and output by reducing public expenditure as a proportion of GDP, and therefore the burden of taxation, by curtailing all government interference in the market economy, except the essential upholding of the rules under which markets operate; and end the power of trade unions to oppose managers' 'right to manage', and their political power to commit governments to Keynesian techniques for managing the economy, interventionist policies, and high public spending programmes.

In Hirsch's view what all this fails to see is that Keynesianism is not a matter of bad economics, as Milton Friedman thinks,[31] or of wrong policy advice which can be corrected by the exercise of political will, however indomitable; nor is the power of trade unions something that can be combated by dreaming about a sudden resurgence of faith in the values of a market order. As Hirsch notes, the importance of Keynesianism, quite apart from its status as technical economics, was that in the circumstances of mass democracy and universal political participation it provided the missing legitimacy for a predominantly capitalist system. It held out the prospect of an economy that was so managed that every citizen could look forward to reasonable security of employment and income, to an improving standard of living, and to widening opportunities. Keynesianism as an economic doctrine proclaimed that these outcomes were within the technical competence of governments to provide and should become its responsibility to ensure. Success in achieving these outcomes became the criterion by which political parties were to be judged by the electorate. If governments now disclaim responsibility for growth and for jobs on the grounds that they cannot guarantee them, how is social order in the widest sense to be maintained?

Sound money policies guarantee one kind of social order by defusing the explosive effects which inflation can have upon a market economy, but at the cost of prolonging and intensifying the slump. It defends existing concentrations of wealth and privilege by increasing inequality and consigning ever larger numbers into long-term unemployment, hence poverty. The plight of this growing surplus population cannot be relieved either by emigration – that avenue has long been closed – or by public spending, for it is an essential part of the doctrine of sound money that public spending should be curtailed and reduced. The grim cycle of monetary squeezes to halt inflation, rising unemployment, falling government revenue, and cuts in public spending, leading to renewed deflation of demand, causes disproportionate damage and hardship to some parts of the economy and some social groups, notably the populations of the inner cities.[32] The more such a cycle is repeated the greater the risk of breakdowns in social order, hence the greater the resources given to security forces to contain them. There is a drift towards a heavily policed democracy; social order for those with jobs and property increasingly entails the repression of those without. In an economy in which competition is increasing for positional goods, the long-term effects of denying access to them, by denying the opportunity to compete for them to an increasing part of the population, must have explosive effects. Liberty in these circumstances can have a high price.

Those who value democracy more than liberty are uneasily aware, however, that there is much resentment against many public agencies, against the remote bureaucracies that administer welfare programmes, and the nationalised industries. There is resentment against the burden of taxation and considerable resentment towards those who are unemployed, particularly if they are Black. There is also little confidence that orthodox Keynesian policies will create growth again.

One solution to this problem has come from the Liberals who have argued over a very long period that the institutional basis of the economy has to be recast if legitimacy is to be restored. In particular they advocate radical measures of industrial democracy based on coownership schemes.[33] Many similar ideas for workers' cooperatives have been put forward in recent years.[34] In Hirsch's terms the value of such reforms would be to give individuals a stake in industrial society not just as consumers of its products but as producers as well. This might moderate at least some of the competitive pressures which the present division between employers and employees, managers and workers, creates.

The main defect of this solution is that it signals a retreat to individualism, even if the individual units are now cooperatives. Leaving aside the enormous practical difficulties of transforming the present economy and its giant enterprises in that direction, such an approach is unlikely to deal with the problem that Hirsch outlined. Western economies suffer from too much individualism rather than too little. According to Hirsch, the political direction in which western capitalist states will have to move if they wish to avoid the dangers of a lurch towards authoritarianism is towards regulation of individual wants, the placing of limits upon individual competition, and the removal of certain goods from competition altogether.

Hirsch does not spell out the implications of this in any detail. But it seems clear that he favoured not a contraction of the present public sector but its extension. Nothing could be more disastrous for social cohesion in Hirsch's model than the present steady drift towards the privatisation of health care and education, since both these goods embody in his terms significant 'positional' aspects. Though he does not state it openly the logic of his position would appear to favour a significant widening not contraction in the number of goods provided publicly and the winning of political consent for the payment of minimum incomes to all irrespective of work performed. This might have the effect of restricting the scope for individual economic striving, at the same time countering the estrangement of those without jobs and property from the political and social order, as well as building in most powerful automatic stabilisers of demand for the products of increasingly automated industries.

Such a programme would mean a more egalitarian society than exists at present and a much larger transfer of income through the state fiscal apparatus than currently exists. The obstacles to it are obvious enough. But a more immediate objection is that it is unnecessary. The doubling of unemployment three times in twenty years has not had the catastrophic effects many prophesied and politicians used to fear. The division and hostility between employed and unemployed has been one of the central supports for monetarist policies. The frustration of expectations about jobs and growth was accepted in the 1970s and early 1980s with remarkable calm. Electoral opinion became highly volatile, but, apart from the 1981 inner-city riots, there was relatively little overt protest about what was happening to the economy. It became common to speak of a politics of declining expectations.[35] Under the Thatcher Government industrial militancy weakened and extra-parliamentary protest was considerably less than it had been under the Heath Government ten years before. Might not the problem of growth breeding inflation simply be solved by a long period of no growth or even declining real output?

The problem, however, is not so easily disposed of. Capitalism has always been an expansionist system, constantly seeking out new technologies, new markets and new needs. As the division of labour has widened and deepened, the whole of industrial society has become a vast interlocking interdependent mechanism, the need for political and social equality of all members of the community has become both a requirement for further expansion and a demand pressed fiercely by the disadvantaged and the organisations representing them. The slump of the 1930s in Britain was also a period of relative quiescence and the continuation of the routines of customary life, but it was succeeded by war and the far-reaching social and political changes of the 1940s which made possible the boom. In periods of slump, restructuring to permit accumulation to proceed extends beyond the economy to social and political institutions as well. From this perspective egalitarian policies which redistribute wealth and enlarge the public sector, though not in themselves sufficient, are nevertheless necessary conditions for recovery to start and be sustained and for the legitimacy of the market order to be maintained. This was the truth which Fred Hirsch saw so clearly and analysed with such precision.

8

The Crisis of Conservatism[1]

The Conservative party has always been one of the great certainties of British politics. It has been so dominant throughout the twentieth century that some observers have begun to speak of this period as the 'Conservative Century'.[2] Between 1945 and 1995, the Conservatives formed majority governments for thirty-two years and eight months – 65.6 per cent of the time. Centre-left governments have been uncommon, and have rarely lasted long. The Conservatives, by contrast, have often enjoyed long, uninterrupted spells in office. They won three consecutive general elections between 1951 and 1964, and four since 1979. Labour by contrast has never lasted in government for two full Parliaments.

At times, this remarkable ascendancy has suggested the kind of dominant single-party system which has been experienced in Japan, Sweden, or Italy. But the dominance which the Conservatives have enjoyed has not rested on any great record of national advance. Apart from the successes in two world wars, it has been associated with failure: economic decline and imperial retreat. The dominance of the Conservatives has rested on their command and understanding of the British state; this venerable institution has sometimes seemed on the verge of foundering, but it has survived into the last decade of the twentieth century with many of its more curious features still intact, the last major *ancien régime* and multinational imperial state left in Europe.[3]

The identity of the Conservative party is inseparable from the history of this state. It has been the state's supremely flexible and adaptable instrument. In the last three years, however, the party has been plunged into the deepest crisis of support it has ever faced. There has even been speculation that it could suffer the fate of the Canadian Conservatives who were reduced to two seats in the 1993 general election. Given the lead which Labour has currently established in the polls, the capacity of the Conservative party to recover before the next election is widely doubted, and many commentators predict that the party could be out of office for more than a decade. Kenneth Clarke, the Chancellor, went still further, baldly stating that if the Conservatives were foolish enough to elect John Redwood as leader in place of John Major it would be out of office for a thousand years.

Are the current difficulties of the party a passing phase or do they reflect deeper problems both for the Conservatives and for the British state? The evidence is contradictory. Many of the former foundations of Conservative hegemony have been eroded, and the Conservative party is deeply divided over Europe and in many ways no longer a coherent or credible governing force. This suggests that the era of Conservative dominance may be coming to an end. But there is no great popular tide behind a radical alternative. The passion and conviction in British politics is still mostly on the right. If the centre-left parties miss this opportunity to reshape the British state, they may find that the future belongs to a new and reinvigorated populist Conservatism.

End of an era?

The present signs of crisis for the Conservatives are plentiful. Electoral support has collapsed, the party has been riven by factions and open conflict, the authority of the leadership has been gravely damaged, and the party has been facing a steep decline in both its membership and its funds.[4] Matters had reached such a low point in 1995 that John Major decided to resign the leadership and stand for reelection, hoping to reassert his authority over the party. His move advertised the deep divisions that had emerged within the party over its future policy and direction.

Major's weakness is partially the result of his own and his party's poll ratings over the last three years. When Major succeeded Thatcher in 1990, the support for both the Conservatives and their leader substantially increased. Thereafter, although the Conservative rating was to decline, Major remained popular, running a long way ahead of his party. This lasted up to, and for a short while beyond, the 1992 election which the Conservatives unexpectedly won. The headline polls had underestimated their vote. Trust in the Conservatives to run the economy better than Labour and an upturn in personal economic expectations were the decisive factors.[5]

All this changed very quickly after the election. The key moment was Britain's forced exit from the Exchange Rate Mechanism (ERM) on 16 September 1992, dubbed 'Black Wednesday'. Since then, the Conservatives have consistently been between fifteen and twenty-five percentage points behind Labour in the polls every month. The previous record for such a gap occurred under the Wilson Government in 1968–69, but lasted only seven months. Since 1992, not only have Labour often risen above 50 per cent support, but in 1994 the Conservatives sank close to 20 per cent, their worst ever showing. Major also achieved the lowest ever leadership ratings, lower even than Margaret Thatcher at the time of the poll-tax riots.

Poll results, particularly mid-term ones, are often dismissed. What has been significant about these results is first the scale of the gap which they register, and second the length of time over which this pattern has persisted. Nothing comparable exists in British polling history. Large-scale events, like the Falklands War, tend to affect poll-ratings for approximately six months. The ERM exit is still affecting ratings three years after it occurred. A structural shift in the electorate's perception of the Government seems to have taken place.

The poll findings have been confirmed by actual election results. The Conservatives no longer seem able to win a by-election no matter how safe the seat. In this Parliament every by-election in a Conservative seat has been lost. The party also suffered heavily in the European Parliament elections in 1994, when its vote fell to 27.9 per cent in Great Britain, and it lost fourteen of its thirty-two seats. In the council elections in May 1995, its national share of the vote was even lower (25 per cent), and it lost sixty councils and two thousand councillors. It was left with control of only eight councils. The party has been unpopular before, and seems in part to be sharing the fate of many incumbent governments around the world. But the scale and persistence of the setbacks is breaking records.

A second sign of disarray has been the factional disputes within the party and the inability of the leadership to impose its authority. Since 1963, the Conservatives have moved from a system in which the leader emerged through a process of consultation and sponsorship to one of election by the parliamentary party. The change was initiated by the disorderly informal contest which developed for the leadership at the 1963 party conference, following the announcement of Harold Macmillan's retirement. The first election held under the new rules, in 1965 when Heath defeated Maudling and Powell, went smoothly, but the elections since then, in 1975, 1989, 1990 and 1995, have been highly charged, dramatic events, which have exposed divisions in the party and left legacies of bitterness. In 1975 and 1990 the incumbent leaders were ousted.

Despite the popular image of him as weak and ineffective, Major is a tough, calculating leader who has used his experience in the Whips' Office to good effect to keep his party together with a mixture of threats and inducements.[6] But he has had to face the most persistent and organised factional revolt in the party this century.[7] The issue has been Britain's role in the European Union, particularly in relation to a single currency and other policies which directly impinge on British sovereignty.[8] Major's overall majority after the 1992 election was only twenty-one, reduced through by-election losses to less than ten after July 1995. In such circumstances, even a small backbench revolt posed severe problems of parliamentary management. The tactics adopted made the leadership look indecisive and opportunistic, and contributed to the general malaise surrounding the Government.

The Conservatives' own explanation of their electoral predicament has focused on policy failures which they believe they can reverse and disunity over Europe which they think they can heal. Their central policy failure has been over the economy. The recession and higher inflation which ended the boom at the end of the 1980s bred great disillusion with the Conservatives and with the Thatcher decade. It helped destroy the Conservatives' reputation for economic competence which for so long had been their strongest card in attacking Labour. The recession was deepened by government policy on interest rates which were linked to those of the European currencies after sterling became part of the European Monetary System in 1990.

At the 1992 general election the severity of the recession, particularly in many of the Conservatives' electoral heartlands in the south and east, looked likely to topple the Government. But at that stage it did not erode the trust of the electorate in the Conservatives' economic competence. Everything changed after Black Wednesday. Although the exit from the ERM released Britain from a straitjacket and actually allowed the adoption of an export-led strategy which helped Britain out of recession and paved the way for recovery, the Government had defended the ERM up to the very last moment as the indispensable plank of its anti-inflation policy. The farce of Black Wednesday, when the Government lost £1.1 billion of reserves and raised real interest rates at one point to 8.4 per cent (a nominal rate of 15 per cent) to defend the exchange rate rather than bow to market pressures, made the Government look incompetent, especially when it was almost immediately forced to reverse the policy.[9]

In British politics, sterling crises have always occupied a special place as symbolic moments of the nation's decline. Before 1995 they could all be blamed, directly or indirectly, on the Labour party. In 1931, the most traumatic of all, when the gold standard had to be suspended, the decision was taken by the newly formed National Government, but the blame for the decision was pinned on the minority Labour Government which had preceded it, and which had split on how to make the economies necessary to keep the confidence of the financial markets. The two devaluations in 1949 and 1967 and the IMF crisis in 1976 all took place under Labour Governments. It helped reinforce the idea that Labour was especially incompetent at managing the economy. If Labour had won the 1992 election as expected, it would have inherited the commitment to the ERM, would have tried to defend the rate, and would have suffered the same humiliation that the Major Government experienced.[10] That would have confirmed the popular view of Labour's economic incompetence and set the party on the way to being another single-term government.

The consequences of the ERM decision and the need to contain the effects of the recession on public finances forced the Government to reverse its election pledges and raise taxes. This decision was extremely unpopular, and some of the specific measures, especially VAT on fuel, were strongly resented. The Conservatives managed to lose their reputation both as the party of economic competence and as the party of low taxes. The general depression of living standards was compounded by large numbers of voters experiencing bankruptcy, unemployment and negative equity on their homes. The experience of the 1990s recession contrasted with the promises of continuous economic prosperity which had been made with increasing confidence by Conservative ministers in the 1980s.

Conservatives agreed that the recession had lasted longer than expected and had been surprisingly deep, but they also concluded that the worst was over, that recovery was in sight, and that the key economic indicators were all pointing in the right direction. They believed that electoral support would be rebuilt once the recovery was seen to be sustained. Voters could once again be made to see that economic prosperity was much more likely to be secured under a Conservative than a Labour government.

But a second factor ruining Conservative electoral prospects was their public disunity over Europe. The constant feuding and the doubts over the leadership made it appear for a time after 1992 that the party had a death wish, and that it contained elements which would prefer electoral defeat to compromise on the European issue. The view of the leadership was that this in-fighting was the single most important reason why the Conservatives were not benefiting electorally from the economic recovery, and determined efforts were made, culminating in

Major's bold decision in June 1995 to force an early leadership election, to reassert authority over the Euro-rebels and reestablish party unity. All Conservatives were aware of the damage that open public divisions had done to the electability of the Labour party in the past and of the difficulty of fighting a general election if the Conservatives did not find a platform on which to unite.

The Conservative leadership hopes that, before the next general election, economic recovery and an outbreak of unity will restore the party to health and give it a chance of clawing back the electoral ground it has lost. Some improvement is virtually certain, and the Conservatives' underlying position is much stronger than the headline polls suggest. There is little marked enthusiasm for Labour, and the number of voters who still identify with the Conservatives suggests that a large part of their support will return to them at the next general election.[11] But it may be too late. The disunity, the staleness and the sleaze which have characterised the party in the last four years are seen as signs that it has been in office too long. The regime has rotted from within, and many Conservatives believe that a spell in opposition would be healthy.

The pillars of conservative hegemony

The causes of the Conservative predicament go much deeper than the short-term reasons for their unpopularity. The Conservatives are threatened not merely by an electoral predicament, from which they may or may not extricate themselves, but with a more fundamental undermining of the foundations of the political hegemony which they have exercised more or less continuously since the advent of the wider franchise in 1885.

Hegemony operates at three levels. At the level of the state, it signifies the fundamental legitimacy and acceptance of the basic institutions and values of a social and political order, including critically those of the economy and the state: these are only questioned in very extreme circumstances – typically those of revolution, invasion or civil war. At the level of government or regime, hegemony signifies that one particular party or faction has achieved a position of leadership and commands the active support, or at least the acquiescence, of leading economic sectors and key social groups. At a third level, the world order, hegemony signifies the political and intellectual leadership of a nation-state whose economic, military, and cultural capacities allow it to take on state functions for the world system as a whole.

A crisis of political hegemony at the regime level need not imply a wider crisis of state hegemony, since it is primarily concerned with particular forms of representation and agency, such as political parties. In Britain, the foundations of Conservative political hegemony were laid in the period between 1886 and 1926.[12] This period saw the creation of many of the political forms which have persisted throughout the twentieth century. The Conservatives mastered the new politics more surely than their main rivals, the Liberals, and by the 1920s it was clear that the main challenger to their political hegemony would be not the Liberals but Labour. The foundations of Conservative political hegemony lay in the development of a statecraft, defined by Jim Bulpitt as 'the art of winning elections and maintaining some kind of governing competence in office'.[13] It was built on the pillars of state, union, property and empire. Its characteristic ideological themes were constitutionalism, unionism, anti-socialism and imperialism.

Conservative dominance was far from assured, however, particularly following their defeat in the 1906 election. The party owed its ascendancy between 1886 and 1906 to the split in the Liberal party over Home Rule for Ireland. The adherence of the Liberal Unionists to the Conservatives ensured the latter's parliamentary supremacy until the Conservatives themselves split over the issue of free trade and tariff reform in 1903. This split was very damaging to the Conservative cause for a time but, by driving the free-traders out, it consolidated the party's identity as the party of Empire, already established through the rhetoric of Disraeli, the Boer War, and the colonial policies of Chamberlain. The Conservatives had defined themselves as the patriotic party while a section of the Liberals were successfully labelled pacifists and little Englanders.[14]

The other two foundations were the state and property. The party was closely identified with the institutions of the British state, particularly the monarchy, the House of Lords, the House of Commons, the law, the Church, the military, the civil service and the universities. It presented itself as the natural defender of Britain's ancient institutions and their privileges. Furthermore, it had always been closely associated with the landed interest but, during the early decades of the twentieth century, it assumed a more general role as protector of all property interests against the threat posed by a rising Labour movement. During the 1920s, the party consolidated a close relationship with the City of London which it has never since lost. Its attitude towards manufacturing was more equivocal. The party always had strong support from some manufacturing sectors, particularly the defence sector, but, in the dispute between free-traders and tariff-reformers, many sectors of British manufacturing which depended on free trade and open markets continued to back the Liberal party. Only later, when the Conservatives appeared as the best political bulwark against socialism, did it come to command the support of all sections of British capital.

Conservative electoral dominance

These four pillars of Conservative political hegemony were consolidated in the early decades of this century, and defined the identity and the appeal of the party. Around these grand ideological themes – the defence of the Union, the defence of the Empire, the defence of the constitution, and the defence of property – a Conservative party was organised which commanded support in all parts of the United Kingdom. Liverpool and Birmingham were Conservative cities, and there was a strong Conservative presence in many others. Northern Ireland, through the alliance with the Ulster Unionists, was a Conservative fief, while there was a strong Conservative presence in Scotland. This was a party which, at its height in the 1930s, polled 55.2 per cent in 1931 and 53.7 per cent in 1935, shares of the vote which gave it overwhelming parliamentary majorities, and reflected its ability to win votes and seats in all parts of the country and from all social classes.

Nevertheless, the success of the Conservatives has not been uninterrupted. Their political hegemony has been challenged in three periods in the twentieth century, by the Liberals between 1906 and 1916, by Labour between 1940 and 1951, and again between 1964 and 1979. We may be on the threshold of a fourth such period. What is significant, however, about these three periods is that the Conservatives, although they suffered serious electoral reverses – particularly in 1906, 1945 and 1974 – always recovered strongly and in each case had reentered government within a decade. Each period of challenge led to the reorganisation of the party and to its reemergence as the dominant force in British politics.

The history of the Conservative party over the last one hundred years can therefore be presented as a series of cycles: 1886–1906, 1906–1916, 1916–1940, 1940–1951, 1951–1964, 1964–1979, and 1979 onwards. The cycles consist of four long periods of almost unbroken Conservative rule, separated by three shorter periods when the Conservatives not only lost office but faced a struggle to reassert their political hegemony.

This pattern of dominance is clear enough, but some have disputed the idea that it amounts to hegemony. Rather, it is sometimes argued, for the first three-quarters of the twentieth century the Conservative party was on the defensive and retreated before the pressure of the Labour movement and collectivist ideas. Hayek in 1960 criticised the British Conservatives for lacking firm principles, and therefore being unable 'to offer an alternative to the direction in which we are moving'.[15] Keith Joseph spoke of the socialist ratchet: each period of Liberal and Labour government in the twentieth century had increased the scope and scale of the state, and each period of Conservative government had failed to reverse it.[16] The cumulative trend of the twentieth century had been towards ever higher levels of public spending and taxation and ever more intrusive state control of individuals.

The hollowing-out of Tory England

A different view of this same process, however, is that part of the success of the Conservative party and the secret of its political hegemony lay in its readiness to develop its own distinctive collectivist and interventionist programme. The Conservative leadership proved sufficiently flexible and far-sighted to reposition the party when it became necessary, and accept changes in the role of the state, justifying them in terms of the Conservative tradition of using the state to promote welfare and security. The Baldwin-Chamberlain Governments of the interwar years and the Churchill, Eden and Macmillan Governments of the 1950s and 1960s fall recognisably into this pattern. If it had been successful, the Heath Government from 1970–74 might well have inaugurated another phase in the development of this tradition. But the defeat of Heath amid industrial unrest and a world economic crisis not only helped discredit his programme but also led to a reaction against that entire tradition within the party. The new line of the Thatcher leadership, although it was strongly resisted by many of the old leadership group, was successfully imposed. Three consecutive electoral victories under Thatcher not only ensured that she became the most dominant leader since Churchill, but also legitimated the new anti-collectivist turn in the party.

The Thatcherites justified their anti-collectivist programme as a return to true Conservatism, and as the only way to rebuild a Conservative political hegemony. Indeed some argued that for the first time the Conservative party was building a genuine political hegemony instead of being content to administer matters within parameters established by its opponents. Earlier generations of Conservative leaders would have been amazed by this. They would have regarded the Thatcherite programme as entailing a huge political risk, endangering Conservative political hegemony by pushing the party out of the mainstream of British politics and sentiment. Some of their heirs in the contemporary party argued that this was precisely what was happening.[17]

These critics of the Thatcherite legacy argue that the real cause of the collapse of support for the Conservative party in the 1990s is directly attributable to what took place during the Thatcher era. The electoral and political success which the Conservatives enjoyed at that time concealed the long-term damage done to their position. From this standpoint, the Major Government represents a return to the more traditional style of Conservative leadership but it has often been trapped by its inheritance.

The bitter internal dispute within the Conservatives over the meaning of the Thatcherite legacy is at the heart of the party's current predicament and its uncertainty over what kind of organisation it wishes to be.[18] Should it reject or build upon the Thatcherite inheritance? Critics of this legacy have contended that neo-liberalism has been corrosive, not just for the Conservative party and its distinctive governing tradition and statecraft, but also for the institutions which have formed the bedrock of Conservative political hegemony in the past.[19] What has been happening in the last twenty years is a hollowing out of Tory England to the point where many of the familiar landmarks have gone and the Conservative party may find it more difficult to rally the kind of support it enjoyed in the past and reestablish its political hegemony. On this view, the Conservative party faces a much deeper problem than a temporary downturn in its electoral fortunes. Each of the four pillars of Conservative political hegemony have been undermined in the recent past, in part by the Conservatives themselves in pursuit of their neo-liberal agenda.

The constitution

One of the great strengths of the Conservative party used to be that it served as the voice of the establishment. It was closely identified with the key institutions of the state and civil society. It was the guardian of the *ancien régime* and the customs and privileges of the various groups within it. It strongly resisted constitutional reform.[20]

The Thatcher Governments certainly continued this constitutional conservatism, blocking any moves to electoral reform, devolution or a bill of rights. It sought to bolster the authority of Parliament, and proclaimed the doctrine of unfettered parliamentary sovereignty. But this constitutional conservatism was accompanied by the deliberate overriding of many long-established constitutional conventions which had softened the impact of executive absolutism made possible by the doctrine of parliamentary sovereignty and the residual prerogative powers of the sovereign. The Thatcher Government made full use of its powers of patronage in pursuit of its ideological programme, deliberately excluding non-Conservatives from many of the quangos it had established to implement government policy. It also reduced the amount of consultation with organised interests and professional bodies over proposed reforms.[21]

In general, this unwillingness to be bound by precedent and convention was characteristic of the Thatcher Government. From the start it was a radical government, not prepared to work within existing constraints where these were blocking the reforms it wanted to enact. From the Thatcherite perspective, the main obstacle to be removed in the pursuit of its programme was the array of special interests represented by the institutions of the state themselves: the culture of dependency and the collectivist consensus which legitimated state intervention and control, and that had its roots in the state apparatus which had grown up in the twentieth century.

To their great surprise, the conservative institutions of the British state began to discover that they were to be one of the main targets of the Thatcherite revolution. The Thatcherites set out to conduct a long march through the institutions. In some cases, such as the monarchy, the Church and the BBC, conflict erupted over ideological criticisms of the direction of government policy. In many others, explicit restructuring of the institutions was sought in order to make them more pliant instruments in the achievement of the Government's aims. In this way, major reshaping of the civil service, the health service, the schools, the universities, as well as the law, the military, and the police, were launched. Sometimes the Government's plans encountered such resistance that they had to be modified or postponed, but in most institutions a substantial reshaping had taken place by the end of the 1980s. The Thatcher Government was responsible for attempting the most far-reaching reform not only of the machinery but of the very ethos of government. The public sector was devalued and delegitimated, subjected to a utilitarian calculus, with market criteria being applied wherever possible to determine the value of particular services.

This radical bourgeois modernisation of the state was something which critics of the British *ancien régime* and its antiquated institutional arrangements had long called for. But it was always a narrow programme. It was not linked to any wider agenda for establishing a more egalitarian civil society, although the Thatcherite media did engage intermittently in wide-ranging attacks on the monarchy, the aristocracy, and more generally on 'grandees'. The tone of Thatcherism was often anti-deferential and meritocratic. The really deserving individuals were those who were self-made, not those who were born to wealth. This lack of deference, both for established institutions and for established status and wealth, was part of Thatcherism's popular appeal, but it also ensured that the Conservatives became thoroughly estranged from many of the establishment elites which formerly had been their natural allies. The anti-Conservative mood which developed throughout the public sector was unprecedented. All parts of the sector felt themselves under attack, and that the ethos of public service had been devalued. The Church and the monarchy, both strong upholders of the ethic of public service, clashed publicly with the Government.

The position was in part remedied by the appointment and promotion of individuals who shared the Government's objectives but there were limits to what could be done. By the end of the 1980s, the isolation of the Conservative party from the establishment for whom it had once been the natural voice was marked. As the principles of the new public management were applied in sector after sector, resistance was steadily overcome, but the cost for the Government was the breakdown of trust among many of its natural supporters.

The Union

The second pillar of Conservative political hegemony, the Union, has also begun to crumble. The territorial politics of the Conservative party has been one of the most consistently successful aspects of its statecraft.[22] Making the political union between the nations of the British Isles one of the basic principles of Conservatism was the policy which, more than any other, reestablished the Conservatives as the leading party at the end of the nineteenth century. The party renamed itself the Conservative and Unionist party to reflect that. In the struggle over Irish Home Rule, the Conservatives became the focus for Unionist opinion, particularly in Ireland and Scotland as well as in major cities such as Glasgow and Liverpool. Playing the Orange card became a key weapon in the Conservative political armoury. The lengths to which the Conservatives were prepared to go was demonstrated before the outbreak of the First World War when the Conservative party encouraged elements of the army to refuse to obey the orders of the Liberal Government to 'coerce Ulster' by making it comply with the provisions of the Home Rule Bill.

Conservative intransigence over Ulster made the break-up of the Union with Ireland much more certain but, when it happened, the settlement was shaped by the Conservatives, and it cemented the alliance between the party and the Ulster Unionists, who dominated the new parliament of Northern Ireland, Stormont, and for fifty years provided a small but very reliable component of the Conservatives' parliamentary majority at Westminster. The Irish crisis and its resolution had long-term consequences for the Conservatives. If the whole of Ireland had remained within the UK and had continued to send representatives to the Westminster Parliament, the balance of political forces there would have been much less to the Conservatives' advantage. A centre–periphery cleavage would have existed alongside the class cleavage, and would have helped create a different dynamic to British politics, one which would have provided significant opportunities for centre-left alliances.

The basis of the Union was different for each of the four nations in the British Isles, and this was reflected in the different arrangements for governing them. Although the UK was a unitary state, its territorial politics showed remarkable diversity. There was no uniform pattern imposed from the centre. This highly flexible system of rule was a crucial component of the *ancien régime* and its legitimacy. So long as the centre retained control over the policy areas to which it attached most significance, it was prepared to allow considerable decentralisation and local autonomy.[23]

The territorial system came under great strain in the 1970s and 1980s. The breakdown of public order in Ulster forced the Heath Government to suspend the Stormont Parliament, impose direct rule, and search for a new political basis for governing the province which involved the minority Republican community as well as the Unionists. These decisions destroyed the alliance between the Ulster Unionists and the British Conservatives at Westminster. After the election of February 1974, the Unionists no longer took the Conservative Whip.[24]

Twenty years on from these events, it is clear that the breach with Ulster Unionism is irrevocable. Under both Thatcher and Major the Conservatives have pursued a strategy of disengaging Britain from Northern Ireland, which has involved intensive negotiation with the Irish Government and secret talks with Sinn Fein and the IRA, culminating in the Downing Street Declaration and the ceasefire announced in 1994. The key passage in the Declaration was the statement that the British Government had no selfish or strategic interest in Northern Ireland, and that if ever the Ulster people wished to separate from the United Kingdom, the British Government would not oppose it. In the House of Commons, Nicholas Budgen asked if the British Government still had a strategic interest in Wolverhampton. The message of the Declaration was not lost on the Unionists. They had to recognise that there was now no party at Westminster which was committed in principle and in all circumstances to the maintenance of the Union.

The same pattern is observable in relations with Scotland. Since the 1955 election, when the Conservatives won 50 per cent of the Scottish vote and 50 per cent of the Scottish seats, support for the party has halved. The rise of Scottish nationalism prompted the Heath Government and the Scottish Conservative party to embrace devolution in the 1970s.[25] This might have halted the erosion of the Conservative vote and allowed the Conservatives in Scotland to build an independent Scottish identity, fighting the other parties for representation in a Scottish parliament. Once Thatcher became leader, however, she changed the party's line to one of total opposition not only to Labour's proposals for devolution but also to any plans for devolution at all, against the opposition of many leading Scottish Conservatives, including Alick Buchanan Smith and Malcolm Rifkind.[26]

Under the Thatcher Government the deterioration of the Conservative position in Scotland accelerated. Although the existence of the Scottish Office provided a buffer, many Thatcherites were keen to impose their policies on Scotland, believing that they would prove as popular as they had in England. Scotland was widely seen by English Conservatives as a burden.[27] The Scots were always demanding subsidies for their industries and extra privileges which were not available to the English regions. In Scotland, Thatcherism came to be viewed as quintessentially English. A series of flashpoints developed: the closing of Ravenscraig steelworks, the imposition of the poll tax – a year before this was done in England – and the privatisation of the water industry.

John Major reaffirmed the commitment to the Union, but with support for an independent Scotland having risen to 35 per cent of the Scottish electorate by 1995, the Conservatives had become a marginal political force, and had no credible strategy for rebuilding their position. They were more than ever the party of England, above all of southern England and its metropolitan heartland. That had always been their core identity but Unionism had allowed them to project themselves as a credible political force throughout the United Kingdom. This was what they had lost.

Property

The third pillar of the Conservative political hegemony was property. The party emerged in the 1920s as the representative of all property interests against the threat posed by the Labour movement at home and by revolutionary socialist and national liberation movements abroad. It developed a particularly close relationship with the City of London.

The identification of the Conservative party with the general interests of capital was, however, accompanied by an identification with the national economy. The blunting of the challenge of the Labour movement was in part achieved through the Conservatives accepting an interventionist role for the state. They became the party of collectivism and of protection, quite prepared to see an extension of welfare programmes and the provision of certain kinds of economic security to particular sectors of the economy. In the 1930s, following the collapse of the gold standard and the dislocation of world trade in the slump, the Conservatives moved to extend intervention much more generally throughout industry and supported many market closing arrangements in order to safeguard profitability and jobs.[28]

At this time, the party also introduced imperial preference, establishing a trading bloc around sterling which covered the countries within the British Empire, as well as some others within the British sphere of influence. The dream of the tariff-reformers at the beginning of the century was thus partially realised. British economic policy aimed to strengthen links within the Empire, so increasing its economic and military security. It was accompanied at home by policies which extended welfare provision.

The Conservatives successfully contained both the political and the industrial challenge of organised labour in the interwar years, blunting militant Labour in the early 1920s, defeating the General Strike in 1926, and weakening the legal position of trade unions. But this was not accompanied by an adoption of laissez-faire policies. The doctrines of economic liberalism had never had much influence within the Conservative party. It had always been a strong defender of the rights of property, protecting them from any form of encroachment, but its dominant tradition had been protectionist, as in the dispute over the repeal of the Corn Laws. In line with its attitude towards government, the party had often been prepared to put the interests of a particular community or group above free-market principles.

This tradition explained why it was relatively easy for the party to recover so quickly after the shock of 1945, to reposition and accommodate itself to the further extension of the state which Labour introduced. So long as the dividing line between public and private sectors was clearly marked, the Conservative party had no difficulty accepting most of Labour's reforms and the new style of economic management which had been introduced. The Keynesian way of thinking about economic problems pragmatically was very much in line with Conservative preferences for the Middle Way and for governing in the light of particular circumstances rather than doctrines.[29]

This One Nation tradition of Macmillan and Heath contained a corporatist bias in the sense that it treated the problem of economic management as governing a political community and therefore of finding policies which could command wide assent, particularly from organised producer interests. At the outset, Heath appeared to be steering a very different course, disengaging the state from many of its responsibilities and adopting a much tougher line towards organised labour. But the difficulties he immediately ran into soon prompted a change of course and a return to an interventionist programme which relied on partnership with the employers and the unions. As we have seen, it was the shipwreck of this policy and the extraordinary political conditions of the mid-1970s which created the conditions for the Thatcherite ascendancy.

In the Thatcher period, the party renewed and consolidated its identity as the party of capital. With Labour moving to the left, the support of all sections of business for the Conservatives substantially increased. The Thatcher Government's success in pushing through tough anti-union measures, combined with the huge shake-out and high unemployment of the early 1980s, broke the back of union resistance to the restructuring of the economy. Tax reductions for high-income earners, alongside deregulation and privatisation, also helped create a financial climate friendly to the City and an economic boom in the late 1980s.

Superficially, the Thatcher decade appeared a huge economic success, and Conservative ministers certainly proclaimed it as such. The party had been elected on a pledge to reverse economic decline, and by the end of the 1980s there was talk of a British economic miracle, and of Britain out-performing all the other economies in the European Union.[30] Yet, although there were substantial improvements in Britain's economic position in the 1980s, such claims proved unfounded.[31] The long and deep recession which began in 1989 punctured the hopes for sustained growth and exposed the limitations of the British economic recovery.

What the Thatcher decade represented was a repudiation of the party's twentieth-century tradition on economic policy, and an explicit abandonment of the national economy as a proper object of government policy. Naturally, there were exceptions to this. Agriculture and defence remained protected sectors and continued to flourish under the Thatcher Government. Certain regions, notably Wales, under *dirigiste* political management, also had a different experience.[32] But for the bulk of the economy, the key stance adopted by the Thatcher Government was expressed in the abolition of all exchange controls and the announcement of the phasing-out of regional aid and industrial subsidies. The Government accepted the shake-out imposed by the world recession which saw the reduction of many industrial sectors and, in several cases, their disappearance. Given the low level of investment over so long a period in so much of British industry, such a restructuring had become almost inevitable. But critics of the Government pointed to the failure to develop a successful supply-side programme to close the gaps in investment, training, finance, and research and development which had crippled British industry in the past. The Thatcherite economic miracle was too dependent on a few sectors, particularly financial services. When the recession came, the economy appeared only marginally better able to absorb it than before 1979.

The main legacy of the Thatcher decade has thus been to remove the identification of the Conservatives with the protection of the national economy, though at the same time it has involved the serious weakening of organised labour as a significant factor in national economic policy. With the shift of the Labour party to a policy agenda which accepts the constraints on national economic management imposed by international financial markets, and the removal of any threat from organised labour, the urgency for business to support the Conservative party as the main defender of their interests has diminished. The Thatcher decade thus saw a loosening of the ties between the Conservatives and their supporters in industry, but also a weakening of the party's ability to project itself as the sole defender of the security of the national economy.

The Conservatives had always favoured, at least rhetorically, the widest possible extension of property ownership but they had often done little to bring it about. In the 1980s the sale of council houses to their tenants and the offer for sale of shares in the former nationalised industries were partly aimed at broadening the base of Conservative electoral support. The evidence shows that it was not very effective at doing this, and that the more competitive environment created as a result increased insecurity – much of which then came to be blamed on the Conservative Government. The enormous financial rewards garnered by a few privileged groups made a sharp contrast with the distress of many new property owners, suffering negative equity in the recession, often through bankruptcy or unemployment. The problem for the Conservatives in the 1990s was that the neo-liberal doctrines to which the party had been wedded for the previous twenty years offered few positive ways of providing relief.

Empire

The fourth pillar of Conservative political hegemony was Britain's external role in the global political economy. For much of the twentieth century this was the Empire. The social imperialism of Joseph Chamberlain and the tariff-reformers advanced a programme of imperial protection to guarantee military and economic supremacy, and help weld the dispersed and fragmented territory which Britain controlled into a cohesive political and economic bloc which could stand against the great continental empires of Germany, Russia, and the United States. In domestic policy the Chamberlainites favoured using the proceeds of the tariff to pay for welfare programmes. The emphasis was on security, creating through the tariff both higher employment and the funds to finance welfare programmes.

The Chamberlainite tradition in the party dominated the perspectives of the leadership until the Thatcher era. The ability to link external and domestic policy, and to provide a positive programme of domestic reform, instead of merely negative and defensive anti-socialism, was a key factor in the electoral appeal of the Conservatives, and the blunting of the class message of its opponents. It was the source of their projection as the party of One Nation. The conception of Britain as an empire, with a global role which went far beyond the British Isles itself, was the basis of an idea of citizenship which legitimated the extended role of the state to ensure basic welfare and security to all citizens.

The Conservatives, however, proved unable to preserve the Empire from disintegration. Instead they had to preside over its decline. Much of the party found it very hard to reconcile itself to this loss, and the leadership strove very hard to postpone it. The policy of appeasement in the 1930s was partly a strategy to avoid British entanglement in another European war because of the consequences for the Empire and the domestic balance of power which many Conservatives feared would follow.[33]

Yet the Chamberlainite tradition proved able to adjust to the loss of empire. The alliance with the United States became the new linchpin of Conservative policy. The hope was that a partnership with the United States would allow the transfer of the parts of the global hegemonic role which Britain could no longer sustain to the larger country, while permitting Britain to remain a great power and protect its global interests. The relationship was always unequal, and the continuing decline in British power after 1945 exposed the limits of British influence. It convinced many in the Conservative leadership that Britain's security in the world order was best achieved by joining the European Economic Community. Although entry into the European Community was bitterly opposed by many of the old imperialists in the party, for Chamberlainites it was a logical step. Their view was that the nature of the world economy created a strategic necessity for Britain to be part of a political and economic network broader than the British Isles. The attraction of the Empire from this geopolitical perspective had been that Britain had been at its centre. The disadvantage of the Atlantic Alliance was that the relationship was so unequal, forcing Britain to gradually disengage from its colonial possessions and military bases. The European Community implied a pooling of national sovereignty and the creation of a partnership in which Britain would be a leading though not a dominant player. Nevertheless the Conservatives under Macmillan and then Heath transformed themselves from being the party of empire to being the party of Europe. Superficially, the motives were to take full advantage of the rapidly growing European market but the real reasons were political: the defence of western Europe and the protection of British security.

With a few exceptions, the Conservative leadership united behind this new project, and opposition within the party was contained and marginalised. It was the Labour party which suffered far more serious splits over its attitude to the European issue, with the Labour leadership changing its position five times between 1961 and 1987. In 1971, the Bill endorsing Britain's entry into the European Community was only passed with the support of sixty-nine Labour rebels.[34] The strength of opposition to Europe in the Labour party arose from the constraints which Community membership imposed on the management of the national economy. The bulk of the Labour movement rejected the European Community and voted 'no' in the 1975 referendum because of the fear that membership would significantly reduce British government sovereignty, incorporating Britain into a capitalist club where neo-liberal ideas would predominate.[35]

Ambivalent attitudes to Europe

One of the successes of the Conservatives has been their ability to project themselves as a national party while, at the same time, accepting Britain's involvement in wider institutions designed to safeguard British interests. During the Thatcher era, the Conservatives renewed their identification as a national party, but they also questioned what

Britain's role in the world should be. Thatcher's ambivalence about the European Union produced a deeply inconsistent policy. The drive to create a single market was promoted, and culminated in the signing of the Single European Act in 1986 which for the first time introduced qualified majority voting to prevent a single country vetoing progress. But Thatcher strongly opposed Britain joining the ERM and succeeding in delaying it for five years. Towards the end of her premiership she became deeply worried about moves towards further integration and the possible creation of a federal union. She stated her position publicly in her speech at Bruges in 1988.[36] Her attempt to sabotage any moves in that direction created open division in the Cabinet, and was the chief reason for the events which led to her resignation, after she had failed to win enough votes to prevent a second ballot in the leadership contest.

John Major inherited a deeply divided party on Europe and has struggled to keep it united. Initially, he gave signals that he would abandon his predecessor's negative attitude, proclaiming that he wanted to see Britain at the heart of Europe. As Chancellor he had been responsible for Britain's belated entry into the ERM in 1990, and as Prime Minister he took charge of the negotiations which culminated in the Maastricht Treaty in 1991. Aware of the strength of feeling within his own party against closer integration, he negotiated two crucial opt-outs from the provisions of the Treaty – from the Social Chapter which detailed workplace rights and social provisions for workers, on the grounds that this would raise British business costs, and from the commitment to participate in the third stage of economic and monetary union, the establishment of a single currency.

Following the conclusion of the Maastricht Treaty, which was presented as a great triumph for British diplomacy, and Major's victory in the 1992 general election, the Government seemed to have a free hand to develop policy in a more pro-European direction, reviving the trajectory of past Conservative Governments which had been interrupted under Thatcher. But there was considerable unease in the party about the constitutional implications of the Maastricht Treaty. Twenty-two MPs voted against the second reading of the Bill in May 1992. After the Danes voted against ratification of the Treaty in June 1992, eighty-four Conservative MPs signed a Commons early-day motion, calling on the Government to make a fresh start and rethink the position on Maastricht.

Following Black Wednesday, there was an explosion of anti-European sentiment in the party. Thatcher, Tebbit, Parkinson, Baker and other formerly senior figures encouraged the rebellion. The party conference in October saw open conflict over Europe. Sixty-five MPS signed another 'fresh start' early-day motion, and ratification of the Maastricht Treaty became the focus for dissidence. A long and laborious parliamentary battle took place, during which the Government narrowly escaped defeat on several occasions. In the vote on the Paving Motion in November 1992, the Government survived by only three votes. Right at the end of the process in July 1993, the Government lost a vote on the Social Chapter by 324 to 316, with the rebellion of twenty-six Conservative MPs. Major's response was to call a vote of confidence and threaten a general election if defeated. The rebels voted with the Government, but its difficulties were far from over. The divisions continued to deepen within the party, and numerous issues, particularly decisions by the European Court, which were accepted as binding by the British courts, and revisions to the rules governing qualified majority voting, became flashpoints. In November 1994 the patience of the leadership snapped and the whip was withdrawn from eight Conservative MPs; a ninth gave it up voluntarily. The rebels then helped defeat the Government over its proposal to put VAT on fuel.

The leadership's problem was partly due to its small majority. But the strength of the Euro-rebels' position reflected the balance of feeling within the party, both inside and outside Parliament. A survey of the parliamentary party at the time of the 1994 European Parliament election showed that, on the key issues that were being debated, the balance of party opinion was closer to the position of the Euro-rebels than it was to the European wing (see Table 1).

After Black Wednesday, Major moved the public position of the party closer to what he correctly perceived to be the centre of Conservative opinion, and his speeches became much more Euro-sceptical in tone, but he also had to keep the support of the majority of his Cabinet and of the group of very strongly pro-European MPs. The difficulty in managing the party was due to the contrast between the leadership and the backbench MPs: the Cabinet was divided two-to-one in favour of a more pro-European policy; the MPs were divided two-to-one against. In addition, substantial parts of the Conservative press, particularly the *Sunday Telegraph*, *The Times*, the *Daily Mail* and the *Sun*, were all urging a much stronger anti-European line. On the business side, although opinion was divided, it was predominantly pro-European.[37]

The depth of the split in the party was a direct result of Thatcher's leadership. She legitimated opposition to Europe in a way which the leadership had hitherto successfully avoided. She suggested that there was an alternative – continuing to give priority to Britain's Atlantic over its European links, pursuing an open-seas, open-trade policy,

Table 1: Backbench Conservative MPs' attitudes to European integration

Statement	Agree	Neither	Disagree
The disadvantages of EC membership have been outweighed by the benefits	59	9	32
An Act should be passed to explicitly establish the ultimate supremacy of Parliament over EU legislation	56	16	28
Sovereignty cannot be pooled	64	6	30
Britain should block the use of Qualified Majority Voting in the areas of foreign and defence policy	87	6	7
Britain should never rejoin the ERM	52	15	33
There should be a national referendum before the UK enters a single currency	55	4	41
Britain should adopt the Social Protocol	5	2	93
Cohesion Funds should be phased out	66	18	16
The EU's budget should be enlarged	11	9	80
The 1996 ICG should not increase the supranational powers of EU institutions	88	5	7
The Commission should lose the right to initiate legislation	61	4	35

Source: D. Baker, I. Fountain, A. Gamble and S. Ludlam, 'The blue map of Europe: Conservative parliamentarians and European integration survey results' in *British Elections and Parties Yearbook 1995*, London 1995.

which cultivated Britain's connections with all parts of the world economy, rather than being exclusively preoccupied with Europe. She pointed to the trade deficit Britain had with the EU and to the location of the bulk of Britain's overseas investments in countries outside the EU. True internationalism, she argued, meant avoiding entanglement with a protectionist, inward-looking, interventionist, high-cost continental economy.[38]

The realism of this policy – to make Britain the Hong Kong of Europe – was much disputed and split the Thatcherites themselves. Those who supported the logic of the free-market policy could see the advantages, not only of completing the single market, but also of putting in place central powers adequate to police it, removing obstacles to its functioning, as well as facilitating its smooth operation through, for example, the stability of a single currency. Other Conservatives, like Michael Heseltine, saw the advantages of extended state powers at European level to develop a coordinated industrial policy. A strong European economy would be the foundation for strong European security and external policy, the means by which European influence could be projected, and the interests of European capital defended against the challenge of North American and East Asian capital.

The opponents of closer European integration have argued that national sovereignty must take priority over economic integration. If national sovereignty is weakened, it is argued, the legitimacy of the state will also be weakened and with it the legitimacy of national political organisations such as political parties. The reaction of the Thatcherites to Europe is in part determined by their concern with what they regard as the fundamental attribute of Conservatism: national identity. They attack the governing elites of Europe for having lost touch with the peoples of Europe, and for embarking on a project of creating a state which has no natural legitimacy, because it lacks its own nation.

Conclusion

The spectacle which the Conservative party presents at the end of the twentieth century is of a force whose ideological tradition has become exhausted. The great crusades of the past – free trade against protection, free trade against tariff reform in the 1900s, capitalism against socialism, the Empire – have all ended. The Conservative party has abandoned its former concern with national protectionism, the Empire has gone, and organised labour is no longer a threat, or even a power to which concessions have to be made. Thatcherism was both an expression of these changes and a catalyst for them. In this sense it was post-imperialist and post-labourist.

Thatcherism played an important part in weakening the pillars of Conservative political hegemony although, at the time of its ascendancy, it appeared to be consolidating and extending them. That is why its legacy remains so controversial. John Major's attempt to return the party to its old political trajectory in British politics encounters constant difficulties. Many of the old landmarks are no longer there, and the party is no longer the disciplined, governing force that it was. It has become infected with ideology and factional disputes.

In the dispute over Europe, the bitterness on both sides has suggested that the party may be heading for a split in which one wing will leave or be forced out. Finding a platform which can unite the party in the run-up to both the election and the 1996 intergovernmental conference will not be easy, although Major may be helped by growing disinclination among other members of the European Union to force the pace of integration.

Splits are rare in British political parties, but when they happen they often create realignments that change the landscape of the party system. So little did the Conservative party look like an effective governing force between 1992 and 1995, that the possibility of such a change cannot be ruled out. The old trajectory of Conservative politics is burnt out and cannot be revived. Thatcher was right in her perception of this. What is not clear is whether her fifteen-year reign over the party has provided the basis for an alternative tradition that can in the future restore Conservative political hegemony. The Thatcherite revolution may not have been radical enough. Many of the old institutions were assailed but few were fundamentally changed. Most are still in place and are hostile towards the Thatcherite project. But the strength of the Thatcherite legacy is that, although it is now strongly criticised from almost every side, there are few coherent programmes for undoing it or going much beyond it.[39]

In this situation, the heirs of Thatcher – Portillo and Redwood – bide their time, confident that eventually the party will fall into their hands.[40] If it is defeated at the next general election, their calculation is that there will be a change of leader and that the party will turn to someone who can offer a combative and distinctive programme, untarnished by identification with the Major years – someone who will reconnect with the heroic decade of Margaret Thatcher. A potent myth and set of symbols is being created, which may make it very difficult for the party to escape from Thatcher's embrace.[41]

The current slide of the party back towards Thatcherism is clearly sensed by the present leadership. It was among the reasons which prompted Major to stand for reelection. Having won the endorsement of his party, mainly because any of the alternatives threatened to plunge it into turmoil, Major used his position to further isolate the Thatcherites within the Cabinet. For the first time since 1979, all the leading ministries, as well as the Treasury team, are composed of Conservatives from the One Nation wing of the party. Major is engaged in one last desperate effort, almost sure that for his wing of the party to stay dominant after the next general election, it needs to win it. The forces of the right are strong and confident, and are busy fashioning an agenda which borrows as freely from Newt Gingrich as from Margaret Thatcher, stressing the themes of economic prosperity, tax cuts, national sovereignty and public order. The policy agenda in Britain has already been shifted once in the last twenty years. The Thatcherite wing of the Conservative party is confident it can be shifted again. They believe that this is the way to restore Conservative political hegemony in Britain: the great task still ahead is the dismantling of the welfare state.

But Europe is a huge obstacle to the consolidation of the party around a neo-Thatcherite agenda. The best hope for the anti-European wing is that the European Union either stalls and makes no further progress, or simply falls apart, as a result of disagreement between France and Germany on the way forward: then the problem might simply disappear. But if it does not, and if the momentum towards integration resumes, then it seems inevitable that the choice John Major has repeatedly sought to postpone will have to be faced. Where does the party stand? Both sides of the argument have no doubt what the answer should be. Their opposing certainties threaten the survival of the party in its present form as a broad-based coalition containing a wide range of opinion and interests. Alan Howarth's defection at the Brighton conference and the reactions to Michael Portillo's speech are reminders of the dangers the party faces. If the divisions over Europe are pushed to the point that the party splits, then the demise of Conservatism as the hegemonic political force is a real possibility.

9

The Thatcher Myth[1]

When Margaret Thatcher died on 8 April 2013 it was more than twenty-two years since she had been ousted as Prime Minister in December 1990. She had been ill for a long time and although she made occasional appearances in public she had ceased public speaking and took no active part in politics. In the time that had elapsed since she was Prime Minister a new generation of politicians had taken charge and the Thatcher decade had begun to seem a distant memory. Yet no sooner was her death announced than for ten extraordinary days Britain was plunged back into that decade. The passions of that era were suddenly reawakened, and many of the same battles were fought out again through the media. It is hard to think of any other British politician in the last hundred years who has excited such extremes of adulation and hostility. Conservative newspapers like *The Daily Telegraph* and *Daily Mail* carried full-page, softly lit portraits of Thatcher treating her as some kind of saint, while at the other extreme there were endless requests for Judy Garland singing 'Ding dong the witch is dead'. In an era of anti-politics and disdain for politicians Thatcher remains an exception. She still divides opinion. She manages to evoke huge loyalty and adoration in one part of the British public, huge dislike and fury in another. There is little middle ground.

This divisiveness was inherent in her style. The words of St Francis she quoted on the steps of Downing Street in 1979 were almost the exact opposite of how she intended to govern, and for the most part did govern. She scorned consensus and saw the world in stark oppositional terms, dividing everyone into friends and enemies. Typical of her approach was her enquiry, 'Is he one of us?', her insistence that since the other side had an ideology the Conservatives must have one as well, and her characterisation of militant trade unionists as 'the enemy within'. Her fierce opinions and her unwillingness to compromise were what enraptured and captivated her admirers and what so infuriated and nauseated her opponents. All kinds of hopes and fears were projected on to her, many of them wide of the mark, but there was enough truth in them to create an unmistakeable political personality, which few people were neutral towards. She not only articulated the values and aspirations of a particular stratum of British society, she embodied them. Although there is no evidence that she ever said it, the remark attributed to her that any man still travelling on a bus at the age of 26 could count himself a failure has been quoted again and again. She never failed to exude a very English sense of status, the moral and social superiority of the people she recognised as 'her people'.

The Thatcher myth

It is hardly surprising that she should have become the subject of a great deal of myth-making. This began as soon as she was elected leader. She became leader by accident; her decision to stand in 1975 against Edward Heath only came about because first Keith Joseph and then Edward Du Cann dropped out, and there was no other plausible standard-bearer from the right of the party. Standing against Heath was high risk, because if she had lost, it would have meant the end of her prospects for advancement within the party. She had no supporters in the Shadow Cabinet, apart from Keith Joseph, and she owed her victory to the fact that many MPs voted for her in the hope they could send a signal to Heath that it was time for him to step down and hand over to Willie Whitelaw or Jim Prior. They famously overdid it, and Thatcher secured a firm lead on the first ballot. The *Daily Telegraph* editorial was headlined 'Consider her courage'. Heath resigned and Whitelaw, Prior and Howe all entered the fray, freed from their oath of loyalty. But it was too late. Thatcher's momentum was now unstoppable. Her boldness in seizing the opportunity to stand against Heath had paid off. It was characteristic of her subsequent career. She was never cavalier about taking risks, and always calculated the odds with as much precision as she could, and was sometimes (for example over the calling of elections in 1983 and 1987) over-cautious. Yet her career was built by taking some very big risks, embarking on courses of action where she could not be certain of the outcome, such as her challenge to Heath, dispatching the task force to recapture the Falklands, and confronting the miners. She was not afraid to play for big stakes, and until the poll tax she proved a lucky politician, and came out on top in all the big confrontations, both those she engineered and those which were thrust upon her.

It was this quality of Thatcher as a warrior, someone prepared to take risks, act on her principles, and face down opponents, which became the heart of the myth which formed around her. Soon after she became leader one of her first major speeches was a passionate denunciation of the USSR and its expansionist ambitions. She was dubbed the Iron Lady in the Soviet media, and she at once took up the nickname, with its resonance of the Duke of Wellington, the Iron Duke. When Enoch Powell jabbed his finger at her in the Falklands debate and told 'the Iron Lady' that how she responded to this challenge would show the metal of which she was made, she gladly accepted the challenge.

How should we think of her legacy? The Thatcher myth still subscribed to by many on both left and right of the political spectrum is that after Thatcher nothing was the same again. The other view is that she did not really make much difference. It was all *Sturm und Drang*. The changes she was associated with would have happened anyway. On this view she is part of the puppet show of British politics, rather than its inner workings. Subscribers to the Thatcher myth were out in force after her death. For them Thatcher transformed British politics, the British economy, and Britain's role in the world. 1979 therefore belongs with 1945 and 1906 as a defining election, because it ushered in a major change of direction in the way in which Britain was governed. The governments which followed Thatcher's, it is claimed, were content to govern within the new parameters she had laid down, rather than challenging them. These interpretations, whether they approve of the changes wrought by Thatcher or strongly disapprove of them, both emphasise her agency. It was the Government led by Thatcher which took crucial decisions to change Britain in particular ways, and which thought through the steps which would be necessary to achieve their goals. Thatcherism was a political project with a strategic intent and long-term ambitions, to which others had to react and adapt. The implementation of the project generated a great deal of resistance, most of it anticipated, and the Thatcher Government was able to defeat most of it. The forward momentum of the project was maintained by successive election victories.

This agency-centred interpretation still captures something about the Thatcher era which does mark it out from many other eras. There was an ideological ferment and some strategic political thinking which were unusual. But as a complete explanation it suffers from two major defects. The first is that the claims made for Thatcher and for Thatcherism are often exaggerated, even in agency terms. They do not make sufficient allowance for the muddle and confusion in which politics is necessarily conducted, and give too much weight to rational calculation and foresight. The particular contexts in which Thatcher and her ministers were obliged to operate, meant that their decisions were often ruled far more by particular circumstances and contingencies than they were by ideological goals and objectives. Many of the policies which were adopted had consequences which were not foreseen; others did not achieve the results which were intended. As always in politics, policies were interpreted retrospectively and stories constructed which gave greater coherence than was intended at the time. All the detailed accounts of the Thatcher Government stress how little Thatcher behaved in the way the myth suggested. She was extremely cautious, always aware of practical obstacles, adept at calculating the balance of forces confronting her, and determining when it was wise to take a step back or find another way. Successful politicians are always opportunists, but Thatcher was particularly good at seizing opportunities and turning situations to her advantage, while presenting herself as always acting out of principle and conviction.

The second objection to the Thatcher myth is that it ignores the structural contexts in which the Thatcher Government operated, by implying that all that mattered were political ideas and political will. What is often lacking from agency accounts is any sense of the comparative international context of British politics, the factors which made certain policy initiatives plausible and viable and ruled out others. Some of the crucial changes with which Thatcher is associated, such as the switch in macro-economic policy or the revival of Atlanticism, had already occurred under Labour. The adaption of Britain to the new dispensation being constructed by the United States would have taken place whichever party was in government, since the proponents of the alternative economic strategy were never likely to prevail. Similarly a major restructuring of the British economy was overdue and could not have been avoided. The specific ways in which the adaptation happened, however, did owe a lot both to agency and contingency, and this is where Thatcher's particular legacy may be found.

Thatcher and British foreign policy

One of the best examples of contingency is the Falklands War, which might well have ended her premiership. As it turned out, victory became the achievement for which she was most remembered and of which she was most proud. The decision of Galtieri and the Argentinian junta to launch an armed invasion of the Falklands was a contingency that was not foreseen. Thatcher's Government had been engaged for two years in negotiations with the Argentine Government over a plan to cede formal sovereignty to Argentina, and then lease the islands back. In this way it was thought both islanders and Argentines would be happy, and another imperial millstone around the neck of the British taxpayer disposed of. The last thing the British Government was looking for was an opportunity to show its military capability and rekindle a sense of pride in British power and British arms. Yet that was the opportunity which presented itself because the junta misread the intentions of the British Government. Thinking the British Government was no longer interested in retaining the Falkland Islands and would not fight to retain them, the Argentines launched their attack. This precipitated a full-blown political crisis in Britain, because it was clear that the British Government had been negligent in not anticipating an attack and had made it more likely, both by negotiating to cede sovereignty of the islands and withdrawing military cover in the Falklands as economy measures in the defence review. The Falkland Islands were a British Overseas Territory with less than two thousand inhabitants a long way away, but their symbolic importance was immense. At the emergency Commons debate on the morning of Saturday 3 April 1982 Thatcher was under enormous pressure to act decisively to regain the islands. Other leaders might have prevaricated and been lost to view. As it was, the course of action which was decided upon, dispatching a task force to conduct a military operation four thousand miles away, was highly risky, since it depended on the goodwill of the United States, and to a lesser extent other states in the region, notably Chile, for it to be logistically possible at all, and even then it could have ended in military disaster, if one of the carriers had been lost or more of the Argentinian missiles had detonated. Thatcher's future was on the line throughout the conflict. She would clearly not have survived as Prime Minister if Argentina had defeated the task force. But she would have also struggled to hang on if the United States had forced Britain to accept a compromise peace before the task force had reached the Falklands. Instead, despite some anxious moments, the reconquest of the Falklands was a complete success, and was accomplished in ten weeks. The US administration, despite being internally divided, ultimately came down decisively in support of its major international ally, against its regional ally. The British lost 255 killed, Argentina 649. The war cost £2.8 billion, and scuppered the defence review which had envisioned a drastically slimmed down navy.

The war transformed Thatcher, and prolonged illusions about the role Britain could play in the world. This became an important part of her legacy. It turned out to be the ideal war to fight – it was short, decisive, and above all it gave the illusion that Britain was once again acting independently. It was the last fling of Britain as an imperial power, and may prove to be the last time the British military ever engages independently in a foreign war against another state. It would have been Thatcher's defeat if the war had gone wrong, but its successful outcome meant that it became Thatcher's victory, and she was idolised by the Conservative media, particularly the tabloids, with the *Sun* leading the way. The return of the fleet to Portsmouth and the victory parade in the City of London, at which Thatcher rather than a member of the Royal Family took the salute, sealed the political gain from this extraordinary episode. It made Thatcher's grip on the Conservative leadership unshakeable, and more than any other event created the Thatcher myth, the idea of the indomitable leader, who stood up for her principles and could not be deflected from her chosen course.

It was the Falklands victory which led to the talk of Thatcher having put the Great back into Great Britain, restored national pride and self-confidence, and ended the years of decline. The reality was more prosaic. It breathed new life into an old conception of Britain as an island nation able to take on all comers, master of its destiny, not in need of foreign alliances and entanglements, particularly not those involving Europe. But the Falklands War proved to be a final hurrah for empire rather than the beginning of a new chapter. The Empire was dead and could not be resuscitated. In the negotiations over ending the rebellion in Rhodesia in 1980, and still more in the negotiations for the return of Hong Kong to China at the end of Britain's one hundred and fifty year lease, the Thatcher Government adopted a very different strategy. There was no question of Britain using the card of national self-determination for the people of Hong Kong, as it had used it to legitimate its retention of both the Falklands and Gibraltar. Britain no longer had the power to prevent the reabsorption of Hong Kong into China. That was the more significant imperial story of the Thatcher years, and it was a post-imperial one. The Thatcher Government refused to extend British citizenship to the citizens of Hong Kong or to allow them democratic institutions so as not to complicate the handover to China or establish costly obligations. It had also revealingly refused to give British citizenship to the Falkland islanders before the invasion. That was hastily changed subsequently. But then there only 1,800 Falkland islanders, as against five million in Hong Kong, and Argentina was not China.

A second area where Thatcher made a significant difference in foreign policy was her role in reviving Atlanticism. This was closely related to the determined stance she took on the need to confront the Soviet Union and resist its expansion. She became one of the main enthusiasts for the new cold war which developed in the 1970s after the era of détente, and lasted until the election of Gorbachev and the collapse of the Soviet Union. The main role was taken by the United States, but Thatcher, particularly through the personal relationship she established with Reagan in the 1980s, was able to breathe new life into the special relationship which had become increasingly troubled in the twenty years after the United States had refused to support the Anglo-French incursion into Egypt in 1956. Harold Wilson had refused to commit British troops to Vietnam in the 1960s while Edward Heath had informed Henry Kissinger, to his considerable dismay, that in future any security proposal from the US to the UK would first have to be discussed with the UK's partners in the European Community, rather than bilaterally. Relations had improved under James Callaghan, an instinctive Atlanticist, and they improved still more following the fulsome backing Thatcher gave to Reagan, sharing as she did his enthusiasm for confronting the 'evil empire' of the Soviet Union and restoring the power of the West. The stationing of Cruise and Pershing missiles in Britain, the willingness to allow the US to use its airfields in the UK to bomb Libya in 1986, the enlistment of Britain in the ideological crusade against communism and (increasingly) Islamic fundamentalism, helped transform British foreign policy, and began the tilt away from Europe and back to the certainties of the Atlantic relationship. Thatcher's increasing scorn for many of Britain's European partners, particularly in relation to defence and security issues, reinforced her instinctive Atlanticism. As she later wrote: 'During my lifetime, most of the problems the world has faced have come, in one fashion or another, from mainland Europe, and the solutions from outside it.'[2]

Thatcher was never subservient to the United States, and had several sharp disagreements over policy. She was particularly incensed when the United States invaded Grenada, a Commonwealth country, without informing Britain in 1983. She was often more hawkish than her US counterparts, particularly in the run-up to the first Gulf War against Iraq in 1990. But the priority she gave to the United States as the ideological, security and economic leader of the West was unquestioned and formed the foundation of her policy. She wanted Britain to be the United States' chief ally and candid friend. The diplomatic, intelligence, military and financial communities which were already closely intertwined since the Second World War provided the sinews for this policy. Thatcher gave it a sharper definition, and it became the template for governments after her, particularly the government of Tony Blair. This renewal of Atlanticism as the UK's most important external relationship was the most striking feature of Thatcher's foreign policy and led to tensions with the increasing Europeanisation of British policy following membership of the European Community in 1973.

Thatcher and Europe

Thatcher's strong Atlanticism made her increasingly sceptical about Europe. This has been seen as one of her most significant legacies to British politics. She made herself very unpopular with her partners by demanding and getting a significant budget rebate. She was strongly opposed to Britain's participation in the ERM, and fought a long battle with senior ministers over it, eventually conceding that Britain should join, shortly before her resignation. At the end of her premiership she became an outspoken opponent of the new plans for federal union being launched by Jacques Delors, the Commission President. After she left office she supported the Maastricht rebels and flirted with the idea that Britain should leave the European Union. Yet this was the same Prime Minister who was an architect of the single market, and agreed to qualified majority voting rules to ensure that one country could not veto the rules necessary to make the single market work. This was the most integrationist measure passed by any British government since the treaty of accession, and under Thatcher Britain became more not less deeply involved in the European Community. Much of Thatcher's hostility to the European Union came only after she had left office. It split the Thatcherites, a number of whom supported the single market and even a single currency as the way to entrench a neo-liberal agenda across the European Union. Thatcher in the end came to pose the issue as a choice between Europe and America, but this was a strange formulation, since the United States had always been keen for Britain to be a full member of the European Community to influence its policy in ways which the United States favoured. But Thatcher's legacy was to reinforce the depiction of Europe as fundamentally opposed to British national interests and its 'special' relationship with the United States. Within a relatively short space of time the Conservative party moved from being the main party supporting a European future for Britain, to being the main Euro-sceptic party, with a sizeable minority wanting to withdraw from the European Union and the single market altogether.

Thatcher's commitment to reversing British national decline linked defence and security with economics. She sought the revival not just of Britain but of the West, and that meant the revival of American leadership. The political and economic difficulties of the 1970s required a new set of policies and strategies, a new sense of resolve. She refused to accept that either the West or Britain were in irreversible decline, and set out to challenge the defeatism of the civil service and much of the British establishment. The setbacks of the 1970s brought forth a political critique on the right of many of the institutions and policies of the post-war western order established in the 1940s and 1950s. There was a revival of the case for freeing markets and reducing the role of government in the economy, curbing the growth of entitlements and the spending commitments which went with them. This had particular applications to each national political system, but it also had implications for the architecture of the international political economy as well. The vision was a strengthened western order.

Thatcher and the economy

In its economic policy the Thatcher Government developed a clear analysis of the causes of British decline, seeing it as the result of trade unions abusing their power, a demotivating tax system, an over-extended state, and a lack of competition in both private and public sectors. At the heart of the strategy was the aim of restoring monetary and fiscal discipline. Controlling inflation became the main policy priority, legitimated by the new fashion for monetarism. As a technical policy monetarism proved a failure, because it proved impossible in practice to control the money supply in the way monetarists advocated. But as part of a shift to a new political economy it was highly successful. It signalled a move away from existing assumptions about macro-economic management, allowing governments to drop full employment as a policy goal, and to concentrate on a stable monetary and fiscal framework which was expected to create the conditions for economic growth. It also helped to insulate government from the demands of spending lobbies, and to prepare the ground for political battles with particular trade unions and other interests demanding government subsidies. The institutional apparatus of quasi-corporatism which had grown up in Britain over the past twenty years was scrapped. The Government set its face against incomes policies, national plans, public enterprise and industrial intervention. It introduced four bills which steadily reduced the legal privileges of the trade unions and made the costs of certain union actions prohibitive. It drastically restricted the powers of local government by capping their expenditure, limiting their freedom to raise extra revenue and abolishing whole tiers of local administration including the Greater London Council. It developed a rolling programme of privatisations which saw the denationalisation of almost all the industries nationalised in the 1970s and the 1940s, as well as many which had been public enterprises for very much longer. It also deregulated some major markets, including the foreign exchange market with the abolition of all capital controls, and it presided over the Big Bang in the City of London in 1986, which swept away restrictions preventing foreign banks from locating in London. The tax system was made much more regressive with the doubling of VAT and the sharp reduction in top income tax rates. As a result inequality soared, and Britain came to enjoy one of the most unequal distributions of income among OECD states.

These changes were significant, and they fitted into the more general shift at the international level to a new policy framework for the western order. This new framework became known as the Washington consensus, although the previous dispensation after Bretton Woods was also a consensus constructed in Washington, since most of the major institutions charged with governing the international economy were based there. What occurred in the 1980s was a shift in this consensus to accommodate new realities, specifically the desire of the United States to be freed from the restrictions of the fixed exchange rate system set up at Bretton Woods and the need to reinvigorate the Anglo-Saxon model of capitalism which was visibly failing in comparison with other models, particularly the German and Japanese. The unleashing of unemployment and bankruptcy, deregulation and privatisation, and spending and tax cuts were designed to reignite the 'creative destruction' and economic dynamism which had always marked the Anglo-Saxon model, shaking out inefficient firms and sectors and making space for new activity. Trust in the spontaneous unplanned restorative qualities of the market was central to the new framework.

The extent of the paradigm shift that was involved can be overdone, however. In the heroic myth of Thatcher she takes on the post-war consensus and its main defenders, the Labour movement, the civil service, the trade unions, local government, as well as the collectivists in the Tory party, and vanquishes them. Those on her side counselling caution or moderation are castigated as appeasers or 'wets', and swept aside. The state is rolled back, and the people set free once more. The traditional British understanding of how the market economy works is restored – sound money, low taxes, individual independence, and a limited state – and although the costs are heavy initially in much higher unemployment, the collapse of much traditional industry, and a sharp recession, from 1982 the economy starts to recover and within two years the economy is booming. By 1987 and Thatcher's third election victory the Government is proclaiming that decline is over, confidence in Britain has been restored, and the enemies of free market capitalism vanquished. The opening of the Berlin Wall two years later appeared to confirm that the new free market dispensation was now irresistible throughout the world. The West led by the United States had triumphed.

The reality was rather different. Some significant shifts took place but they hardly amounted to the grand rollback of the state which was proclaimed. The Thatcher Government did not significantly reduce the level of government spending in its eleven years. It restructured spending in some areas but it failed to make many inroads on the entitlement state. Health, education and welfare were not privatised. What did occur were sustained attempts to create quasi-markets in the public sector through the adoption of the techniques of the new public management, with varying degrees of success. New sectors were created in the economy, particularly in financial services, but unemployment remained permanently much higher than it had been in the twenty boom years after 1950. The policies of the Thatcher Government greatly exacerbated the problem of welfare dependency, by creating a permanent class of workless citizens who could not be absorbed into the new economy. The greater flexibility in the labour market which resulted from the trade union reforms did not solve this problem, but it did contribute to the spread of low-paid, temporary, part-time and insecure jobs in the economy. The changes in economic policy introduced by Thatcher worked by creating the conditions for the boom in the 1990s and early 2000s, taking advantage of the favourable international circumstances. But the deep-seated problems of the British economy in terms of a chronic lack of skills and investment were not solved, and the economy became increasingly unbalanced, with the hothouse growth of the South East, based on the powerhouse of the City of London. The over-dependence of the British economy on the financial sector was a liability which was exposed in the 2008 financial crash.

Thatcher and British politics

The third aspect of the legacy is narrower, and concerns the impact of Thatcher and the Thatcher decade on the British party system and the conduct of British politics. Thatcher is venerated now as one of the most important leaders the Conservatives have ever had, but in many ways she was not a normal Conservative leader, but an outsider, like several other major Conservative leaders, notably Disraeli and Churchill. She was an outsider partly because of her gender and partly because she challenged the Conservative establishment, and in many areas was a deeply unconservative figure. She seemed never satisfied with what had been achieved and was always pressing for further reforms. When Prime Minister she sometimes gave the impression that she was campaigning with the people against the government of which she was head. Her instincts were often populist; she rarely saw issues through the lenses of the establishment, but always from the perspective of the people, her people. She understood how a broad stratum of Middle England felt because she felt the same way. It was one of her greatest strengths as well as one of her greatest weaknesses. It ensured that she inspired intense devotion among many Conservative party members, as well as among tabloid proprietors and editors. She had a much more supportive press than any Prime Minister in the last fifty years.

Yet although she aspired to be a leader for all the nation, in practice there were many parts of the nation she did not understand and did not succeed in reaching. She wanted to capture the inner cities for Conservatism, to win back the great Northern cities, and to make Scotland a Conservative and Unionist stronghold again. But during her time in office the Conservative party lost even more ground in these areas. The narrowness of her appeal and her divisiveness was one of the things which worried many of her colleagues, as did her increasingly autocratic behaviour after 1987. Those in the party who urged that the Government should consolidate the gains it had made and seek to lower the political temperature were peremptorily brushed aside by Thatcher, but she always found it difficult to find allies who were both able and reliable to carry through her project. She did have some, particularly Norman Tebbit and Nicholas Ridley, but most of her Cabinets were populated by Conservatives who did not share her Manichaean view of the world, or her enthusiasm for permanent revolution. Some key ministers who had been loyal Thatcherites fell out with her over substantive policy issues – management of the economy in the case of Nigel Lawson, and Europe in the case of Geoffrey Howe. The resignation of those two ministers paved the way for the rebellion in the parliamentary party which would oust her.

The way in which she fell was even more dramatic than the way she first captured the leadership, and contributed to her myth. Forced to submit to an election under the party's rules she did not lose the vote on the first ballot. She had 52 more votes than her challenger, Michael Heseltine. But she needed a lead of 54 to avoid a second ballot. Although she at first declared that she would contest the second ballot ('We fight, we fight to win'), support ebbed away from her in the next twenty-four hours. So dominant had she been that her inability to win on the first ballot damaged her authority beyond repair. When she spoke to members of her Cabinet individually, a majority professed loyalty to her, but many of them told her they expected her to lose and that she would hand the leadership to Heseltine. Reluctantly she accepted their assessment and resigned. Thatcher subsequently described the behaviour of her Cabinet as treachery with a smile on its face, and another part of the Thatcher myth was put in place. But again the myth is not quite right. For once in her political career Thatcher uncharacteristically blinked. Her nerve failed her and she gave up the fight. She could have accepted Alan Clark's advice to go down with all guns blazing, but she chose not to do so. She had a majority of 52 on the first ballot, none of her Cabinet colleagues were willing to oppose her openly, yet she walked away rather than risk defeat.

Her decision had a big impact on the Conservative party. The party has struggled with the legacy she left them. No Conservative leader since Thatcher has been able to establish the kind of authority she had, partly because they are all measured against her. Although John Major was her choice as successor and prevailed over the 'assassin' Michael Heseltine, she soon despaired of his leadership, and let it be known that she had been deceived in him. The only successor she really warmed to was Tony Blair. He shared her view of the priority which should be given to the Atlantic Alliance and to fighting international terrorism, and she came to regard the creation of New Labour as one of her most important achievements. The transformation of the Labour party into a pro-market, Atlanticist party was remarkable. For a brief period at the beginning of the 1980s it had been neither.

David Cameron after he became leader in 2005, following three consecutive defeats under Michael Howard, William Hague and John Major, did try to move the party away from her legacy, but he has faced persistent hostility from a minority of the party, which has repeatedly rebelled against his leadership, aided by a significant part of the Conservative press and Conservative commentators. The issues are Europe above all, but also immigration and the economy, as well as the liberal agenda Cameron has espoused on the family and gay marriage. The Thatcherite opposition within the Conservative party yearns for a new Thatcher figure they can rally round, although in some respects they have also begun to reject Thatcher's legacy. Many Conservative Euro-sceptics are opposed to Britain getting involved in any wars or humanitarian interventions which are not directly related to Britain's national interests. They are sceptical of the benefits of the special relationship with the United States. The vote against military intervention against Syria in August 2013 was a clear instance of this new isolationist mood in the party, one shared fully by UKIP. Thatcher made abundantly clear in several of her writings after she left office that she favoured military action against Syria, Iraq and all other dictatorships in the Middle East which were opposed to the West and sponsored terrorism against it. In taking the stance he did on Syria and support for the United States, Cameron was following in the footsteps of Thatcher and Blair, but a large part of the Thatcherite wing of the party repudiated his stance.

The Thatcher myth is something no Conservative leader can now ignore. Tribute has to be paid to her memory and achievements, as David Cameron did most eloquently at the time of her death. Announcing that the funeral would be a 'ceremonial' funeral, similar to those held for the Queen Mother and Princess Diana, he intended to signal how strongly the Government wished to honour her memory. No other Prime Minister had been granted such an honour, and Cameron may have hoped such a gesture would forestall criticism from his Thatcherite critics in the party and the media. If so it was only partly successful. The *Daily Mail* immediately labelled the decision not to grant Thatcher a full state funeral a disgrace, and invited its readers to sign a petition calling for Downing Street to think again.

Churchill was the only twentieth-century British Prime Minister granted a state funeral. A state funeral requires a vote in Parliament to authorise it, and the attendance of the monarch, although Queen Victoria refused to attend Gladstone's. A vote in Parliament would not have been unanimous and therefore potentially embarrassing, so the Government avoided it. The Queen decided to attend the funeral in any case, the only time apart from Churchill that she has attended the funeral of one of her Prime Ministers. There was some puzzlement as to why she did so, an honour not given to any Labour Prime Minister, not even Attlee. Some suggested it was because Margaret Thatcher was the first woman Prime Minister. She had already been given the final vacant plinth in the lobby of the House of Commons, her statue standing with those of Churchill, Lloyd George and Attlee as one of the four great Prime Ministers of the twentieth century. But another explanation is that it was because Thatcher, like Churchill, was a war leader. Thatcher's only war was the ten-week Falklands War, but it stood out as a victory won by the British armed forces acting on their own, possibly for the last time. Burying Thatcher was also the final, delayed burial of imperial Britain. Her legacy preserved it a while longer but now it is gone.

When the myth is stripped away Thatcher is still the dominant figure in her era, but her achievements are more qualified and provisional, in the way that political achievements always are. Her legacy has been shaped as much by the unintended as by the intended consequences of her actions. Her intransigence over devolution to Scotland helped create the conditions which led to the collapse of support for Conservative Unionism north of the border, the reestablishment of a Scottish Parliament, and the steady advance of the SNP pledged to taking Scotland out of the Union altogether. Her enthusiasm for free markets assisted the rise of a more individualist and permissive culture associated with forms of individual autonomy which undermined social conservative values. Her support for the European single market created the conditions for the surge in immigration which started during the boom of the 1990s. Her solutions for British economic problems created a deep-seated dependency culture. Setting the banks free unleashed the financial revolution which culminated in the spectacular crash of 2008. There are many other examples. Perhaps the greatest of all was that she divided the Conservative party against itself, destroying it as a credible governing party for thirteen years, the longest period the Conservatives had been out of office in the modern democratic era. Even now in 2014 Conservative party hegemony is not yet restored. Thatcher partly succeeded in remaking the main opposition party in British politics in her own ideological image, but she also helped destroy the old Conservative party which had dominated British politics for so long.

At the Carlton Club meeting in 1922, which broke up the Coalition, Stanley Baldwin said Lloyd George was a dynamic force, a terrible thing in politics. He had already destroyed the Liberal party and Baldwin feared he would in time destroy the Conservative party too. Thatcher was another dynamic force, and many of the consequences of her decade in office still shape British politics.

10

Theories of British Politics[1]

> One sure sign of an ill-conducted state is the propensity of
> the people to resort to theories.[2]
>
> Edmund Burke

Courses on British politics, like courses on English literature, have
become embedded in institutions of higher education. They sometimes
seem as natural and inevitable as the weather. But are there good
intellectual reasons rather than expedient ones why students should
be asked to study *British* politics rather than the politics of some other
country? What do political scientists study when they study British
politics? Is Britain chosen because it is a unique phenomenon, with its
own institutions and special characteristics? Or is it chosen because its
politics provide case studies which can contribute to general theories
of comparative politics? Britain may have its local peculiarities but are
these better understood as manifestations of a unique political entity
or of a set of universal concepts?

A glance at the available literature reveals that there is no longer
any consensus on the answers to these questions. The current variety
of approaches and perspectives stems from the influence on the
development of the discipline exerted by intellectual traditions in other
countries, notably the United States, as well as from the response of
political scientists to developments in British politics during the last
two decades. One consequence has been to make writing on British
politics more self-conscious about theory and methods. In the past
much of the writing was deliberately atheoretical and this tradition
continues. But it is under increasing challenge.

The textbooks have become quite diverse, both in the range of topics
they include and in their methodological and ideological orientation.[3]
There is no longer a single body of knowledge or interpretation to

which the student is directed. The cause is partly the sheer volume of writing on British politics but more fundamentally it stems from the fact that there is no longer a single 'organising perspective' which guides teaching and research.

This loss of an agreed core disturbs many political scientists, who look back to a time when there was broad agreement on what British politics was about. Yet the degree of consensus is easily exaggerated. There have always been theoretical debates about how best to study British politics and much variety of methods and topics.

W.H. Greenleaf has distinguished a number of different traditions.[4] They include: writing on constitutional arrangements, the machinery of government and representation; detailed case studies of particular institutions; and research on the determinants of the political behaviour of voters, politicians and public officials. He noted a lack of writing on the ideological dimension of British politics and little analysis of the impact of foreign affairs on the conduct of domestic politics or the development of institutions and ideas. He also detected an absence of 'an explicit organising perspective of an adequate historical kind'.[5] Accounts of British politics, he argues, tend to become entrapped in a mass of detail and fail to provide a set of analytical distinctions that would allow a coherent picture of the whole to be drawn. His own work is an extended attempt to remedy this deficiency.

Organising perspectives in Greenleaf's sense are theories that operate at the most general level. They provide a framework for analysis, a map of how things relate, a set of research questions. Such perspectives are not normally testable or falsifiable, yet it is hard to imagine how the study of politics could proceed very far without them. The problem with organising perspectives arises when there is more than one of them. If all political scientists worked within the same framework, their allegiance to a particular theory of politics would only be observable to an outsider.[6] It is when there are rival theories that the problem begins. On what basis is one organising perspective to be preferred to another?

Organising perspectives have to be distinguished from theories which present distinct hypotheses that may in principle be falsified. Theories in this latter sense have become increasingly important in the study of British politics, especially as the impact of behavioural methods of analysis have spread.[7] The framing of hypotheses about the nature of political behaviour and political processes and the collection of systematic evidence to test their validity have transformed our knowledge of the working of many parts of the political system.

The need for general theories of British politics is still resisted by many British political scientists. They prefer to work at a less abstract level, concentrating on the detailed examination of particular institutions and problems, or the testing of relatively precise theories about specific political behaviour. But it is hard for political scientists to avoid general theories altogether. Even when it is not acknowledged, an organising perspective will always be implicit in the way the research is framed and the conclusions are drawn.

Greenleaf is in favour of making organising perspectives explicit, in order to make our understanding of British politics more coherent. The dangers are apparent. A discipline could quickly drown in a welter of general theorising, unconnected to historical or empirical research. Greenleaf attempts to block this by stating that only organising perspectives of an adequate historical kind will do. To be 'adequate' an organising perspective must employ historical methods of enquiry and have as its purpose the depiction of the character of the British political tradition. Greenleaf wants to exclude from the study of British politics organising perspectives that utilise non-historical methods, models and theories. He believes that the defence of the traditional understanding of British politics requires a more coherent and explicit statement of its organising perspective.

The British School

This traditional understanding treated the relationship between political ideas and political practice that had emerged in the course of Britain's development as a unique political tradition. By reflecting on its character the political scientist could clarify the nature of contemporary political problems. Comparative studies were not ruled out but they tended to be used for illustration rather than to test general hypotheses about the workings of all political systems. This approach had three key elements: a constitutional doctrine, a conception of the state, and an interpretation of British history. All highlighted the special character of British political arrangements in comparison to those which existed elsewhere. It helped give rise to the notion of a British political science and a British School.

The constitutional doctrine was distilled by Dicey at the end of the nineteenth century.[8] The key to the British constitution was parliamentary sovereignty. This sovereignty was unlimited in the sense that there was no division of sovereignty. There was no authority higher than Parliament to which appeal could be made. The courts might interpret decisions of the Parliament in particular ways but they could not formally overturn or block them. There were many conventional restraints on what Parliament might and might not do but no constitutional ones. In principle, Parliaments might do as they pleased. They could pass retrospective legislation and overturn laws passed by previous Parliaments, since no Parliament could bind its successor.

As the supreme legislative body the task of Parliament was to pass laws. The willingness of citizens to obey these laws and public servants to enforce them was seen to depend on Parliament being representative of the political community. The boundaries of the political community and the forms through which representation was organised were frequently controversial but the important principle that became established was that Parliament was both sovereign and representative. As the seat of sovereignty it was independent of the people. Its members were representatives not delegates. Yet as representatives they had to be accountable to the people. Accountability was enforced through regular elections. Government therefore rested on public opinion. With the widening of the franchise, so the public whose opinion counted was enlarged and the importance of understanding how public opinion was shaped increased.

Since Parliament was the ultimate source of sovereignty all other branches of the state were subordinate to it. The state as such was not a term much used in British political science until recently, in part because students of British politics drew a distinction between continental states which were separate legal entities with an independent legal personality and the British concept of parliamentary government.[9] In Britain parliamentary sovereignty meant that the public agencies which made up the state were subordinate to the will of Parliament and were obliged to enforce its decisions. The central institutions of British government were a machinery at the disposal of the parliamentary majority. The British system at its best was celebrated for providing both responsible and representative government and maintaining a balance between them.[10] The Cabinet, the prime minister and the civil service formed an executive which was subject to parliamentary scrutiny and approval but retained its capacity for independent action, leadership and decision. Its dependence on Parliament and Parliament's dependence on the electorate ensured that new demands and interests would always have to be accommodated and that British political institutions would remain flexible and responsive.

This Westminster model with its elaborate conventions for the conduct of parliamentary business, the institutionalisation of opposition and the rules of debate, became not only a notable British export but the key element in the British School's account of British politics.[11] Understanding British politics meant understanding the workings of

British parliamentary government. Underlying this Westminster model of how British government worked was a particular interpretation of British history which owed much to Burke and the Whig historians. It emphasised the continuity which British institutions had enjoyed since the Glorious Revolution of 1688. Britain's success in maintaining economic advance, overseas expansion and political stability was credited to the excellence of British political institutions. Among their virtues were the balance achieved between the different elements of the constitution, the supremacy of Parliament, the flexibility and foresight of the governing class and the resulting responsiveness of British institutions to new demands and pressures.

The emergence of a political leadership which was prepared to seek compromises and pragmatic solutions to conflicts of interest was a distinctive feature of the old constitutional regime in England. A political system which had first emerged in an agricultural society dominated by the landed gentry was gradually adapted to cope with the very different requirements of an industrial society and popular sovereignty. The traditional interpretation of British politics saw British history as a story of liberty, the establishment of a set of political institutions which fostered compromise and tolerance, promoted individual liberty and ensured that government remained limited and accountable.

This interpretation reflected a particular kind of political science. In the nineteenth century, political science was not a separate discipline but an interdisciplinary field of enquiry, in which history, philosophy and law were intermingled. The 'noble science of politics' praised by Macaulay in the nineteenth century was inductive, discursive and reflective.[12] Its practitioners believed in developing a political science which would be a science for legislators. The materials of this science were the historical records of politicians and political systems in the past. Discursive historical and philosophical reflection on the past would yield knowledge useful for the education of future political leaders. It was a broad and loosely defined area of study, whose remit ran very wide. Political economy and sociology were as much part of its subject matter as law and history, since all contained knowledge which was relevant to the education of legislators and rulers. It was orientated to practical problems rather than to knowledge of the political system for its own sake. It therefore tended to be prescriptive and make judgements, proclaiming its values and priorities openly.

A discursive political science which was sensitive to the nuances of history and saw its role as transmitting an understanding of a unique political tradition was sharply opposed to that other tradition in modern social science, represented among others by the utilitarians, which received its fullest expression in the development of economics. Its basis was abstraction and deductive models, the construction of hypotheses and universal generalisations. What such a science of politics might look like had been sketched by James Mill in his *Essay on Government* (1820). Mill's purpose was to contribute to the founding of a deductive, universalising, single-discipline science of politics.

Ever since Macaulay ridiculed Mill and denounced his ahistorical method, the dominant tradition in British political science has sought to resist deductive models and positivism whenever they have been proposed. It has clung instead to the analysis of British political institutions as a unique blend of theory and practice rather than as an instance of a general theory of political behaviour. Deductive models made much greater progress in economics, as a discipline emerged which focused on the analysis of choice under conditions of scarcity and led to the stripping-out of discursive and historical elements from classical political economy. Political science successfully retained its historical and philosophical methods.[13]

What these methods yielded was a widespread consensus on the character and the merits of British political institutions. The leading practitioners of political science were convinced that change needed to be evolutionary and gradual and that there were strict limits to what could be achieved through political action. Study of the past revealed both the achievements of English political institutions and the difficulty of improving upon them without endangering their survival. What was celebrated was the practical wisdom embodied in England's constitutional arrangements, a quality demonstrated by the continuity of British institutions which was in sharp contrast to the interruptions and disorders common elsewhere.

This Whig perspective on Britain's political arrangements was put to severe test in the twentieth century because of the emergence of mass democracy and the growth in the size and scope of government. The nineteenth-century ideal of the constitutional state had assumed a government limited in its powers and responsibilities. But the doctrines of parliamentary sovereignty and popular government implied that if parliamentary majorities could be assembled in support of collectivist doctrines there could be an unlimited expansion of government.[14]

The advance of collectivism divided the British School. Some believed that the advent of mass democracy and the rise of parties like Labour, which did not understand or accept the basis of the British political tradition, would lead to the loss of liberty and limited government. For Michael Oakeshott the rationalism inherent in modern ideologies threatened the survival of the British political tradition by sanctioning wide-ranging reforms of British institutions and a major increase in the responsibilities and powers of government.[15] Only gradual, piecemeal, pragmatic change could preserve Britain's unique political identity. Oakeshott's pessimism about the possibilities of accommodating the rising Labour movement without sacrificing limited government was a distinct and influential position which was to reemerge in the 1970s[16] but it did not reflect majority opinion among students of British politics. Many viewed the extension of public responsibility, the enlargement of the franchise and the rise of mass parties as a new and positive stage in the evolution of British institutions. The high point of this mood is perhaps Samuel Beer's *Modern British Politics* published in 1965, which celebrated the political settlement reached with Labour and the establishment of a new set of collectivist values as the basis for British politics.[17]

The methodology of the British School

One of the key methodological influences on the British School has been idealism. Ideas, rather than interests, behaviour or circumstances, are treated as the most important component of political action. Institutions are understood as the expression of human purposes, which in turn reflect ideas. As an organising perspective this has proved very powerful. British politics becomes the study of theory and institutions and the constant interaction between the two. Many studies of British politics belong to this tradition, including those of Dicey, Laski, Beer and Greenleaf,[18] but it is not the only methodological tradition. There has always been writing that has given much greater weight to interests or institutions than ideas. These alternative approaches emphasise the gap between political rhetoric and political achievement. Attention is directed to what political actors do rather than what they say. Ideas are more often viewed as providing legitimation for political behaviour rather than explaining it.

This realist tradition has always been well represented in British political science. It often affects a debunking style, puncturing belief that politics is a benign or lofty pursuit of the public interest. Politics is concerned with power, with who gets what, when and how. Ideas are viewed as instruments in that struggle, not as prime movers. Leading figures in this tradition include Bagehot, Ostrogorski, McKenzie and, more recently, Jim Bulpitt and Keith Middlemas.[19] All are concerned with understanding political action within specific institutional contexts, in which the course of politics is determined by the response of political agents to information about the constraints and circumstances they face. All tend to draw a contrast between appearance and reality, as Bagehot did in his distinction between the dignified and the efficient parts of the constitution. Key areas for enquiry become the character of political management and where the real sources of power lie within a political system or institution.

This debunking realist tradition of analysis has always been an important corrective to the idealist emphasis on the importance of ideas in understanding politics. It is present also in the British Marxist tradition, whose representatives have not been numerous but which include Harold Laski (in his later works) and Ralph Miliband. In place of the emphasis on politics as political management within particular institutions, the Marxists shift the focus to what Ralph Miliband has called 'capitalist democracy'. They study the tension between the promise of popular power brought by universal suffrage and the denial of that promise in practice. Politics in a capitalist democracy is about how pressures from below for change are constantly deflected and contained by those in control of the state. Such a perspective again suggests particular areas for enquiry, such as the processes by which the radicalism of successive political and industrial leaders of the Labour movement have been weakened as they have become involved in the running of the state.[20]

Although these alternative perspectives exist and continue to flourish, it can be argued that they were always internal critiques of the assumptions of the dominant paradigm rather than independent alternatives. Even Marxism is not an exception. Writers in the British Marxist tradition have produced a powerful anti-Whig and anti-pluralist account of British politics but they base it not on a comparative political theory but on an alternative historical interpretation of the British political tradition, which continues to treat it as a unique historical formation. Ralph Miliband, for example, argues that there has been no crisis of the political regime in Britain since 1688.[21] Where his approach and that of Keith Middlemas differ from Beer or Dicey is that both see the containment and management of conflict as the fundamental purpose of the state.

Criticisms of the Westminster model

The apparent success of British institutions in adapting to the demands of mass democracy was reflected in the ascendancy in the 1950s of the liberal democratic perspective, a clear descendant of its Whig forerunner. At the heart of this perspective was the Westminster model of parliamentary and Cabinet government. There were some dissenting Marxist and Conservative voices but the majority of the political science profession were largely sympathetic to the political regime created in the twentieth century. Rodney Barker notes that:

> the English tradition has been empirical, reformist, and collectivist, a combination which has placed political scientists both conceptually and practically within the limits set by the present order, rather than with both feet, or even one foot, outside them.[22]

Political scientists as a result made little effort to theorise the state. Change came when many became dissatisfied with the Westminster model as an adequate account of modern British politics and government. Influenced by American and European models, political scientists began to experiment with theories and approaches that allowed different questions to be asked.

There has been a considerable ferment in the discipline during the last twenty years. Mainstream political science texts have been criticised for focusing on the liberal–democratic constitution and formal institutions, reflecting a narrow conception of politics and of power. In an influential modern text, John Dearlove and Peter Saunders advocate a political science that pays attention to the non-democratic aspects of British politics, to the substance and the outcomes of public policy, and to the role which the British capitalist economy plays in the world market.[23] Such a political science would have to be pluralist in its methods, combining the insights that come from a range of different methods and models, including mainstream political science, the New Right, Marxism and political sociology. They argue that no single theory can explain everything. Different perspectives allow different questions to be posed, although not all perspectives are equally valid. Such views reflect the present proliferation of approaches to the study of British politics. The theoretical assumptions about the state, about politics, and about history that underlie the liberal–democratic perspective and the Westminster model have all been challenged. They have led to the elaboration of many different models and theories to explain different aspects of British politics.

Politics

Influenced by American models and methods, behaviouralists in Britain have since the 1950s argued that a focus on behaviour and processes offers a much faster route to the construction of theoretical models that can explain and predict political phenomena.[24] Behavioural approaches revolutionised understanding of electoral behaviour, through the collection of systematic evidence about how voters actually behaved and the framing of models and theories to make sense of the data. These models had a profound effect upon the ways in which political scientists understood the party system, stimulating interest in the alignments, solidarities and choices that shape electoral behaviour, as well as in the strategies and calculations of party leaders seeking to win votes.[25]

Behavioural methods have also, through their insistence on the collection of data and construction of explanatory models, assisted the development of studies of the policy-making process, in particular the analysis of outputs and of policy implementation. They also exposed the limits of political scientists' knowledge about behaviour even in key institutions like Parliament. This emphasis on observing and measuring what political actors actually do helped stimulate, for example, Philip Norton's studies of dissent in the House of Commons.[26]

The behavioural school introduced new rigour into British political science and widened the range of research questions but had no alternative organising perspective to propose. Leading advocates of behavioural approaches, such as Richard Rose and Dennis Kavanagh, have not departed very far in their textbooks on British politics from the liberal–democratic perspective of the British School.[27] They have devoted their energies to exposing what they see as the limited conception of political action and behaviour associated with the traditional theory and institutions approach.

What behavioural methods have also done, however, is to advance the study of mass political behaviour and widen the definition of things political. The Westminster model had concentrated on the political elite and the central political institutions of the state. British politics was equated with British government. The breach in the wall made by behaviouralism has been followed by other methodological approaches. The political has come to be defined in much broader ways, to embrace other areas of social life such as gender, race and class. Politics has come to be understood as an aspect of all social relations, rather than as an activity centred on the institutions of government.[28]

Underlying such approaches is an organising perspective for the study of politics which is far removed from the Westminster model and any historical method: the concept of a social system, another American import. Political life is understood through the common structures and processes which define all political systems, not in terms of the special features which define a particular national tradition. Easton's abstract models of the political system have had only a limited influence in Britain but they have systematised thinking about the policy-making process and helped widen the research agenda.[29] Other approaches have benefited from this. The development of feminist analysis and the study of the politics of race, for example, have been aided by the much wider conception of the political which behaviouralism and systems analysis introduced. They raise questions about the nature of power and how participation is structured in the political system. It becomes legitimate for political science to investigate which groups are excluded from the political process and how, rather than to be exclusively concerned with the workings of the central institutions of Westminster and Whitehall.

The state

The reluctance of British political scientists in the past to analyse the British state directly rather than through the structures of parliamentary government is fast disappearing. There is now an abundance of theorising about the state, much of it critical of the pluralist conception that is implicit in the Whig perspective.[30]

In the Whig perspective the state is enlightened, neutral, representative, parliamentary and national. All these assumptions have been questioned. New Right exponents have criticised the idea of the state as an enlightened state, omniscient and omnicompetent, which can be trusted to act in the public interest.[31] Marxists and neo-pluralists have disputed the notion that the state is neutral between the interests of major social interests.[32] The view that Parliament remains the key institution for representing interests and opinion has been rejected by the theorists of corporatism.[33] For elitist and neo-pluralist theorists the central role accorded to Parliament and Whitehall neglects other parts of the state system, including the military and security services, and the vast realm of sub-central and territorial government.[34] Finally the assumption, perhaps most deep-rooted of all, that what is being analysed is a unitary nation-state, has been questioned both by studies of territorial politics and by analyses of Britain's economic and political role in the world system.[35] The questioning of these core assumptions has liberated analysis of contemporary British politics in many directions and allowed the development of new theories and models.

History

Whig history too has had to suffer some hard knocks. Historians began the task of demolition some time ago but Whig optimism in progress and the benign character of British political institutions lingered on in the liberal-democratic perspective of the 1950s and 1960s. The fresh burst of praise which British political institutions received at this time was soon to be eclipsed by the political writing of the 1970s, when numerous political scientists, including S.E. Finer, S.A. Walkland and Nevil Johnson wrote scathing critiques of the working of key aspects of the constitution.[36]

Reinterpretations of British history also suggested that formal continuity might well conceal major change. Hall and Schwarz have argued that the British state has been radically transformed on several occasions in the last three hundred years.[37] The history of Britain as a multinational state has begun to be explored in much greater detail,[38] prompted in part by the upsurge of nationalism, particularly in Scotland, and the renewal of conflict in Northern Ireland. Comparative political science models developed elsewhere, such as Lijphart's concept of consociational democracy, have been used to analyse the politics of Northern Ireland,[39] while theories of internal colonialism have attempted to map the complex network of relations between different parts of the United Kingdom.[40] British politics looks very different when it is viewed not from the centre but from the periphery.

New theories of British politics

One major reason for the questioning of the traditional model of British politics was the influence of American and European political science upon a British political science community which was becoming less insular. The other was the influence of events on the way the British political system was perceived. Chief among these have been the political crises of the 1970s and the Thatcher Government of the 1980s.

In the 1970s Britain was no longer an imperial power and was beset by problems, notably poor economic performance and the renewal of sectarian conflict in Ulster. Repeated failure to find solutions to these problems cast doubt on the effectiveness and adequacy of Britain's political institutions. The crises of the 1970s have left a deep mark on the study of British politics. They shook liberal-democratic complacency severely. British political institutions suddenly had as many critics as formerly they had had admirers. The debates on Britain's political institutions took place in the 1970s against a background of polarisation between the two leading parties, the loss of significant support by both to third parties and growing volatility in the electorate. In the 1980s, analysis of developments in British politics has focused on the changes in policy, ideology and institutions associated with the Thatcher Government.

The weakening of the hold of the liberal–democratic perspective encouraged experiments with other theories, and some fierce controversies, but no new dominant organising perspective has emerged to take its place. New Right, neo-pluralist, Marxist and elitist theories currently contend with the pluralist and idealist theories that used to dominate. The opposition between liberal–democratic and Marxist perspectives has tended to weaken, as both have become internally more diverse. Methodological differences have become as important as ideological differences. Political scientists tend to define their work in terms of subject areas which are distinguished partly in terms of institutions, partly in terms of problems, and partly in terms of methods. Five such subject areas are currently of particular importance: ideology and the role of ideas; the constitution and party politics; public policy; political economy; and political behaviour. Threading through these subject areas are a number of major historical themes, reflecting long-standing problems and issues in Britain's political development. They include the maintenance of institutional continuity, the growth of government and relative economic decline.[41]

Ideology and the role of ideas

The analysis of the role of ideas in British politics has had to explain the ideological changes of the 1970s and 1980s, the rise in influence of the New Right and the waning of collectivism. Greenleaf's work represents the traditional approach. He continues Dicey's project by interpreting changes in the role of government in terms of the ideological clash between two general doctrines – collectivism and individualism (or libertarianism as he prefers to call it). He sees libertarianism and collectivism as the two poles of the British political tradition, the two voices that are never silenced, and which define the space within which political argument and action move. Unlike Dicey, who seemed to view the triumph of collectivism as inevitable because of the extension of the franchise, Greenleaf argues that there are cycles of influence and that the dominance of one strand in the tradition is only ever temporary.[42]

Other theories of the ideological changes in British politics have regarded them not as cyclical but as marking an important discontinuity, a movement to a different stage in political and social development. One variant of this approach uses the American concept of the political culture. Samuel Beer for example, adapting his theory of political modernisation to the events of the 1970s in Britain, argued that the fundamental cause of the political upheaval of that decade was a major change in the political culture. There had been a shift from collectivism towards neo-liberal individualism.[43]

The concept of political culture is frequently linked to evolutionary theories of modernisation and a stages theory of political development. The emergence of a new stage of post-industrial society is reflected in the emergence of post-industrial values.[44] Ideological change in Britain is taken as one instance and an important cause of this wider system change. A different theory of ideological change, developed by Stuart Hall utilising Gramscian political analysis and discourse theory, has sought to explain the role of New Right doctrines in the rise of Thatcherism through the concept of authoritarian populism.[45] All these theories have had their critics. It has been alleged that there is no evidence that the British political culture has substantially altered,[46] while Stuart Hall is criticised for putting too much emphasis on ideological factors rather than political and economic factors in the explanation of Thatcherism.[47]

A further theory of the role of ideas in British politics and the rise of Thatcherism is the cultural thesis of British economic decline, associated in particular with Martin Wiener and Corelli Barnett, but also with Tom Nairn.[48] Decline is explained by the ascendancy within all classes of attitudes and doctrines which have created a culture relatively hostile to commercial and industrial success. Thatcherism is then explained as the attempt to break these attitudes and create a new enterprise culture.

Constitutional and party politics

Writing on all aspects of the constitution has flourished in Britain in the last twenty years. Much of it has been critical, concerned to account for what is seen as the failure of the system to deliver either representative or responsible government. There have been theories attributing the problems of British politics to the harmful effects of adversary politics, the overloading of government, the economic consequences of democracy, elective dictatorship, the unfairness of the electoral system, and the drift of power to the centre.[49]

The deficiencies of Britain's constitutional arrangements were pointed out sharply by Conservative politicians such as Lord Hailsham and by academics like Nevil Johnson. A few years later, suffering under the rule of a different party, intellectuals of the left began to diagnose similar faults in the constitution.[50] Another strand of writing focused on the challenge posed to Westminster by the emergence of strong nationalist parties in Wales and Scotland, discussing the possibility that the UK might be on the point of breaking up.[51]

Writing on the political parties has produced theories of adversary politics and Jim Bulpitt's analysis of the 'high politics' statecraft of the Conservative party, which proposes a theory of the character of political management and how politicians make calculations in the light of the information available to them.[52] There is now a wealth of writing on the party system but as yet no synthesis that ranks with Beer or McKenzie.

What has been lacking in the new constitutional literature, with a few exceptions,[53] is major new work on the relationship between law and politics. Dicey is still often cited as the major authority on the constitution. The two disciplines have drawn apart and there has been little interchange. With the prospects of rapid change in legal and constitutional codes as the result of closer integration with the European Community, and the emergence of programmes such as privatisation which have important legal and constitutional implications, this relationship may change and new interdisciplinary research between law and politics may emerge.

Public policy

Institutionalist approaches were once subjected to fierce attack from behaviouralists but more recently have been staging a recovery. The renewed enthusiasm for studying behaviour within institutional contexts rather than abstracting it from them is in part due to the placing of problems related to the growth in the size and the scope of government at the front of the concerns of political science. An extensive literature has emerged on the extended state, the state as it exists beyond the Cabinet and Parliament, and also beyond Whitehall. Theories of the relations between the subsystems of government and the centre have emerged as the focus for vigorous research into the actual process of policy formulation and implementation, spurred on by the conflict between central and local government in Britain during the 1980s.[54]

Among the most influential theories in this literature have been the theories of corporatism and the theories of the policy-making process – in particular the theories of policy networks and policy communities.[55] Pressure groups are increasingly analysed within this context, as well as the traditional context of Parliament and the political parties. There is also a rapidly developing literature on the core executive.[56]

Public policy theories of British politics have tended to be far more sceptical than either the theories of ideological change or the theories of the constitution and party politics about the scale of the changes achieved in the 1970s and 1980s. The slow, incremental nature of change and the continuities in policy which exist between governments formed by different parties are emphasised, as well as the haphazard, inconsistent, and intermittent nature of party and parliamentary influence. This emphasis partly reflects the increasing use of neo-pluralist and New Right theories of the policy-making process.[57] Many of these models are American political science models. Their appearance signals a further shift from the old assumptions of the Westminster model.

Political economy

The political economy literature also gives ideas and political parties a relatively small role in their explanations. Theories of political economy tend to be deductive, moving from a few postulates about behaviour and interest to models that predict how political agents will act, irrespective of the ideas they hold. What they seek to identify are the structural constraints on action. The key problem which political economy theories have tried to explain is the relative decline of the British economy. The method employed is always comparative, seeking to analyse what is distinctive about the British case.

One notable New Right contribution has been Mancur Olson's theory of the rise and decline of nations.[58] Olson reasons that the more developed and long-established a democracy, the more the logic of collective action ensures that a dense network of interest groups will emerge whose purpose is to protect the interests of their members, fighting for subsidies and other political privileges, and seeking to offload as many costs as possible onto other groups. This theory suggests that democracies succumb to institutional sclerosis at a certain stage of their development, and that this hinders the adaptation that is required to remain economically competitive. It also suggests how too much institutional continuity can become dysfunctional and why governments continually grow.

A vigorous institutionalist and comparative political economy has also arisen, exemplified in the writings of Keith Middlemas, Alan

Cawson, Bob Jessop, Wyn Grant, Peter Hall and David Marquand. Marquand explains British decline as the consequence of the absence of a developmental state, which could have modernised the British economy and British society in ways that were accomplished elsewhere. The constitutional and political preconditions for such a state never emerged, and the political forces in favour of creating them were successfully resisted.[59]

Theories of British decline have also been derived from Marxist political economy, and world systems theory has also provided important explanations of British decline. The consequences for British domestic politics of Britain's place within a world system of formally sovereign nation-states and an increasingly interdependent world economy have been a major focus of this work. An extensive literature has emerged on the economic and political consequences of the relationship between the industrial and financial sectors in Britain. Britain's divided capitalism reflects the special role which Britain has occupied within the world economy.[60] The main thrust of these theories, including those of the New Right, is pessimistic about the prospects for political decisions transforming the performance of the British economy. The forces determining economic outcomes give politicians very little scope for altering the long-term trends.

Political behaviour

These theories emphasise the social context of politics. The focus is on the determinants of mass political behaviour and mass political attitudes. Behavioural methodologies have been dominant and the main subjects of attention have been the explanation of why people vote as they do, what explains levels of political participation and why social movements rise and fall. In much of this literature the emphasis is placed on trends and structures which are not amenable to political influence. Like the public policy and political economy models, these approaches tend to emphasise the limitations of politics and the small scope for choice and individual will.

The different theories of voting behaviour, which include the sociological model, the party identification model, the rational choice model and the dominant ideology model, have had a profound effect on how party competition has been understood.[61] Many of these theories were developed through the incorporation of insights from related disciplines such as economics and sociology. More recently, political geographers have begun to have an important impact on electoral studies, with theories of the spatial effects of voting.[62]

A new diversity

At the end of the 1980s Britain's institutional continuity was still intact, although its political institutions were less celebrated. There had always been critics of Britain's institutions within the traditional British School but it no longer dominates studies of British politics as it once did. As the discipline has become more professionalised, so the idea of political science as a science for legislators, an internal conversation within the political elite about the objectives of government and the best means to achieve them, has receded. The insularity of British political science has declined and British political scientists are now more likely to speak of the peculiarities of British institutions than of their uniqueness. Research into the workings of political processes in Britain has become more firmly established, comparative studies have revived and prescriptive writing on the problems of representative and responsible government has diminished.

A more diverse and fragmented study of British politics is the result, but the critical tradition of the old British School has not been extinguished. Research in British politics still tends to be driven by problems rather than theories but the problems now derive less from the character of Britain's political tradition than from comparative political science and contemporary history. The interest in the constitution, in the role and scope of government and in British decline all raise issues for comparative analysis and stimulate comparative research.

The Westminster model has weakened but it has not disappeared, nor has it been replaced by a coherent alternative. Instead the range of possible perspectives has widened and the variety of methodological approaches has increased. Marxism was once the main challenger to the Westminster model; today the principal challenge comes from neo-liberalism. It has emerged as a major organising perspective for thinking about contemporary problems of British politics. Among its distinctive features are suspicion of the state, faith in markets and hostility to any processes that extend the sway of politics over individual choices and behaviour. Politically it has been associated from the start with the New Right and as such became fashionable in Britain in the 1970s and 1980s. But it is not intrinsically tied to any single ideological position, and its insights and modes of reasoning have been widely employed in political science.[63]

Theories of the state

Yet the New Right model is far from gaining the ascendancy which the Westminster model once enjoyed. There are instead a wide range of different theories which explain the decline of Parliament, the growth of government and the relative decline of the economy. They include the developmental state, libertarianism and collectivism, divided capitalism, institutional sclerosis, overloaded government, and adversary politics. It is impossible to go back to one theory of British politics. In theory as in practice it has become a contested terrain.

What is likely to emerge in the future is a greater emphasis on comparative and interdisciplinary studies. New theories of British politics will be needed to make sense of Britain in the context both of the European Community and of the wider Europe of the 1990s. New connections between politics and law, and politics and geography, will aid the process of theory construction.[64] Assistance will come also as British political science becomes more integrated into American and European political science. In the past, many models for understanding British politics have come from American and European political science. Some have felt that British political science has been too American in its approach; others that it has not been American enough. On balance, American and European models have been an important and valuable stimulus: in electoral behaviour, in public policy, and in political economy. They have helped correct the insularity of the British tradition, which still has its strengths, particularly in historical analysis and the analysis of ideas. Partly because of this, British political scientists have often been reluctant to develop any kind of theory – historical, constitutional, institutional or behavioural. That now seems to be changing.

There remain large gaps in our knowledge of British politics and in our understanding of how it has developed and how it is likely to develop, but the science of British politics has now become a much more powerful engine of research. The pluralism of methods and theories is a strength rather than a weakness, contributing to a fruitful debate and exchange of ideas across perspectives and across disciplines.

The Constitutional Revolution in the United Kingdom[1]

Radical breaks and turning points are always hard to discern at the time. What looks like change can appear at a later date as continuity. How will historians come to assess the first term of the Blair Government elected in May 1997? Will they see it as marking the beginnings of a decisive change in the territorial constitution of the United Kingdom? Or simply the rearrangement of familiar furniture? Certainly in formal legal terms the territorial constitution of the United Kingdom underwent a radical change after 1997, more radical than anything that had happened since the secession of the Irish Free State in 1922. The programme of devolution which unfolded after 1997 was from the beginning the centrepiece of a much wider programme of constitutional reform on which the Government embarked.[2] Following referendums in Scotland and Wales in the autumn of 1997, The Scotland Act 1998 and The Government of Wales Act 1998 were passed, allowing the first elections to be held for the new institutions in 1999. In 1999 also, the Good Friday Agreement on Northern Ireland's constitutional future appeared a major milestone in the peace process in that province.

Early judgements on the significance to be attached to the devolution programme differed. There were sceptics who thought that the constitutional reforms introduced by the Blair Government were largely cosmetic and left the traditional constitution intact.[3] From this perspective the measures of devolution did not live up to the rhetoric, and far from decentralising power they were just another ruse by which Westminster continued to hold sway. Many constitutional conservatives on both right and left, however, were initially extremely alarmed by the changes, and in particular the implication of the devolution proposals for the governability and even the territorial integrity of the United Kingdom. Immediately following the reforms there was no shortage of books with titles like *The Death of Britain?*[4] and *The Abolition of Britain.*[5] On this side of the political argument the Blair Government was viewed as a set of constitutional vandals and tinkerers with no sense of the fragility and importance of the precious organism which had been temporarily entrusted to their charge. Constitutional reformers by contrast welcomed the steps that had been taken, but did not think they went nearly far enough. They believed, however, that change was at last under way, and that a momentum had been released which would eventually lead to further change. The accumulation of anomalies and the working of the new institutions themselves would create pressure for further reform.[6]

Beyond these immediate controversies the devolution process raises larger questions about the nature of political change, the expression of political identity and the function of constitutions. Three long-standing debates are particularly useful for thinking about these issues – the first on the historical roots of the British state and the British constitution;[7] the second on Britishness and national identity;[8] and the third on the consequences of different institutional arrangements, including the many forms of federalism, for democracy and public policy.[9]

This essay assesses the devolution programme of the Blair Government by placing it within these wider historical, comparative and institutional contexts. Power in the UK state has historically tended to be concentrated rather than dispersed. Devolution is not a new issue, but formal devolution of powers has generally been resisted. The Blair reforms raise many questions. Do the changes introduced by the devolution measures enacted after 1997 mark a shift in this pattern, a deviation from the historical path of development, with wider implications for the nature of the UK state? Or are they merely an alteration of form without substance? Do they represent continuity, rupture or reform of British institutions? Do they open the way to recasting the British state on federal lines, or to the formalisation of Britain as a federacy? Will they so unhinge the state as to lead inexorably to its breakup? Why did proposals for devolution succeed in the 1990s when they had failed so often before?

Historical and comparative context

Attempts to understand the territorial constitution of the United Kingdom must start with the peculiarities of the British state as they emerged in a long and generally evolutionary rather than revolutionary process. These peculiarities are inseparable from the role played by

England in this development.[10] The British state began as the English state, and the expansion of this state throughout the territorial space of Britain and Ireland created the United Kingdom. The Union was an extension of the English state, a particular form of English empire and an expression of English sovereignty. The distinctive English perspective on the state crystallises in the sixteenth century, a seminal time of state formation, and is well captured in the Preamble to the 1533 Act in Restraint of Appeals declaring that 'this realm of England is an Empire ... governed by one Supreme Head and King'. Ireland and Wales were forcibly incorporated into this empire. Scotland successfully resisted at first but later negotiated the terms of its incorporation in 1707. The Scottish Parliament was dissolved, and the supremacy of the Westminster Parliament and the Kingdom of England, now renamed the Kingdom of Great Britain was proclaimed.

One of the fundamental ways of classifying constitutions is according to whether they concentrate or disperse power,[11] ranking them both on a federal/unitary dimension and on an executive/parties dimension. On these criteria both the English and, after 1707, the British state appear to have a constitution which is unitary, characterised by executive supremacy and single party majority governments with few checks on their power. All other institutions have tended to be subordinate, or made subordinate to the executive. This includes both chambers of the legislature, the monarchy, the Church, the civil service, the universities, the judiciary, the central bank, as well as the institutions of territorial government.

But as many scholars have argued, Britain has never been a pure type of unitary system in which all power is concentrated and centralised. Because the supremacy of the executive in the United Kingdom is unquestioned it can choose to grant autonomy to various subordinate bodies, and this autonomy can be quite extensive, so long as it does not interfere with the core preoccupations of the centre.[12] This is what makes the British state so peculiar to many outside observers. Its institutional arrangements have in practice permitted varying degrees of autonomy and dispersal of power, while its formal constitutional doctrines have always asserted the unqualified supremacy of the executive. When governments exercise that supremacy, the fragility of other institutions is often apparent, and the absence of formal constitutional obstacles to the centralisation of power in the hands of the executive of the day only too apparent. The degree of power and authority vested in the executive in the UK is only tolerable if exercised within the conventions that have been established over the last three hundred years. But none of these are obstacles to a determined executive – not even some of the most venerable principles such as habeas corpus and due process.

The constitution of the British state is both majoritarian and flexible; majoritarian in the sense that a simple majority in the House of Commons confers full authority on the executive. The winner takes all in this system, the largest minority being rewarded with a majority of the seats in Parliament. The simple plurality electoral system normally ensures disproportional, sometimes wildly disproportional representation of votes, as in the 2005 general election. The constitution is flexible because there are in principle no constraints on what this majority can do. The doctrine of parliamentary sovereignty means that no Parliament has the authority to bind its successor and can legislate in any manner it chooses. In practice there are numerous conventions and practical constraints which limit this flexibility. But compared with many written constitutions and federal systems, the autonomy of the British executive and its freedom from formal restraint are marked. Since 1688 sovereignty in the British state has rested with Parliament, or more precisely Crown-in-Parliament. It is not backbench MPs who exercise sovereignty, but the executive of the British state, which rules through Parliament and is dependent upon Parliament for its legitimacy.[13] The civil wars of the seventeenth century resulted in the Crown losing the ability to rule without the support of Parliament, and the powers and prerogatives of the Crown were gradually transferred to the executive. Parliamentary government is different from the monarchical government which it replaced but it is still a form of executive government, which gives prime importance to the formation and sustaining of a strong executive, and secondary importance to reflecting or representing the electorate.[14]

One of the most important practical constraints is the informal territorial constitution. In a unitary state all powers are vested in a central authority rather than dispersed or divided as in a federal system. The British state would appear to be a unitary state in the supremacy it gives to the executive, but in practice this centralism is heavily qualified by the different arrangements which emerged for governing England, Scotland, Wales and Ireland, subsequently Northern Ireland. These arrangements are not formally federal arrangements; at best they are quasi-federal, but they mean that the United Kingdom has never been a pure type of unitary state. The term which best captures the kind of quasi-federalism which has developed in the United Kingdom is *federacy*, used to denote a large political unity to which smaller units are federated, even though the larger unit is not itself a federation.[15] The basis of the British federacy is that from the outset Britain has been a multi-nation state rather than a single-nation state. Four separate nations have been joined to it, and the British nation and Britishness have been an addition to the national identities of England, Wales, Scotland and Ireland. But Britishness never replaced the primary identities, unlike in some other modern nation-states, and despite attempts at different times to promote assimilation, it was never pursued wholeheartedly, and for the most part the British state was content to use the separate national identities as the basis for an elaborate and differentiated system of territorial governance.

The key to this was England. It was the size and importance of England which made such a loose arrangement possible. From the start the imbalances and asymmetries in the relationships between the four nations and the British state were marked. England was always the dominant partner, because of its population (never less than 60 per cent of the whole, and more recently 85 per cent) and because of its greater wealth. The four nations were therefore very unequal, and were governed differently. In addition there was a double asymmetry in the relation of the Westminster state to England, because of the dominance of London, as the political, administrative, financial and cultural centre, and little significant regional devolution. London acquired a greater dominance within its national territory than any other major European capital. Scotland and Wales in particular came to enjoy more autonomy than the regions of England.

The British constitution combines a single ultimate source of authority with considerable variation in the territorial arrangements for its component nations and regions, which is why the UK has sometimes been described as a union-state, or even a state of unions, rather than as a unitary state.[16] The series of unions between England and the other nations within the British Isles eventually created the United Kingdom, but each of these unions was different, and this was reflected in how they were governed. The formal devolution of powers to the other nations through the establishment of separate Parliaments and Assemblies has highlighted the oddities and anomalies of this 'union-state'. What has also struck observers is that large parts of the British political class from both left and right have always been averse to putting the internal arrangements of the United Kingdom on a formal federal footing. Yet in the wider empire beyond the shores of Britain the Westminster government promoted and sanctioned numerous federal schemes in territories over which it had jurisdiction – in Canada, Australia, the West Indies and parts of Africa. It was only in its empire within the British Isles that federalism was fiercely resisted by important elements of the British political class, fearing that it might destroy the foundations of the British state.

These peculiarities of the territorial constitution of the United Kingdom arose as part of the process of the expansion of the English state and the kind of empire which it established, radiating out from the English core. The United Kingdom was never a federation; other nations, both in the British Isles and then in many other parts of the world, were incorporated through force or by treaty. There was always great variety in the ways these territories were governed, and different opportunities for their citizens to participate in the British state, but there was never any question that it was the British state which enjoyed supreme authority throughout its territories. Other parts of the Empire could seek to operate on the inside to influence the policies of the British state, but when relationships irretrievably broke down, as they did with the American colonies in the eighteenth century and with Ireland in the nineteenth and early twentieth century, the British state proved quite inflexible in dealing with these problems, unable in the end to share power or pool its sovereignty in a way that satisfied the legitimate aspirations of either the Americans or the Irish. One of the big questions about the present devolution programme is whether this has changed. Are the English now ready to make the United Kingdom a federation, in the way that so many other former parts of the Empire became federations with Westminster's blessing? Or will Britain remain at best a federacy, a strong English core, with more explicit quasi-federal arrangements for the other nations?

Political and institutional context

The project of Great Britain which emerged after the Treaty of Union with Scotland in 1707 was the forerunner of the later project of Greater Britain – the attempt to unite all the English-speaking dominions of the Empire into a single state. But there was one crucial difference. By the time the project of Greater Britain was being discussed, the weakness of England, and in particular the impossibility of simply relying on the supremacy of the centre, was apparent. Many of the advocates of imperial union as a result also became federalists, believing that the way to preserve the Union was to disperse and divide power, and allow self-government and autonomy to any part of the Empire which wanted it, in the hope that in this way the unity of the whole could be preserved.[17]

The idea that the British Empire might evolve into a federation, a network of states which governed themselves in most things, but still accepted common membership in a British state, had important implications for the way that Britain itself was governed, in particular the four home nations. Many of those active in the imperial union movement did not shrink from the consequences. They advocated Home Rule for Ireland, and by extension Home Rule for Scotland and Wales also. This became known as Home Rule all round, and many prominent Liberals were attracted to it, including Winston Churchill. As Home Secretary Churchill made a speech at Dundee in 1910 in which he called not only for Parliaments for Scotland, Wales and Ireland but twelve elected assemblies for England. The move to Dominion status of first Canada, then Australia, New Zealand and South Africa concentrated minds in England, and made the constitutional arrangements for the governing of the home nations seem anachronistic. This wing of imperialists hoped that a federal solution for Britain if adopted in time might persuade the Irish to remain British, and might become the blueprint for a wider federal union embracing the English-speaking Dominions as well as in time other British colonies overseas.

The federal option was, however, strongly opposed by the Conservative and Unionist party for the United Kingdom, and specifically for Ireland, on the grounds that to cede sovereignty in this way would rapidly lead to the breakup of the United Kingdom, and to the loss of the institutional forms which had served Britain so well for the previous two hundred years. This intransigence did not in the end prevent an Irish secession, but it did ensure the retention of part of Ulster within the United Kingdom after the rest of Ireland had departed. The failure of Home Rule for Ireland effectively ended the debate on Home Rule for the rest of the United Kingdom for several decades, especially since in the aftermath of the First World War, it quickly became clear that there was no prospect in any case of a wider imperial union, because the Dominions were opposed to it. Other issues came to dominate domestic politics. The rise of Labour following the introduction of universal suffrage made the choice between capitalism and socialism the fundamental question of domestic politics for the next sixty years. Other issues, including devolution and the constitution, tended to be buried.

Devolution and territorial politics became major issues once more in British domestic politics in the 1960s. The Scottish National Party (SNP) and Plaid Cymru emerged for the first time since they were founded in the 1920s as serious electoral forces, while the renewed outbreak of disorder in Northern Ireland destroyed the relative calm which had descended over the province after devolution of power to the

Parliament at Stormont in 1921. The suspension of Stormont in 1972 by the British Government and the imposition of direct rule brought the Irish question back into British politics in a major way. At the same time the surge in nationalist feeling, particularly in Scotland, appeared for a short while to be sweeping all before it. The SNP polled 30.4 per cent of the Scottish vote in the 1974 November general election, winning eleven parliamentary seats.

The immediate reason for the renewed interest in devolution by the major parties was the urgent need to respond to Welsh and Scottish nationalism, and to slow their advance. But this devolution debate took place in a very different context from the earlier devolution debate before 1914. At that time devolution was discussed in the context of Empire and a possible federal imperial union of the English-speaking peoples. By 1970 the Empire was no more, and although the post-imperial transition proved long and tortuous, there was no possibility of going back. Devolution was now discussed in the context of Britain's likely membership of the European Community, and the numerous models of federal and devolved regional government elsewhere in Europe took on a new relevance, especially given the possibility that Europe itself might develop as a federal union. It had a particular impact on the handling of the problem of Northern Ireland, and the renewed violence there, because with both Ireland and Britain members of a larger association, the European Community, some of the old tension in the relationship between them disappeared, and the need to fight over the status of Northern Ireland was weakened. The coming together of the two governments was to be one of the decisive aspects of the eventual breakthrough that led to the peace process and broke the constitutional impasse over Northern Ireland's future.

In the twentieth century the Union was sustained by Empire and by welfare. The Conservatives were particularly associated with the first, and Labour with the second. These were both transnational projects, expressed in common institutions and programmes, which came to define what Britishness meant. Both Conservatives and Labour believed in a strong British state in which all the different nationalities could participate fully. Institutions like the British Army and the National Health Service were therefore crucial in making the case for the existence of Britishness over and above Scottishness, Welshness and Englishness. The distinctive character of the British state as a federacy depended on sustaining a strong sense of Britishness in all four nations. The weakening of Empire from the 1960s onwards, and of welfare from the 1970s onwards were very disorientating for the British polity and its major parties. The basis of a Unionist appeal was undermined, and the purpose of the Union openly questioned by increasing numbers of voters.

The Conservatives were the first to respond to this, and their initial conclusion under the leadership of Edward Heath was radical. The Wilson Government had set up a Royal Commission on the Constitution, but even before it reported, Heath seized the initiative by declaring in 1968 at Perth, the old Scottish capital, that the Conservatives supported the creation of a Scottish assembly. Consistent with his thinking about Britain's place in the world which had led Heath to be a firm proponent of entry to the European Community, the downscaling of Britain's relationship to the United States, and the abandonment of the former imperial framework, Heath saw constitutional reform in the United Kingdom, including devolution to Scotland and Wales and new regional English authorities as measures necessary to modernise the country and bring it more into line with some of its European neighbours. At that time a significant section of the Conservative party in Scotland and its leadership agreed with him. As with Europe, it was the Labour party which was more divided over the question of devolution, since many socialists remained convinced that territorial and constitutional questions were irrelevant, a digression from their chief task, which was implementing programmes of social justice across the whole of Britain. By introducing diversity devolution would mean a move away from creating common standards and common experience for all British citizens.

The industrial and political turmoil of the early 1970s meant that there was no immediate progress on plans for devolution. This had to wait for the Labour Government which held office between 1974 and 1979. A major reason for the decision of the Labour leadership to implement a scheme of devolution in Scotland and Wales was the growing nationalist threat in Scotland and Wales, two areas which were key to Labour's prospects of winning an overall parliamentary majority at Westminster. There remained many people in the Scottish Labour party, however, who were not reconciled to devolution. The Liberals were keen supporters, but the opponents were now joined by the Conservatives, who under their new leader, Margaret Thatcher, abandoned plans for constitutional modernisation, and fell back on an intransigent defence of the status quo. Pro-devolution Scots, including Malcolm Rifkind, the future Foreign Secretary, resigned from the Shadow Cabinet in protest. The bill to hold referendums on the proposed new assemblies was eventually passed, but the Government's loss of an overall majority in Parliament meant that the rebels in its ranks were able to amend the legislation, crucially inserting a clause which only made the result of the referendum valid if 40 per cent of the electorate voted for it. In Scotland a majority of those voting did vote yes, but the 40 per cent threshold was not passed. In Wales there was a sizeable 'no' vote. Shortly after the Callaghan Government lost a no confidence vote at Westminster, partly because the nationalist parties saw no reason any longer to sustain it in office, now that devolution was dead. The new Conservative Government under Margaret Thatcher had no interest in reviving it, and devolution was quietly buried. The old territorial settlement was back in business.

Despite its strong defence of the old constitutional state, and its opposition to any measures of reform, the Thatcher Government is often seen as the catalyst which created an unstoppable momentum for devolution, because of the way it relentlessly centralised power and drove through policies in areas such as Scotland which had not voted for them. The need for devolution and self-government to protect regions from the depredations of the Westminster elective dictatorship, when this was controlled by a party few in Scotland had voted for, now became widely recognised. A broad-based movement in Scottish civil society emerged to press for the restoration of the Scottish Parliament and the return of self-government.

This reputation of the Thatcher Government is more myth than reality. Scotland and Wales were in fact protected from the full force of the Thatcherite policies that were applied in England. In Wales, Peter Walker ran a distinctly non-Thatcherite administration at the Welsh Office.[18] For much of the 1980s the Scottish Secretary was George Younger, who used his office to gain concessions and subsidies for Scotland in the time-honoured fashion.[19] Only later were fatal mistakes made, particularly over the new local tax, the community charge, dubbed by its opponents the poll tax. But even here the poll tax was introduced because of the very strong demand from Scottish Conservatives for the abolition of the local property tax known as the rates, and not because Scotland was being used as a test bed for policies that were to be introduced in England. Nevertheless as so often in politics the perception mattered more than the reality, and the intense unpopularity of Margaret Thatcher in Scotland did give an enormous boost to the campaign for Scottish self-government, culminating in the establishment of the Scottish Convention and the issuing of the Claim of Right.

In the 1990s two of the Unionist parties in Britain, Labour and the Liberal Democrats, became strongly committed to devolution for both Scotland and Wales. The third Unionist party, the Conservatives, remained firmly opposed, and under John Major its opposition if anything hardened. By posing as the defenders of the old constitutional state and warning that devolution would lead to the breakup of Britain and Scottish independence, the Conservative position was entirely clear and consistent, but their support in Scotland continued to weaken. The party which had had a majority of the Scottish seats in 1955 ended in 1997 with no seats at all. It also lost all its seats in Wales. During the 1990s the initiative passed decisively to the proponents of reform. Nevertheless the reasons for supporting change varied. The number of committed federalists were relatively few, and mostly to be found in the Liberal Democrats. Labour's motives were more mixed. Devolution was supported partly because the Labour movement in Scotland had now come down decisively in favour of it, and partly as a reaction to the Thatcher years and the impotence of the Labour party at Westminster. Almost a quarter of the seats Labour won at the 1983 general election were in Scotland.

Neil Kinnock at first followed a strong tradition on the left of the party in dismissing devolution, but after assuming the leadership he became a convert to it, and under his successor John Smith, the party embraced it as a major principle. When John Smith died in 1994, the new leader, Tony Blair, did not attempt to change the commitment, and although some doubted his enthusiasm, it remained an important part of his discussions and understanding with Paddy Ashdown, the leader of the Liberal Democrats, before the 1997 election.[20] Once elected, Labour lost no time in carrying its pledges into effect. Referendums were held in Wales and Scotland in 1997, the legislation to create the new Parliament and Assembly passed in 1998, and the first elections were held in 1999. At the same time the Government secured a renewed IRA ceasefire and began the process of negotiation that led to the Good Friday Agreement.

Evaluating devolution

The scale of the changes to the territorial constitution introduced after 1997 are impressive, but the substance has been questioned. In particular the trajectory of the reforms has been the subject of much debate. Is a real break in British constitutional arrangements in prospect, or will path dependency reassert itself? As mentioned at the outset there is no shortage of those who believe that the changes are largely illusory. The reforms have not delivered self-government, or federal institutions, or done much to limit the continued supremacy of the Westminster executive. From this standpoint the reforms look like a clever device to appease pressure from nationalists wanting full separation and from constitutional reformers wanting to decentralise power. The devolution settlement is another tactic by the Westminster executive to set up new institutional arrangements which appear to devolve powers to subordinate bodies, but which in reality give away nothing of importance, and certainly nothing which at Westminster is regarded as the preserve of 'high politics'. This is centralism again, clothed differently to be sure, but still centralism.

Constitutional conservatives are dismayed by the changes, and although they have to acknowledge that so far their dire warnings of the breakup of the United Kingdom have not come true, they also think that the United Kingdom is in danger of drifting apart.[21] As in many federal systems the granting of greater autonomy to different regions can lead to a growing divergence in their political culture and political economy. In the case of the UK, constitutional conservatives fear that the sense of being British will be undermined by the new arrangements, and that more and more people will no longer acknowledge a British identity in addition to their primary national identity. But they are also aware that reversing the constitutional changes will be very difficult, and most Conservatives, including crucially younger Conservatives, are now reconciled to it.[22]

The British Parliament has the power to abolish the Scottish Parliament and the Welsh Assembly by a simple majority vote in both Houses, but since both were sanctioned by referendums, it would be politically difficult to abolish them without the sanction of a further vote by the people. In this way several of the constitutional measures introduced by the Blair Government appear to be entrenched, and not subject to a simple exercise of parliamentary sovereignty at Westminster. The people of Wales and Scotland have a veto over the removal of the institutions that have been granted them by the Westminster executive. Like earlier reforms such as the granting of universal suffrage, there are some changes which the British Parliament can in practice not reverse. Even those minor parties in the 2005 election, such as the United Kingdom Independence Party (UKIP) and its splinter party, Veritas, which were viscerally opposed to devolution and to separate representative institutions for Scotland and Wales, conceded in their manifestos that until the Scots and Welsh wish to give up these institutions, they cannot be taken away.

The constitutional reformers are divided over the reforms. Some incline to the sceptic position, and are disillusioned with what has so far been achieved. The limited powers, particularly of the Welsh Assembly, are cited. The defeat of the proposal in a referendum in 2004 to set up an assembly for the North East of England region is ascribed to the very limited powers which the Government was proposing to confer on it. The apparent indifference of the Government to the many anomalies and inconsistencies that have arisen in the implementation of the devolution programme, and the refusal of ministers to put their reforms into a wider context of democratic renewal, make many reformers fear the worst. But some remain optimistic, arguing that despite the many hesitations and mistakes of the Government, the devolution programme has been rolled out, the institutions are in place, and some significant changes in policy and also in the style of representation and of government have taken place. Furthermore they believe that the logic behind devolution will gradually build pressure for further changes, and that eventually the momentum will become unstoppable.[23] This rests on the belief that once citizens have experienced self-government they will not want to give it up.

The reforms were not announced as part of a grand new constitutional settlement, but have emerged piecemeal, with solutions being tailored to particular circumstances and pressures. This has led to criticism that there is no overall design or direction to the reforms, and many anomalies that will have to be dealt with at some time in the future. That may be so, but it should be remembered that the British constitution, like many constitutions elsewhere, has always been riddled with anomalies yet has survived. A successful constitution may need anomalies, and may need to tolerate asymmetries. Part of the success of the British constitution has been its flexibility, and its ability to avoid the application of rigid rules. The United Kingdom is never likely to adopt a tidy, rational and consistent constitutional document of the kind which many constitutional reformers such as the pressure group Charter 88 have advocated.[24] The degree of tolerance of the British for muddle, ambiguity and inconsistency has always infuriated reformers. It has generally meant that reform when it takes place happens slowly, incrementally and haltingly. The degree to which this sets the United Kingdom apart from other states should not, however, be exaggerated. Many other federal and non-federal systems tolerate asymmetries for the sake of political peace. Conservative disquiet at the reforms was often because they shed too much light on things that were better left obscure and unstated.

The great unresolved questions of the post-1997 devolution settlement are whether it is the starting point of a much larger change, or merely the end of an old song, the completion of a process begun much earlier; whether the momentum towards Scottish and Welsh independence has been halted or merely slowed; whether the Good Friday Agreement has solved the constitutional problem in Northern

Ireland and in doing so has provided the basis for a lasting peace; and whether under the new dispensation England can continue for long without either regional assemblies or an English parliament.

Northern Ireland is often discussed quite separately from the rest of the United Kingdom, partly because it is perceived as distinct in so many ways, and partly because its problems are regarded as unfinished business from the 1920s. The basis on which six of the original nine counties of Ulster were allowed to remain within the United Kingdom when the rest of Ireland seceded was always unsatisfactory, since it was designed to maintain the Protestant ascendancy which necessarily excluded the Catholic population of Ulster from full participation. It succeeded in this for forty years, but when it was challenged in the 1960s the Stormont regime quickly unravelled and the Westminster executive had to take back direct responsibility for the province. Ever since then policies of military containment of the IRA and other paramilitaries have gone hand in hand with the search for a political solution. This solution has been slow to emerge but the process was begun under the Thatcher Government with direct talks with the IRA and culminated in the signing of the Good Friday Agreement in 1999. What is significant about this agreement is less the details of power sharing but the underlying constitutional agreement between the Irish and British Governments, in which the Irish gave up their constitutional claim to jurisdiction of Northern Ireland, and the British accepted that Northern Ireland was only de facto part of the United Kingdom and that its constitutional future was a matter for the people of Ireland and not for the people of Britain.[25] This echoed the famous statement from the Major Government in the earlier Downing Street Declaration that the British Government had no selfish or strategic interest in Northern Ireland, in response to which a Conservative MP, Nicholas Budgen, pointedly asked in the House of Commons whether the British Government had any selfish or strategic interest in Wolverhampton (his constituency). The decision by the British Government to abandon its claim to sovereignty over any piece of Ireland, while defending the right of the majority of the population in Northern Ireland to continue to choose to be part of the United Kingdom, was the key advance. It enabled the leadership of both sides of the sectarian divide in Northern Ireland to claim victory and to recommend to their supporters that they share power with their historic enemies. This process is still not complete, but by 2005 it appeared tantalisingly close, and the IRA ceasefire seemed increasingly unlikely to be broken.

Devolution will only be restored in Northern Ireland if there is a lasting agreement on power-sharing, but this will not be devolution as it is practised elsewhere in the United Kingdom. The split between the two communities means that the minority rejects Britishness and British identity, while the majority still cleaves to it. If power-sharing returns, it will make Northern Ireland still less like the rest of the United Kingdom rather than more like it, and it is hard to see how the province could ever become a building block for a new federal system in the United Kingdom. With its separate parties and institutions, divided loyalties, and its relationship to Dublin it will remain apart. Power was devolved to Stormont in the 1920s for reasons of political expediency, but ultimately the policy failed. When devolution was revived, it was done under very different conditions, and in a way which loosened British links and claims.

Scotland and Wales are very different, in that the Scottish nation and the Welsh nation which the nationalist parties seek to mobilise to demand self-determination and self-government, do not have to share their national space with another nation, as in Northern Ireland. Unionists in Wales and Scotland have no difficulty in claiming to be Welsh and British or Scottish and British at the same time. In Northern Ireland, British is the primary identity for Unionists, while Irish is the primary identity for nationalists. The problem for the Scottish and Welsh nationalists was that although they had achieved substantial electoral support since the 1970s they had yet to make a decisive breakthrough. Devolution did not immediately create a new momentum towards independence. The decline in the numbers of people in Wales and Scotland identifying themselves as British as well as Scottish and Welsh has continued, but this decline in Britishness had not been associated with any increase in support for nationalism. In the 2005 election the SNP gained two seats but its share of the vote fell (to 17 per cent) behind both Labour and the Liberal Democrats and only just ahead of the Conservatives. In Wales Plaid Cymru lost both seats and votes. The Unionist parties breathed a sigh of relief. But particularly in Scotland it was to be the calm before the storm.

Conclusion

How far the constitutional changes since 1997 represent the beginning of a new chapter or the end of an old one was disputed. For some of those who had long hoped for the emergence of strong independent self-governing nations in Wales, Scotland, and England, the results of devolution were disappointing. They had not produced a genuine move towards either federalism or independence, but for the moment they had dampened nationalist ardour. There was some pressure, particularly in Wales, to take more powers from Westminster, and the Labour Government promised legislation, but there was little desire for more far-reaching measures. After the first decade of devolution how stable this would prove to be was uncertain. It was widely acknowledged that the real test of the devolution arrangements would come when a different party was in power in Edinburgh or Cardiff to the one in Westminster, creating a new nationalist dynamic, as had happened in Canada in Quebec.[26] If Quebec were ever to vote to leave Canada, the impact would be felt around the world, since up to now there is no clear example of the successful secession of a minority region from a state which has become a full democracy. There have been federations which have been dissolved, such as the Federation of the West Indies, but within established democracies the complex trade-offs between interest and identity and the concessions made to intending secessionists tend to inhibit breakaways.

One of the biggest impacts of devolution was expected to be on England, but again the effects were initially small. Conservative columnists like to quote the writer G.K. Chesterton, warning menacingly that the people of England 'never have spoken yet', but the English have proved difficult to arouse. The emphatic rejection of the proposal for an elected assembly in the North East of England in 2004 killed the Government's plans for a gradual extension of assemblies throughout England. Similarly the ideas of the Conservative leader, William Hague, before the 2001 election of 'English votes for English laws', and his floating of the idea of establishing a possible English parliament, made little headway at the time.[27] The anomaly of Scottish MPs after devolution voting on matters in the Westminster Parliament affecting England, while English MPs were unable to vote on such matters in Scotland, was indefensible. Yet there was no great sense of grievance among English people about this state of affairs, or about the imbalances in funding and representation which the territorial constitution continued to authorise. It suited the Labour Government to maintain the status quo, since so much of its majority depended on its Scottish MPs. From a party point of view the Conservatives had everything to gain from playing the English card. In 2005 they had a slight advantage in votes over Labour in England (although a big deficit in seats). Scotland and Wales remained major areas of Conservative weakness, and Conservatives were aware that their electoral prospects would be considerably strengthened if either or both of them were no longer represented in the Westminster Parliament. But under William Hague and his successors the Conservatives remained a Unionist party, and resisted the calls of those who want the party to be the champion of an assertive English nationalism.[28]

Vernon Bogdanor has argued that the reforms have shifted Britain towards a form of quasi-federalism.[29] The desire for greater self-government also chimes with the drive towards a regulatory state, in which many functions which would once have been carried out centrally are devolved to subordinate bodies.[30] In response to these pressures the constitutional basis of the United Kingdom has changed in a federal direction, yet in comparative terms it remains a federacy rather than a federation. The supremacy of the Westminster executive has been qualified, but not removed.[31] In 2006 the new system had still to be fully tested, but its architects hoped that it had established a new equilibrium in Britain's constitutional affairs. A further shift towards federalism or towards breakup was possible but in the years before the financial crash and Brexit looked unlikely. In Lijphart's terms the United Kingdom had become less centralist and less unitary than it had been, but it was still a long way from a political system which is truly federal and decentralised, and many doubted that it ever would be.

What's British about
British Politics?[1]

Britain is a settled polity. It has been a full democracy for almost one hundred years, and it has representative institutions and a continuous political tradition stretching back to the seventeenth century. During that time its external fortunes have risen and fallen but it has not experienced either internal revolution or external invasion and occupation. Many have argued that it is this experience which has made Britain special, the essential context for understanding its politics, and its success in managing orderly and peaceful change.

Britain is also a troubled polity. The unity of the United Kingdom was first broken when Ireland separated in 1921, and in recent decades it has been threatened again by the conflict in Northern Ireland and by the rise of the Scottish National Party (SNP) to dominate the politics of Scotland. It only narrowly lost the referendum on independence in September 2014, and the issue has not been closed. Britain held another referendum, on its future within the European Union, in June 2016. By a narrow margin (52:48) Britain voted to Leave, but there were different votes in the four nations of the UK. England and Wales voted to Leave, while Scotland and Northern Ireland voted to Remain. Britain's external standing and global reach have declined sharply in the last hundred years as its empire collapsed and its industrial pre-eminence receded. Trust in the integrity and competence of its political class has weakened too, because of the 2008 financial crash and its aftermath, inconclusive military interventions such as Iraq and Libya, political scandals and anxieties about immigration. The mismatch between representative institutions and grassroots democracy has steadily grown, with anti-system and anti-politics insurgencies challenging established elites.[2]

Does any of this make British politics distinctive? Does Britain's experience stand out from the experience of any other European state of similar population and resources in the last seventy years?

Every nation-state in the modern world claims that its own experience is special, and has developed its own national myth. That makes states different but does it make them distinctive? Or are all modern states just variations on a common theme? If we look closely, are not all states that have reached a certain stage of economic and political development pretty similar, and the way they conduct their everyday politics essentially the same? The evidence from Eurobarometer indicates that while there is considerable variation of attitudes within member states, it is much less than might be expected.[3]

This essay explores these issues by examining some of the main features of the British state which are said to make British politics distinctive – its multinational character, its highly centralised institutions, its uncodified constitution, its imperial legacy, its Anglo–liberal political economy, and its liberal political culture. Each of these is examined to see whether or not these features truly mark out Britain as distinctive or whether they are merely variations on patterns found in many other countries.

Long-term social and economic trends – industrialisation, secularisation, rationalisation, globalisation and regionalisation – shape the contexts and constraints within which all politicians have to operate and reduce their autonomy. They are often seen as inexorable forces which lead states to become increasingly alike, ironing out national differences and idiosyncrasies, and obliging governments to behave in very similar ways. Because modern states share many of the same problems they often gravitate to similar solutions. They learn from one another, they compete with one another, they imitate one another. In this way they become more like one another.

If politics is a universal and necessary aspect of human experience, an activity which arises whenever human beings form associations, managing the conflicts of interest which arise among them, then we might expect politics to be much the same everywhere, with the same patterns and underlying logic. If this were so there would be nothing particularly distinctive about British politics, nothing especially 'British'. Politics in Britain would be fundamentally the same as politics in France, politics in the United States or politics in Egypt.

What makes politics distinctive in different places and different times, such as Britain in the twenty-first century, is that politics arises to manage the clash not just of different interests but different beliefs and different perspectives, and in doing so helps create and sustain a common world of values, institutions, rules and discourses, making it possible for human beings to cooperate with one another. These common worlds are more than just a matter of common interests but also involve common identities and common institutions.[4] Understanding politics through identity focuses on who we are and where we belong, distinguishing between friends and enemies, those who are included and those who are excluded from a political community. Understanding politics through institutions focuses on the rules and discourses which create an order, establishing a set of assumptions and prescriptions which define the context in which political activity takes place. Both these understandings of politics anchor politics in a specific time and space. In the modern era the most common site for politics has been the nation state, defined by notions of sovereignty and territory, and supplying a framework for a common world, a community of fate. Such a community is formed when all its members are inescapably bound together because they share a common identity. They belong to an *order* which is distinctive and exceptional. The peculiarities of each nation–state shape its politics.

A multinational state

From this perspective Britain (and all other bounded national political systems) is a specific configuration of identity and interest, which creates an order which is distinctive but not unique. There are differences, but also many commonalities. One of the most distinctive aspects of British politics has always been the notion of Britishness which is rooted in the territorial politics of its multinational state.

Several other European states have territorial politics as complicated as the United Kingdom, among them Belgium, Spain and Italy. In all those states significant minorities claim a separate national identity and assert the right to self-determination and the establishment of their own state. The desire of many Scots to secede from the United Kingdom is not so different from the desire of many Catalans to secede from Spain. The norm in Europe has been for states to express a single national identity, but a number of European states like the UK remain multinational. Where Britain's multinational state is different from others is that it came into existence before the modern era of national self-determination and popular sovereignty. Scotland's accession to the Union in 1707 was the result of agreement rather than annexation, and so created a union-state,[5] which was different from either a unitary state or a federal state, the two main forms of European state in the modern era, because it was founded on the union of two independent nations.

One of the things that makes British politics distinctively British has been the internal dynamics of Britain's union-state, which include the asymmetry of the governing arrangements of its different territories, nationalist insurgencies against Westminster rule, and the way the party system has been shaped by territorial as well as class cleavages in the modern era. The trumping of the Labour party's class appeal by the new identity politics of the Scottish National Party (SNP) in 2015, depriving Labour of one of its most important electoral strongholds, is the most recent example of this.

Most other European states made determined efforts to weld their citizens into a single nation, actively suppressing regional institutions, languages and cultures, making the nation the focus of loyalty and identity, the primary imagined community within a territorial space, and the state its expression. In many parts of Europe the nation was deemed to exist before a state had been created to represent it, and often that meant altering boundaries to bring the two into alignment. In the Kingdom of Great Britain and then after 1801 in the *United Kingdom* of Great Britain and Ireland the position was rather different. The state had been created first, and although some effort was put at first into building a unified British nation to underpin it, the separate cultural identities of the four nations did not disappear but flourished alongside one another within the same state.[6] The United Kingdom became (accidentally) an early experiment in multiculturalism and multinationalism. There were other much larger multinational states in Europe, notably the Austro-Hungarian Empire and the Russian Empire, but the British multinational state is unusual for surviving into the democratic era.

The establishment of the British state as a union between more than one nation was the key fact in the emergence of Britishness. It exists because a British state exists. There was no prior British nation which could give it legitimacy. Instead a British national identity had to be created alongside separate Scottish, Irish, Welsh and English national identities. British national identity was originally a product of the union of Scotland and England. This new union-state contained within it the annexed territories of Wales and Ireland. It took them much longer to be accorded the privileges Scotland enjoyed from the beginning. Ireland did not even appear in the name of this new state – Great Britain. A new British identity and British institutions gradually emerged in the course of the eighteenth century.[7] The monarchy had been British since the Union of the Crowns in 1603, now it was joined by Parliament and the army. The British (Scots, English and Welsh) were also united by being predominantly Protestants against the Catholic monarchies of

Europe, although Protestantism itself was internally divided, and the Scottish Kirk remained very different from the Church of England. The pursuit of colonies and commerce also came to unify the new nation, but many things remained separate. The Bank of England, for example, which had been established in 1694 just before the Union, was never renamed the Bank of Britain, although in time it came to preside over a UK–wide currency union.

Over the next two hundred and fifty years the new state became adorned by new British institutions from the British Museum and the Royal Mail to the BBC and the National Health Service. The British built the richest and most powerful state in the world and set international standards in many different fields. Their soft power, the cultural appeal of the British way of doing things, the spread of the English language, went alongside the hard power of their gold and guns. The inventions which poured from Britain were not only technological and industrial, but also included new sports and games and a remarkable range of social and cultural organisations which came to be copied in many other countries, as well as dress, manners, hobbies and much else which came to define the modern world.[8]

World leadership after 1815 for a time made Britain seem more exceptional among other European states than it really was.[9] In the democratic era Britain was unable to defend its Empire or even its Union against the claims of national self-determination. The loss of Ireland from the Union in 1921 foreshadowed the much larger dismemberment that was to come after 1945 with the withdrawal from the great majority of Britain's overseas possessions, and which compelled Britain to readjust its position in the world, becoming in the process a normal European state again. Empire along with the creation of a welfare state had helped define Britishness and keep the Union together. But with the Empire no more, apart from a few scattered outposts, and with the push to devolution fragmenting the sense of a common citizenship with the same social and economic rights, defining Britishness had become much harder by the beginning of the twenty-first century. Since the 1970s in particular the identities associated with the four nations which make up the United Kingdom have become more salient.[10] At one time most English people thought of themselves interchangeably as English and as British. The Unionists in Northern Ireland gave their primary identity as British. The Scots and the Welsh were more equivocal but large numbers still embraced both identities. That position has changed in recent years, particularly since the big push to devolution began in the 1990s. Now a majority of Scots identify themselves as more Scottish than British, and within that majority around 25 per cent refuse the label of British altogether. In England too attitudes have begun to change, although less dramatically. There is now a significant number of the English who give their primary identity as English (17 per cent) and another 12 per cent who consider themselves more English than British. 44 per cent still think of themselves as equally English and British.[11] But this is no longer a majority position.

The nature of Britishness is changing and British politics as a result is becoming more fragmented. The United Kingdom is less united by the activities of its state than it was in the past, whether through the promotion of empire or the welfare state, and with the weakening of these bonds of unity the identity which this state promoted is weakening too. British politics is still distinctively British because the British state and its core institutions continue to exist, but it is distinctively British in a new way. It is the increasing exclusiveness of the separate national identities rather than the way they are integrated into a harmonious whole in which they complement Britishness rather than compete with it, which has come to characterise British territorial politics.[12]

A centralised state

Britain is often seen as more centralised than other states, partly because its constitution concentrates rather than disperses power, and is unitary rather than federal, and partly because of London, which is much more dominant than capital cities in comparable states. Only Paris comes close. London's dominance can be measured by many indicators including the concentration of wealth, of finance, of media, of the arts, of politics, of sport, of tourism, of transport links, of infrastructure spending, of employment and of government agencies in the capital and its immediate hinterland. As a global city London has its own distinct political economy, and has become noted for its high levels of immigration, its cosmopolitan culture and the spiralling cost of its housing. It tends to suck talent and resources from the rest of the country, but although the imbalance has long been recognised, rectifying it has proved difficult.

The centralisation of decision-making in London can be observed in the way the British state manages public spending. In many respects the British state operates as other European states do. The size of the state falls within the European range, towards the middle or low end. Public spending was below 10 per cent of national income before 1914, stabilised at around 20–25 per cent in the 1920s and 1930s, following the big increase in the First World War, before rising sharply again in the Second World War and stabilising at around 38–42 per cent in the post-war period. It has occasionally risen higher than this, as a result of the severe recessions in 1974 and 2009, resulting in fiscal squeezes to bring public spending back into line with the shrunken economy. Politically it seems very difficult to push the percentage of public spending higher or lower than the post-war average. The Thatcher Government talked about rolling back the state but the size of the state did not alter very much. The composition of public spending was changed, but not the overall amount. It proved much harder than expected to make significant inroads into the state, except for short periods.

The reasons for this can be found in the functions which modern states carry out. The original functions of the state were preserving external defence, internal law and order, maintaining sound money and protecting property rights. In the twentieth century the state gradually assumed major roles in stabilising and regulating market economies to prevent slumps and promote growth and prosperity; second in providing social protection and social investment through welfare, education and health programmes; and third in investment to promote technological innovation, provide better infrastructure and foster faster growth. States have as a result become multi-purpose, multi-agency, and multi-layered, with highly complex systems of governance and coordination.

These features are true of all states and have been made necessary by the way modern economies and societies and democracies work. All advanced economies for example have developed welfare states. They vary in their generosity, and this is reflected in the proportion of national resources devoted to them and therefore in the fiscal regime which underpins them. As Esping-Andersen observed, by the end of the 1980s three distinct worlds of welfare capitalism had emerged based on the strength of the different class coalitions in different countries.[13] The British welfare state had become distinctly less generous than either the Nordic social democratic welfare states or than the conservative welfare states of central Europe. Britain belonged to a cluster of liberal residual welfare states, although even within this group there were important differences. While income support in Britain has over time become much less generous than many other welfare states, Britain has retained some universal services free at the point of use, most notably its National Health Service. All three models of welfare capitalism in Esping-Andersen's schema are recognisably welfare states. The politics of the welfare state in Britain, as in other residual welfare states in the Anglo–American world, has come to discriminate between the deserving and the undeserving poor (strivers and shirkers) by focusing on squeezing the benefits of those deemed capable of working, while protecting those of groups deemed deserving, such as pensioners, and also protecting the universal services. Difficult though this is to do in practice (many of the working poor receive tax credits), this is a distinctive pattern when compared with many European welfare states, but it is not a unique pattern. Britain shares it with several other liberal market economies.[14]

While the core functions of the state do not differ very much from what is found elsewhere, the degree of centralisation of the British state and some key public services like the NHS is distinctive. Most taxes are collected centrally, the Treasury has control of all budgets, there is very little hypothecation of taxes (tying taxes to particular programmes), and very little autonomy for local bodies. Many taxes are spent locally, but the priorities are established centrally. More than two thirds of the resources available to local government are collected and allocated centrally. Only around 15 per cent of local government revenue is raised through the council tax, and even this is subject to government control. The pattern is very different in most other European countries, where local autonomy is buttressed by a much greater degree of fiscal autonomy. This used to be the case in Britain but successive governments have found it useful to control spending priorities from the centre, and not allow any real devolution of powers. Even in the case of Scotland and Wales one of the most contentious issues has been the extent of fiscal devolution they should be given by Westminster. The UK has long been one of the most centralised states in Europe, but devolution has begun to change this, and more decentralisation is expected. How far this will challenge the dominance of Whitehall and London is unclear. Up to now this dominance has been a distinctive feature of British politics. Controlling the levers in Whitehall has been the main focus of political competition, and much less energy has gone into local politics. All parts of the UK have been subordinated to London.

An uncodified constitution

A second distinctive feature of British politics is the particular combination of representative and responsible government which Britain developed over three centuries and which became known as the Westminster model.[15] Even after the transition to democracy in the twentieth century, the aristocratic and monarchical elements in the British constitution were still pronounced, in part because in contrast with almost all other democracies, Britain never adopted a formal codified constitution. Several important aspects of its state were adopted in pre-modern and pre-democratic times, particularly the prerogative powers retained by the monarch as head of state, but exercised by the Prime Minister; the unelected second chamber, the House of Lords; the doctrine of parliamentary sovereignty, Crown-in-Parliament; and the first-past-the-post electoral system. The gradual evolution of this aristocratic polity into a democratic one left many features of the old British state intact. In comparative terms this has placed Britain among western democracies as concentrating power rather than dispersing it, majoritarian rather than pluralist, and centralised rather than decentralised.[16] Despite the devolution of some powers to Wales and Scotland since 1997 and changes to the voting systems for many subordinate bodies in the UK, this characterisation still holds good for Westminster itself.

The doctrine of parliamentary sovereignty for example implies that there is no higher authority than Parliament. Its sovereignty is potentially unlimited. Popular sovereignty, although a de facto reality since universal suffrage, is not formally acknowledged in Britain, as it is in all other democracies. It is recognised indirectly in the supremacy of the elected chamber of Parliament, the House of Commons, over the unelected chamber, the House of Lords, since the Parliament Act of 1911. Perhaps surprisingly for the country that gave birth to Magna Carta, constitutional doctrine still maintains that there is in principle no law which a Parliament cannot change, because no Parliament can bind its successors. In practice there are a host of conventions, procedures and organised interests in the state and outside it which prevent Parliament acting despotically. But the principle of unfettered sovereignty remained the cornerstone of the legal authority of the British state.

This has begun to change, in ways that may ultimately make British politics less distinctive, but during the process of transition emphasise just how different British political institutions are from other democracies. These changes include membership of the European Union, devolution to the Scottish Parliament and the Welsh Assembly, and the passage of the Human Rights Act. There are now things which a British Parliament is in practice unable to change, and legal parameters it has to work within. In theory the British Parliament could still dissolve the Scottish Parliament and the Welsh Assembly and rescind the devolution settlement. It could also in theory repeal by a simple majority vote the acts which established universal suffrage. In practice there are some changes which once made become politically irreversible. There is no prospect, for example, of devolution being overturned, except in response to an extreme emergency. That means the sovereignty of the Westminster Parliament is now qualified. It has to acknowledge the sovereignty of the other representative assemblies in the United Kingdom. There may not yet be a constitution in the way the rest of Europe understands it, but as Vernon Bogdanor has argued,[17] a new constitution has gradually emerged, which marks a break from the traditional Westminster model. In this sense British politics is becoming less idiosyncratic and more European, but there is still a considerable way to go. House of Lords reform has taken a hundred years already and is still not complete. With 826 unelected members it has become by a considerable margin the largest and the least representative second chamber anywhere in the democratic world, but is playing an increasingly important part in policy-making.[18]

Britain used to be celebrated for its success in combining representative and responsible government in contrast to less happy lands.[19] What is now distinctive about British politics is that its traditional constitution is increasingly a source of instability rather than stability, whether it is the asymmetry of its devolution arrangements, the lack of a body to oversee the arrangements between the different parts of the UK and adjudicate conflicts, or the mismatch between votes and seats delivered by the first-past-the-post electoral system.

Britain has long enjoyed a greater degree of institutional continuity than most other European states. There has never been the occasion in the recent past for a wholesale rewriting of the British constitution, starting again from a blank slate and a constitutional convention. The British disposition is to muddle through, seeking only incremental change, and dealing with the unforeseen consequences of piecemeal change as they arrive. The untidiness of British constitutional arrangements does not bother most of the British, who accept the often complex, arcane and convoluted practices by which Britain is governed as natural.

Traditionalists bemoan the loss of the old uncodified constitution, and its dense patchwork of laws, conventions and precedents.[20] Reformers are in despair at the slow pace of change. There is endless tinkering and adjustments to the present arrangements but little sense of direction or what a desirable constitutional order for the UK should now be. Key constitutional arrangements, such as whether there should be two classes of MP in the Westminster Parliament, are in flux and open to question. Legitimacy has drained away from Parliament and the political class, in part because of scandals like the parliamentary expenses scandal in 2009. Yet although some argue that the amount of corruption in the UK has increased,[21] it remains lower than in many other states, and far below the levels of the early nineteenth century. A greater cause of declining legitimacy is the way in which Parliament no longer represents the current multinational and multiparty reality of British politics. British politicians were once distinctive for the ability to manage the orderly evolution of its political institutions. But with so many unresolved constitutional questions and anomalies which recent reforms have created, that ability is now in question.

A post-imperial state

A third distinctive aspect of British politics arises from the role Britain plays in the international state system, and in particular Britain's continuing ambivalence between Europe and America.[22] Britain's capacity and global reach may have declined in the last seventy years but British politics is still shaped by Britain's experience as an empire and a leading great power for more than two hundred years. It is responsible for many policies which are characteristic of the British polity, such as the debates on whether Britain should or should not retain a nuclear deterrent, whether it should continue to spend a larger proportion of its national income on its armed forces than other European states, and whether as a permanent member of the UN Security Council or as an ally of the United States it should be willing to deploy its troops abroad.

Britain became the closest ally of the United States in forming the western alliance and reconstructing the post-war international market order, and has been willing on several recent occasions to support US military interventions and also to conduct military interventions of its own.

British political culture since the Second World War has been noticeably more willing to celebrate its military and favour military action than has been the case in most other European states. The European country Britain most resembles in this respect is France, another former European imperial power. Britain spends the same proportion of its national income (2 per cent) on defence as France, which is double that spent by Germany, Italy or Japan. But in Britain there is something else as well. Its experience in the Second World War of successfully resisting invasion and occupation and then being part of the victorious coalition against the Axis powers has become the most important single component of a reworked national story, Britain standing alone against impossible odds. As a result seventy years since it ended British culture at all levels is still saturated with references to the Second World War. This is not the case anywhere else in Europe apart from Russia. The British political elite from right to left is still deeply preoccupied with geopolitics and Britain's international status and international influence. British politics is constantly convulsed with arguments not on whether Britain should intervene but on how it should intervene, militarily or in some other way.

Britain's past history and inherited commitments are used to justify a continuing role in the international state system which is often in danger of outrunning the capacities of the British state to fulfil. Although it had to accept the absolute decline in its power, the British political class still had great difficulty in adjusting to it and finding an appropriate role to play. This was captured by Dean Acheson, one of the key architects of US foreign policy after 1945, who observed in 1962 that Britain had lost an empire and not yet found a role. He argued that Britain could no longer expect to play a role apart from Europe, maintaining 'a special relationship' with the United States and aspiring to be a broker between the United States and Russia, based primarily on being the head of a commonwealth which had 'no political structure, or unity, or strength'. British policy he argued had become as weak as its military power.[23]

The British political class came to accept this criticism. After the failed Suez intervention in 1956, British governments were already aware that a special relationship with the United States was no longer available on the old terms, and that it was increasingly impossible to stand apart from Europe. Britain therefore attempted to join the new common market which was emerging in Europe, which it finally achieved in 1973. The special relationship entered a new and relatively troubled phase, but then was reinvigorated in a new form, particularly under the premierships of Margaret Thatcher and Tony Blair.

The attempt to combine these two roles has made Britain's position distinctive but also contradictory. Britain never fully committed to membership of the European Union. Despite a referendum held in 1975 which confirmed Britain's membership, and the general election defeat of the Labour party in 1983 when its manifesto pledged to withdraw from the EU, Britain's relationship with Europe was not settled. It remained contentious in British politics and frequently divided both major parties. There is Euro-scepticism in many European countries, and many populist anti-system parties which like the UK Independence Party (UKIP) want to sever ties with the EU, but nowhere else was the mainstream political class and the mainstream media as divided over their country's membership of the EU.

British ambivalence towards Europe made Britain an awkward partner. Britain proved reluctant to participate as a full member of the

European Union, seeking optouts from key European initiatives such as the Schengen treaty on open borders and the euro single currency. Yet Britain was also reluctant to disengage completely, because British governments were unwilling to accept relegation to a second tier of European states within the EU. At the heart of this problem was the unresolved tension between Europe and America as the main focus of Britain's identity and loyalty following the end of empire. Churchill's vision of Britain as the intersection of three circles, Empire, Anglo-America and Europe, contained the assumption that the Empire, with the British Union at its core, was the fundamental one. Britain had strong ties with the United States and the rest of the English-speaking world, and equally strong ties with Europe, but Britain because of its empire and global reach had no need to be absorbed by either. It could deal with both as an independent power.

When the withdrawal from empire began some seized on Europe as a surrogate, but the attraction of Europe was always counterbalanced by the special relationship which British political leaders aspired to enjoy with the United States.[24] British leaders, with the exception of Edward Heath, when forced to choose between Europe and America always chose America. French leaders by contrast have always given priority to Europe. The nature of Britain's special relationship with the United States has been distinctive and sets Britain apart from the rest of Europe, as was shown clearly in the 2003 invasion of Iraq. Other European states, such as Spain, supported the invasion, but many others did not, even though they were members of NATO and the western alliance.

The unwillingness to contemplate a European future is not primarily a yearning for isolationism. The supporters of disengagement from Europe often desire not less but more involvement with the outside world. They argue that Britain has a different political economy from the rest of Europe, which is criticised for being too inward-looking, too protectionist, too bureaucratic, and too regulated. Britain by contrast is said to thrive on having access to markets and cultures around the world. It is a global power not a regional power. By disengaging from Europe Britain can open itself once again to the fastest growing markets around the world, such as China, India and Brazil as well as renewing its links with Australia, New Zealand, Canada and the United States, creating a new kind of network commonwealth.[25] This would certainly make Britain distinctive at least in comparison with the rest of Europe. But the enthusiasm of the other proposed members was always limited. The United States in particular was keen that Britain remained within the European Union, since a Britain detached from the EU was less valuable as an ally to the United States.

In its post-imperial phase the British political class has not wanted Britain to abandon its global reach and global status. Britain remains committed to its membership of the UN Security Council, and the maintenance of worldwide interests and responsibilities. Political leaders across all parties believe Britain should provide leadership, if not military then moral, to sort out conflicts around the world. To sustain such a role presumes either a very close relationship with the United States or a much closer union with Europe. The first has occurred whenever a particular national security emergency means that the US needs to hug Britain close. This has happened less often than sometimes supposed. Only two British Prime Ministers have received the Presidential Medal of Freedom since it was inaugurated in 1963, Margaret Thatcher and Tony Blair, and only two have received the Congressional Gold Medal, Winston Churchill and Tony Blair. Many British Prime Ministers have not formed a close relationship with American Presidents, yet most of them have wanted it. British politicians of both parties have found it easier to identify with the United States than with Europe, and this Atlanticist orientation continues to mark Britain out from other European states. In forty years of EU membership the British economy became increasingly integrated with the European economy, in terms of flows of goods, capital and labour, but this did not lead to a shared European identity and solidarity, except among the younger generation. Many British might accept that the British are *in* Europe but not *of* Europe, and certainly not run *by* Europe. Most British people continue to think of Britain not as part of Europe but standing outside it.

An Anglo–liberal political economy

A fifth distinctive aspect of British politics arises from its political economy. This has been shaped by the particular role Britain has played in the global economy since the seventeenth century. Britain emerged as an entrepreneurial commercial society and then the first industrial society, using naval power to protect its trade and expand its colonies. Some of the things that used to be most distinctive about Britain's political economy, such as its status as the first industrial nation, have become less marked or disappeared altogether. Whatever their initial starting points modern capitalist economies have steadily converged. Little now separates the performance of the French and British economies. Similarly Britain was once very distinctive for the size of its working class, the extent of its urbanisation and the small proportion of its population engaged on the land, and British politics was dominated for a hundred years by the struggle to contain the rising labour movement, and this produced, especially after the exit of the Irish Republic from the UK, a more polarised class politics than in any other comparable modern state. But with the transition from an industrial to a service economy the salience of class as a basis for political allegiance and party politics has declined markedly in Britain in recent decades, as it has elsewhere.

What makes British political economy distinctive today is not its former status as the workshop of the world but the importance of its financial and commercial sectors. One million people now work in financial services in the UK, as many as once used to work in the mines. The City of London, and the role it plays in British politics, is greater than in any state of equivalent size. The financial sectors of some other countries such as Switzerland are even larger in relation to their host economies, but the populations are much smaller. The importance of the City in the UK stems from the rise of London in the nineteenth century to become the leading centre for financial, shipping, and insurance services for the rest of the international economy. This cluster of expertise survived long after the disappearance of the economic and military power which made it possible, and has revived in spectacular fashion since the development of the Eurodollar market in the 1960s. Successive British governments were willing to allow the City of London to act as though it were an offshore financial centre, free of many of the regulations which other jurisdictions, including the US, imposed on their financial centres. One of the main reasons why the 2008 crash hit the UK economy so hard was because London had become such a key international financial centre, and its banks were leading players in the practices which burst the boom and western prosperity and almost caused the collapse of the international financial system.[26]

The policy of giving the City free rein and ensuring that it remained ahead of other financial centres was established under Labour and Conservative governments in the 1960s and 1970s, and received a major boost with the Big Bang in 1986, which removed many restrictions on the entry of foreign banks into London. The encouragement given to the development of financial services was a bipartisan policy and during the long boom between 1993 and 2008 the major parties competed with one another in supporting light touch regulation and removing obstacles to London's success. The crash forced revaluation and some reforms, but the British political class remains very wary of hobbling the City of London and UK financial services, since this is such an important part of the UK economy, and one of the main areas where the UK is competitive internationally. So despite popular anger at bankers there have been few moves to change fundamentally how the banking system operates.

Britain's variety of capitalism, the Anglo–liberal model,[27] places it in the liberal market rather than the coordinated market group.[28] The importance of finance in the UK is a key component of the British model. All actual political economies are hybrids, including elements from several models rather than just one, but there remain important ways in which the political economy of the UK is distinct from most other members of the European Union (Ireland is closest to it), and this has important political effects, not least the repeated reluctance of the UK when a member of the EU to participate in further European integration. Distinctive aspects of British political economy since the Thatcher reforms of the 1980s include: flexible labour markets and weak trade unions; a system of corporate governance which treats the company as a private association rather than a public corporation; a hybrid welfare state which while retaining some universal features such as the National Health Service has steadily moved to a residual conception of welfare; and since the 1980s a sharply widening gap in both income and wealth inequality, highlighted in particular by the pay and bonuses of CEOs and bankers.

Many of these trends date in particular from the 1980s and the changes introduced by the Thatcher Government, but the broad pattern, with some variations has continued since. The UK economy shed its image of relative decline in the 1990s, overcame its long-running sterling problem, and embarked on the longest period of continuous expansion in its history. It became one of the most successful economies in the neo-liberal era, partly because successive governments were willing to embrace the logic of the changes in the rules governing the international economy which the United States promoted after the structural crisis of the 1970s. One of the consequences was to make London and the South East of England the main beneficiaries of this policy, and by the time of the 2008 crash the economy had become very imbalanced, with the dominance of London over all other regions ever more pronounced. The 2008 crisis initially hit Britain much more severely than most other European countries because Britain was at the heart of the financialised open liberal market economy which had been so dominant for thirty years, and London was one of its two leading financial centres. The economy began finally to recover in 2013, despite or because of the austerity programme pursued by the Coalition Government. It was helped by a further rise in house prices and household debt, but investment, productivity and wages remained low, and the balance of payments deficit continued to increase. It had reached 5 per cent of national income by 2015. Despite plans to rebalance the economy and create new export led growth, the distinctive patterns of the British political economy in 2015 were very familiar from the past.

A liberal political culture

Ideology and culture are often the most idiosyncratic features of a state, but also the hardest to pin down. Is there anything distinctive about British ideological traditions and political culture which mark them out as especially British? Britain's ideological traditions are part of wider families of ideas which shape the discourses and institutions in many countries. Trying to disentangle Britain from broader European currents of thought is no easy task, but there are some important aspects of ideological discourse in Britain that are distinctive.

The first of these is the strength of the Anglo–American community of ideas and political discourse. This has been a predominantly liberal tradition, which has influenced all other ideological doctrines, and helps explain the liberal forms which both conservatism and socialism have assumed in Britain, in contrast to many other countries. This liberal tradition is Anglo–American, and often the terms of ideological debate on both right and left in the UK are Anglo–American rather than European. This is partly the result of the common language, but it also reflects the way that English political traditions and ideas shaped the American experience, and made debates in Britain part of transatlantic debates rather than merely British debates. This has been true ever since the American War of Independence, the French Revolution, and closer in time the New Deal and social democracy which resulted from the Great Depression and the neo-liberalism which arose in the 1970s and influenced the Thatcher Government and the Reagan administration.

A second important context shaping British ideological discourse has been the nature of the party system. The first-past-the-post electoral system has forced parties seeking to form governments to form broad ideological and interest coalitions. Partly as a result of this the two main British parties in the last hundred years (Conservative and Labour) have been unlike centre-right and centre-left parties in the rest of Europe. The Conservative party was obliged to become a party which drew fifty per cent of its support from the urban industrial working class rather than rely on the votes of those working on the land. Conservative ideology tended to be pragmatic and not doctrinaire, organised around the defence of key institutions – Crown, Church, Union, Empire,

Property – rather than a set of abstract ideas. The priority given to the pursuit of power and being in government meant that the party was usually able to sideline its diehards and became throughout the twentieth century Britain's default party of government, the most successful centre-right party in any western democracy. The Labour party was also distinctive from social democratic parties elsewhere, particularly because the party was created by the trade unions and they retained the dominant say until relatively recently in the governance of the party. This meant that one of the strongest influences on the ideology of the party was labourism, the defence and protection of the interests of the trade unions, and this contended with various currents of socialism, but the party even under Tony Blair never fully became a social democratic party on the European model, based on individual membership.

The liberalism of British political culture is bolstered by certain institutions, notably the universities, and the BBC. The BBC has been under sustained attack for some time by Conservative newspapers, which want to cut off its funding from the state, for a mixture of ideological and commercial reasons. The newspapers, particular those on the right, are noted for their stridency and their partisanship, which often reflects their ownership. The particular character and ideological leanings of the British media have always been a distinctive part of British politics, but newspapers are dying in a digital age, and new forms of communication are arising to take their place.

In terms of its broader political culture Britain has been subject to the same trends towards the secularisation and individualisation of politics which can be observed across western Europe. On some specific issues such as capital punishment and gun laws Britain appears much more European than American. The same is true of secularisation which has advanced much further in Europe with declining church attendances than in the United States. In Britain the trend has been particularly marked, but it has been a common European experience. The Protestant–Catholic divides in Europe and within Britain itself have become less important. Britain, like many other European countries, has also experienced a decline in solidarity and since the onset of the crisis the emergence of more punitive attitudes to the poor. In recent decades Britain has become a much more multicultural country, as a result of high levels of immigration, and also a much more socially liberal country with legislation to extend equal rights to minorities which suffer discrimination. The acceptance of same-sex marriage in 2014 was a notable milestone. These too are common trends across Europe. In Britain they have been particularly marked.

Where British political culture is different from that in most European countries is the large numbers of British people, particularly English people, who do not identify themselves as European. This is not the same as xenophobia which, while it undoubtedly exists in Britain, is not noticeably greater than in other countries. But the British are much more 'anti-European' than other European peoples. This remains a distinguishing feature of British politics. Over recent decades Britain has become much more European, with young people in particular identifying as European. But as the Brexit referendum showed many in the older generations still define their identity *against* Europe. That attitude contributed to the vote to leave the EU in 2016. The result was narrow but still decisive. In the future the attitude towards Europe will change as the generations change and a new pro-European majority emerges. When that happens, British governments will again seek a closer association with Europe. The Scots may not be willing to wait that long. Being anti-European is primarily an English problem. The Scots have much less difficulty than do many of the English in reconciling their Scottish identity with a European identity. One Union, the Union with Europe fell apart in 2016. But Scotland and Northern Ireland voted to Remain, and that has created new strains within that much older Union, the UK. British politics may not be 'British' for much longer.

Epilogue: Last Thoughts

On rereading the essays collected here and others which are not included I accept I was wrong in many particular judgements I made at the time on how events would turn out, although I was careful not to make predictions and recognised that the outcome might be different from the one I considered most likely. Sometimes the contingencies involved made the outcomes extremely uncertain. They really could have gone either way. Take elections. No one was in any doubt that Tony Blair would win in 1997, 2001 and 2005, or that Margaret Thatcher would win in 1979, 1983 and 1987, or Boris Johnson in 2019. Elections which were much harder to call were 1970, 1974 (February), 1992, 2010, 2015 and 2017. Some of these I called right but most wrong. I did not expect Theresa May to lose her majority in 2017 or Harold Wilson to be defeated in 1970. I thought that 1992 and 2015 would both result in hung parliaments. I was also wrong about the Brexit referendum. I expected that the result would be close but that Remain would narrowly win. I thought the argument 'why risk it?', the safety first argument would be strong enough among Conservative voters to give Remain victory. In the event 58 per cent of those who had voted Conservative and for David Cameron in 2015 voted Leave and against him in 2016. That was the real surprise of the referendum, not the Leave vote in Labour seats in the North of England. They voted in 2016 as their parents and grandparents had voted in 1975. It was the defection of so many Conservative voters in England to Leave that tipped the balance.

I also did not anticipate how devolution would allow the SNP to dominate politics in Scotland. In the essay on the constitution, Chapter 11, which was written in 2006, the Labour party and the Liberal Democrats seemed likely to keep control of the Scottish Parliament for a long period. Yet within a few years the SNP had not only achieved a majority in Holyrood, they had also destroyed Labour as a parliamentary force in Scotland. The explosive force of nationalism was shown yet again. The devolution settlement which had been designed to prevent the SNP from ever getting a majority in Scotland completely failed in that respect.

On Conservatism I am happy to let most of my judgements stand. In some of my earliest writings on the party, especially the postscript to *The Conservative Nation*, I was too struck by the depth of the party's crisis in 1973, too little focused on how it might reinvent itself. Viscount Hinchingbrooke a former Conservative MP, and a strong critic of Heath's leadership, wrote a review of the book in which he praised the analysis but took issue with my conclusion, noting that the Conservative party had always been protean and would find a way to survive. He was correct, and the postscript was not in line with the analysis in the rest of the book. Ever since I seem to have been writing about just how protean the Conservative party is able to be. The latest example of its extraordinary versatility is the programme on which it fought the 2019 election. Repudiating what remained of its Thatcherite legacy and embracing a Chamberlainite policy of state intervention and large-scale public expenditure in the cause of 'levelling up', it promised to repair the damage that had been done to so many communities in the North of England in the Thatcher years. Some of these communities voted Conservative for the first time in 2019, apparently believing that a government which promised to deliver a proper Brexit would address their concerns and redistribute wealth from the South to the North.

In the debate on Thatcherism I was rather more cautious than some at the beginning, emphasising the difficulties in the way of implementing a radical policy. This is very much the theme of the essay on 'Thatcherism and Conservative politics' (Chapter 6). It reflects just how difficult the first two years of Thatcherism were. There was nothing inevitable about its subsequent triumph, and in 1981 it still looked as though it could be a short-lived administration. Ian Gilmour certainly thought so, declaring when he resigned from the Cabinet in 1981 that the Government was heading straight for the rocks. The real threat to the Conservatives was not the Labour party which was consumed by internecine strife, but the emerging alliance between the SDP and Liberals which was carrying all before it, winning by-elections and scoring over 50 per cent in some polls. As so often, events intervened. The Falklands War changed the political mood, and gave Thatcher's leadership a boost she never lost. The even split between Labour and the SDP-Liberal alliance at the 1983 election gifted her a landslide victory on 43 per cent of the vote and prepared the way for the radical phase of the Thatcherite project.

Sceptics about the concept of Thatcherism often argued that there was no Thatcherite project and that the Government made up things as it went along, like previous Conservative governments. I agreed that the Thatcher Government was often cautious and pragmatic in its tactics, but that did not prevent it having at the same time a strategic purpose which had been forged in the ferment of right-wing ideas in the 1970s. Thatcher had to struggle against many obstacles not least that of her own party and she was never able to appoint the kind of Cabinet of true believers which Boris Johnson did after his election as leader. But she ensured that Thatcherites controlled the key departments, particularly the economic departments. The Thatcherites had a revolutionary zeal and an intellectual conviction which their opponents in the party lacked. I once attended a closed session of the Conservative Centre for Policy Studies in 1989, just after the celebration of Thatcher's first ten years as Prime Minister and just a year before the end, and heard Thatcher declare in answer to her party critics urging her to consolidate her reforms rather than press on with new ones: 'Stop? Stop? We haven't even started yet.' The assessments I made of Thatcher and Thatcherism in 'The crisis of Conservatism' (Chapter 8) and 'The Thatcher myth' (Chapter 9) still seem to me the right ones.

In the debate on decline I was always careful to distinguish between Britain's absolute decline as a great power, and the relative decline of its economy. In describing and analysing the different explanations I wanted to show how they fed into political narratives which then framed these events as crises to which there had to be a political response. The idea of British decline was central to Thatcherism, but also to the social democratic prospectus of the modernisers in the Labour party and the Conservative party, as well as to the Labour left's alternative economic strategy. No one disputes the absolute decline which was involved in the withdrawal from empire and from Britain's former dominant role in finance, industry and trade. But there is disagreement as to whether there was a relative economic decline at all, and if so when it started. This is an important question but rather different from what I was concerned with – the framing of decline as a political issue and the political consequences of that. In 'Explanations of British decline' (Chapter 2), written in 1999 at the height of the new world order prosperity, I suggested that the decline was now over. It no longer featured in political debate. That may have been premature. The incompetence of the May and Johnson Governments' handling of Brexit and the COVID-19 pandemic, and the deep institutional and governance failures they have revealed, shows signs of reigniting the debate on British decline, driven by fears about Britain's economic prospects and political isolation outside the EU, and fears that Brexit may be followed by the breakup of the United Kingdom.

On Brexit although I and many others, including Nigel Farage and it seems Boris Johnson, were wrong about the result of the referendum I think my general analysis, particularly of the civil war in the Conservative party and its importance for British politics, has been borne out. An article which I wrote with David Baker and Steve Ludlam for *Political Quarterly* in 1993 at the height of the divisions over the Maastricht Treaty was entitled '1846 … 1906 … 1996? Conservative splits and European integration'. It argued that the Conservative party was likely to split over membership of the European Union as it had done twice before over fundamental issues of political economy and national identity.[1] This argument was drawn on in 'The crisis of conservatism' (Chapter 8) two years later. After another twenty years of festering divisions civil war broke out anew after 2010, leading David Cameron ultimately to concede an in/out referendum, with a simple majority deciding the outcome. The polarisation and the turmoil caused by the issue of Europe destroyed David Cameron as it had destroyed John Major and helped to destroy Margaret Thatcher. It went on to destroy Theresa May. Boris Johnson ended the civil war in the party by purging his Cabinet of Remainers and withdrawing the whip from many of his MPs, forcing the deselection or withdrawal of many of them as Conservative candidates. The party was also purged of its free traders in the early 1900s during the ascendancy of the tariff-reformers who wanted protectionism to promote imperial union. Winston Churchill left before he was pushed, crossing the floor to join the Liberals.

As a political issue Brexit came to be posed by many Brexiters as a fundamental geopolitical and political economic choice between Europe and America which Britain had to make. This was before Trump muddied the choice. In 'The European disunion' (Chapter 3) I commented that the cost for Britain of leaving the European Union made it an unlikely prospect. But that was before the great surge of populist nationalism after the 2008 financial crash. Many people voted for Brexit aware it could make them poorer. Affirming their national identity had become more important to them than the economic costs of separation from the EU. It is one of the reasons that Brexit has made a future vote by Scotland to leave the United Kingdom more likely, even if still far from certain.

In 'The free economy and the strong state' (1979) (Chapter 5), I talk about populism and its significance for the new radical right in harnessing support, and in 'The crisis of conservatism' (1995) (Chapter 8), I argue that the future may belong to a new and reinvigorated populist Conservatism. That finally did come about in 2019.

One of the distinctive features of populism is its impatience with representative government and the rule of law. It is sometimes said that Brexiters are champions of parliamentary sovereignty, but that is incorrect. Some are but others are champions of state sovereignty and the pre-democratic power of the executive which the American colonists rebelled against. This is the doctrine of Crown-in-Parliament which seeks the full exercise of prerogative powers, the heart of the Westminster model described in 'Theories of British politics' (Chapter 10). The actions of the Johnson Government in sidelining Parliament both in relation to Brexit and to COVID-19, ruling by executive decree, fit into that tradition. At the same time it followed the pattern established by the Trump administration, breaking rules and conventions to centralise power. Populist regimes always claim to be democratic. It is just the checks and balances of liberal constitutions and any restraints on their power which they abhor.

Absences and omissions

There are other absences and omissions in these essays. They are unavoidably euro- and western-centric given their subject matter. As the geopolitical balance of the world continues to shift, Europe and the West as a whole will come to play a smaller part. The world's concern with what went on in one corner of the globe will diminish. Every nation, every region likes to imagine itself as special and as unique. Europe's story and Britain's story within Europe are important stories, but they are only stories among many others. I do not claim any priority or privileged status for them in the understanding of our world. They are a piece of the jigsaw, nothing more.

Another very big omission in these essays is that they are for the most part conducted within a political economy frame which gives priority to certain types of power and inequality rather than others, class rather than gender or race. I have tried to rectify this in recent work by emphasising the importance of households as well as markets and states in political economy, but I accept there are questions I would frame differently if I were starting again. One of the big changes in political economy and in the academy in recent years has been the acceptance that all forms of inequality are important and that we need theories and frameworks that can do justice to them. Feminist political economy has begun to transform the discipline with its new research programmes and research questions.

Race has been another area of neglect in writing on British politics. David Olusoga's *Black and British* is a telling exposure of how absent black lives and the slave trade have been in normal tellings of Britain's story and in the analysis of contemporary Britain.[2] The history of Britain is often told as though the empire had never existed, as though three million Africans were not transported by British slave-traders with the support of the British state in the seventeenth and eighteenth centuries, or that somehow this had nothing to do with Britain, because it all happened faraway from British shores. When the slave trade is remembered it is to celebrate that Britain was one of the pioneers in abolishing it in 1807. William Wilberforce is rightly regarded as a national hero for his role in this, but what is forgotten is the strength of the opposition in Parliament from slave-traders and plantation owners and other national heroes like Horatio Nelson to what Wilberforce was doing. Britain was not the only country involved in the Atlantic slave trade but it was one of the most important, and between 1640 and 1807 it played the leading role. Of the three million slaves who were transported, it is estimated that 13 per cent of them (400,000) died in the crossing. The enormity of what was done and the consequences which flowed from it are still little recognised by conventional histories.

The amnesia in British culture runs very deep. Michael Oakeshott's elegant defence of civil association as Britain's political tradition and his disparagement of less happy lands subject to 'lordly rule' never addressed the lordly rule that Britain imposed on the colonial territories it seized and on enslaved people it transported as Perry Anderson has pointed out.[3] Britain finally abolished slavery throughout its empire in 1834, compensating the slave-owners handsomely for their 'property'. But the end of slavery did not mean the end of racial subordination and doctrines of Anglo-Saxon racial superiority. These were rife in Victorian Britain and throughout the Empire. Deep cultural prejudices against other races came to be instilled in the British and influenced attitudes to the arrival of Black and Asian immigrants in the 1950s and 1960s.

A succession of politicians from Oswald Mosley, to Enoch Powell and Margaret Thatcher defined immigrants as the problem, and helped create the climate in which racial attacks, racial abuse and racial discrimination became everyday experiences for Black and Asian citizens. Powell gave voice to attitudes and feelings which were outside the mainstream debate by presenting himself as the only politician who was really listening to the people and prepared to take their side. He claimed to be representing ordinary working people who had never been asked to approve the policy of mass immigration and who now no longer felt at home in their own country because of the numbers of Black and Asian immigrants. Stuart Hall used to gently remind the English: 'the immigrants are here because you were there'.[4] He argued that there could no understanding of Englishness without understanding its imperial and colonial dimensions, the expansion of England overseas over four centuries. Lest we forget.

Despite recognising things that might have been done differently I have never regretted making the study of British politics my primary interest. Even though I quickly learned that British politics is best understood not as a unique national story but by comparing Britain with other states and appreciating the much broader geopolitical and political economic contexts in which that story unfolded. British politics has always been fast-moving, full of drama and the unexpected. The twists and turns over sixty years have been extraordinary, and the most recent chapter one of the most extraordinary of all, with a Conservative Government (or as Margaret Thatcher might have said, echoing Neil Kinnock, a *Conservative* Government). announcing in September 2020 that it intended to break international law by overriding the provisions of a treaty it had signed only eight months before.

This epilogue was written during the COVID-19 lockdowns of 2020 which interrupted normal politics and normal life. The fog surrounding the future of British politics and world politics was even denser than usual. All we can do is peer into the murk as best we can and hope we can make out the shape of something approaching solid ground.

Notes

Introduction
[1] Andrew Gamble, *The Western Ideology and Other Essays*, Bristol: Bristol University Press, 2021.

Chapter 1
[1] This essay was first published in Colin Hay and Daniel Bailey (eds), *Diverging Capitalisms: Britain, the City of London, and Europe*, London: Palgrave-Macmillan, 2019, pp. 17–42.

[2] Michael Heseltine, https://www.theguardian.com/politics/2017/mar/08/michael-heseltine-keep-opposing-Brexit-disastrous-eu-referendum-lords

[3] Boris Johnson, https://www.theguardian.com/politics/2017/feb/22/boris-johnson-accused-of-bad-taste-for-calling-Brexit-liberation

[4] Jeremy Green, 'Anglo–American development, the Euromarkets, and the deeper origins of neoliberal deregulation', *Review of International Studies*, 42:3, 2016, pp. 425–449.

[5] John Parkinson, *Corporate Power and Responsibility: Issues in the theory of company law*, Oxford: Clarendon, 1993.

[6] Keith Joseph, *Solving the Union Problem is the Key to Britain's Recovery*, London: Centre for Policy Studies, 1979, p. 5.

[7] Conservative Party, *Election Manifesto*, London: Conservative Party, 1987, p. 5.

[8] Gordon Brown, *Budget Speech*, 17 March 2004.

[9] David Coates, *Models of Capitalism*, Cambridge: Polity, 2000, pp. 246–7.

[10] Geoffrey Owen, *From Empire to Europe*, London: Harper Collins, 2000, pp. 460–1.

[11] Andrew Gamble, *Between Europe and America*, London: Palgrave-Macmillan, 2003.

[12] David Coates, *Models of Capitalism*.

[13] Peter Hall and David Soskice (eds), *Varieties of Capitalism: The institutional foundations of comparative advantage*, Oxford: OUP, 2001, p. 16.

[14] Paul Addison, *The Road to 1945*, London: Pimlico, 1994.

[15] T.H. Marshall, *Citizenship and Social Class*, Cambridge: CUP, 1950.

[16] Peter Burnham, *Remaking the Postwar World Economy: Robot and British policy in the 1950s*, London: Palgrave-Macmillan, 2003.

[17] David Edgerton, *England and the Aeroplane: An essay on a militant and technological nation*, London: Macmillan, 1991.

[18] Roger Bacon and Walter Eltis, *Britain's Economic Problem: Too few producers*, London: Macmillan, 1976.

19 Andrew Shonfield, *British Economic Policy Since the War*, Harmondsworth: Penguin, 1958.

20 Andrew Shonfield, *Modern Capitalism: The changing balance of public and private power*, Oxford: Oxford University Press, 1965.

21 Stuart Holland, *The Socialist Challenge*, London: Quartet Books, 1975.

22 Richard Heffernan, *New Labour and Thatcherism: Policy change in Britain*, London: Palgrave-Macmillan, 2001.

23 Will Hutton, *The State We're In*, London: Cape, 1995.

24 Stephen Blank, 'The politics of foreign economic policy', *International Organisation*, 31:4, (1977), pp. 673–722.

25 Ben Clift, Andrew Gamble and Michael Harris, 'The Labour party and the company', in John Parkinson et al (eds), *The Political Economy of the Company*, London: Hart, 2000, pp. 51–82.

26 Paul Pierson, *Dismantling the Welfare State?*, Cambridge: CUP, 1994.

27 Gøsta Esping-Andersen, *Social Foundations of Post-Industrial Economies*, Oxford: OUP, 1999.

28 Matthew Watson, 'The politics of inflation management', *Political Quarterly*, 74:3, (2003), pp. 285–297.

29 James Bennett, *The Anglosphere Challenge: Why the English-speaking nations will lead the way in the twenty-first century*, Lanham, MD: Rowman & Littlefield, 2004.

30 See the speech by Michael Howard, then Leader of the Conservative party, to the *News Corporation Conference in Cancun*, Mexico, 19 March 2004. It is summarised in 'The European disunion', Chapter 3 in this collection.

31 Michael Kenny, and Nick Pearce, *Shadows of Empire: The Anglosphere in British politics*, Cambridge: Polity, 2018.

32 Guiliano Bonoli, Vic George and Peter Taylor-Gooby, *European Welfare Futures*, Cambridge: Polity, 2000.

33 Andrew Gamble, *Crisis Without End? The unravelling of western prosperity*, London: Palgrave-Macmillan, 2014.

34 Rob Ford and Matthew Goodwin, *Revolt on the Right: Explaining support for the radical right in Britain*, London: Routledge, 2014.

35 Daniel Hannan, http://www.conservativehome.com/thecolumnists/2016/11/daniel-hannan-i-got-it-wrong-the-pundits-got-it-wrong-so-what-really-lies-in-store-for-the-united-states.html

36 Economists for Brexit, www.economistsforBrexit.co.uk

Chapter 2

1 This essay was first published as 'Theories and explanations of British decline', in Richard English and Michael Kenny (eds), *Rethinking British Decline*, London: Macmillan, 1999, pp. 1–22.

2 See, for instance, Nicholas Crafts, *Britain's Relative Economic Decline: 1870–1995*, London: Social Market Foundation, 1995; David Coates, *The Question of UK Decline: The economy, state and society*, Hemel Hempstead: Harvester Wheatsheaf, 1994; David Coates and John Hillard (eds), *The Economic Decline of Modern Britain: The debate between left and right*, Brighton: Harvester Wheatsheaf, 1986; David Coates and John Hillard (eds), *The Economic Revival of Modern Britain: The debate between left and right*, Aldershot: Gower, 1987; Alan Sked, *Britain's Decline: Problems and perspectives*, Oxford: Oxford University Press, 1987; and

Andrew Gamble, *Britain in Decline: Economic policy, political strategy and the British state*, Basingstoke: Macmillan, 1994; 1st edn, 1981.

3 Nicholas Crafts, *Britain's Relative Economic Decline*.

4 See Paul Krugman, 'Competitiveness: a dangerous obsession', *Foreign Affairs*, vol. 73, no. 2, (1994), pp. 28–44.

5 Martin Wiener, *English Culture and the Decline of the Industrial Spirit 1850–1980*, Harmondsworth: Penguin, 1992; 1st edn, 1981.

6 Aaron Friedberg, *The Weary Titan: Britain and the experience of relative decline 1895–1905*, Princeton: Princeton University Press, 1988.

7 Bernard Semmel, *Imperialism and Social Reform: English social-imperial thought 1895–1914*, Cambridge, Mass.: Harvard University Press, 1960.

8 Donald Watt, *Succeeding John Bull: America in Britain's place 1900–75*, Cambridge: CUP, 1984.

9 Henk Overbeek, *Global Capitalism and National Decline: The Thatcher decade in perspective*, London: Unwin Hyman, 1990.

10 Peter Jenkins, *Anatomy of Decline: The political journalism of Peter Jenkins*, London: Phoenix, 1996; 1st edn, 1995.

11 David Marquand, *The Unprincipled Society*, London: Cape, 1988.

12 Correlli Barnett, *The Audit of War: The illusion and reality of Britain as a great nation*, London: Macmillan, 1986; and Correlli Barnett, *The Lost Victory: British dreams, British realities 1945–1950*, London: Macmillan, 1996; 1st edn, 1995.

13 Andrew Shonfield, *Modern Capitalism: The changing balance of public and private power*, Oxford: Oxford University Press, 1965.

14 Sidney Pollard, *The Wasting of the British Economy: British economic policy 1945 to the present*, London: Croom Helm, 1982.

15 The cultural thesis is discussed sceptically in David Edgerton, *England and the Aeroplane: An essay on a militant and technological nation*, London: Macmillan, 1991; and W.D. Rubinstein, *Capitalism, Culture and Decline in Britain 1750–1990*, London: Routledge, 1994; 1st edn, 1993.

16 See Correlli Barnett, *The Lost Victory*.

17 See Martin Wiener, *English Culture*.

18 W.D. Rubinstein, *Capitalism, Culture and Decline*.

19 Will Hutton, *The State We're In*, London: Cape, 1996; 1st edn, 1995, p. 112.

20 Frank Blackaby (ed), *Deindustrialisation*, London: Heinemann, 1979.

21 Perry Anderson, 'The figures of descent', *New Left Review*, vol. 161, 1987, pp. 20–77.

22 Geoffrey Ingham, *Capitalism Divided? The city and industry in British social development*, Basingstoke: Macmillan, 1984.

23 Hamish McRae, *The World in 2020*, London: Harper Collins, 1994.

24 W.D. Rubinstein, *Capitalism, Culture and Decline*.

25 Eric Hobsbawm, *Industry and Empire: An economic history of Britain since 1750*, Harmondsworth: Penguin, 1968.

26 Paul Kennedy, *The Rise and Fall of the Great Powers: Economic change and military conflict from 1500 to 2000*, London: Unwin Hyman, 1989; 1st edn, 1988.

27 Peter Cain and Anthony Hopkins, *British Imperialism: Volume Two, Crisis and Deconstruction 1914–1990*, London: Longman, 1993.

28 Michael Barratt Brown, 'Away with all the great arches: Anderson's history of British capitalism', *New Left Review*, vol. 167, (1988), pp. 22–52.

29 On 'overload' see Antony King, 'Overload: problems of governing in the 1970s', *Political Studies,* vol. 23, (1975), pp. 284–96. And on 'club government' see David Marquand, *The Unprincipled Society,* pp. 175–208.

30 See Tom Nairn, 'The crisis of the British State', *New Left Review,* vol. 30, (1981), pp. 37–44.

31 Bernard Elbaum and William Lazonick (eds), *The Decline of the British Economy,* Oxford: Oxford University Press, 1986; Michael Dintenfass, *The Decline of Industrial Britain 1870–1980,* London: Routledge, 1992.

32 Charles Feinstein, 'The benefits of backwardness and the costs of continuity', in Andrew Graham (ed), *Government and Economies in the Post-War World: Economic policies and comparative performance, 1945–85,* London: Routledge, 1990.

33 Giovanni Arrighi, *The Long Twentieth Century: Money, power, and the origins of our times,* London: Verso, 1994.

34 Mancur Olson, *The Rise and Fall of Nations: Economic growth, stagflation and social rigidities,* New Haven: Yale University Press, 1982.

35 Geoffrey Maynard, *The Economy Under Mrs Thatcher,* Oxford: Oxford University Press, 1988.

36 John Ruggie, 'Territoriality and beyond: problematizing modernity in international relations', *International Organization,* vol. 47, no. 1, (1993), pp. 139–174.

37 Nicholas Crafts, *Britain's Relative Economic Decline.*

38 See W.D. Rubinstein, *Capitalism, Culture and Decline in Britain.*

39 Paul Hirst and Grahame Thompson, *Globalisation in Question: The international economy and the possibilities of governance,* Cambridge: Polity, 1996.

40 Jonathan Michie (ed), *The Economic Legacy 1979–1992,* London: Academic Press, 1992.

41 Paul Krugman, 'Competitiveness: a dangerous obsession', *Foreign Affairs,* vol. 73, (1994), pp. 28–44.

42 Andrew Gamble and Anthony Payne (eds), *Regionalism and World Order,* London: Macmillan, 1996.

Chapter 3

1 This essay was first published in *The British Journal of Politics and International Relations,* 8:1, (2006), pp. 34–49.

2 John Kampfner, *Blair's Wars: A Liberal Imperialist in Action,* London: Free, 2003; Peter Riddell, *Hug Them Close: Blair, Bush, Clinton and the 'special relationship',* London: Politicos, 2003.

3 Stephen George, *An Awkward Partner: Britain in the European Community,* Oxford: OUP, 1994.

4 Hugo Young, *This Blessed Plot: Britain and Europe from Churchill to Blair,* London: Macmillan, 1998; Andrew Geddes, *The European Union and British Politics,* London: Palgrave-Macmillan, 2004.

5 Norman Davies, *The Isles: A history* London: Macmillan, 1999.

6 Andrew Gamble, *Between Europe and America: The future of British politics,* London: Palgrave-Macmillan, 2003.

7 The original Claim of Right was an Act of the Scottish Parliament in April 1789 asserting the right of Parliament to determine to whom the Crown should be offered and under what conditions.

[8] Stefan Collignon, *The European Republic: Reflections on the political economy of a future constitution*, London: Kogan Page, 2003.

[9] Andrew Moravcsik, 'Brussels diary', *Prospect*, October, 2005, p. 58.

[10] John Fischer, 'From Confederacy to Federation – Thoughts on the finality of European integration', in Mark Leonard (ed), *The Future Shape of Europe*, London: Foreign Policy Centre, 2000, pp. 7–20.

[11] Stefan Collignon, *The European Republic: Reflections on the political economy of a future constitution*.

[12] Mark Leonard, *Network Europe: The New Case for Europe*, London: Foreign Policy Centre, 1999.

[13] Larry Siedentop, *Democracy in Europe*, London: Allen Lane, 2000.

[14] Zygmunt Bauman, *Europe*, Cambridge: Polity, 2004.

[15] Ben Rosamond, *Theories of European Integration*, London: Macmillan, 2000.

[16] Neil MacCormick, *Who's Afraid of a European Constitution?*, London: Imprint, 2005.

[17] Dick Leonard and Mark Leonard (eds), *The Pro-European Reader*, London: Palgrave-Macmillan, 2002.

[18] Martin Gilbert, *Winston Churchill: Volume 8: Never Despair 1945–65*, London: Heinemann, 1988, p. 407.

[19] Ron Chernow, *Alexander Hamilton*, London: Penguin, 2004.

[20] Tony Giddens, 'A Third Way for the European Union?', in Mark Leonard (ed), *The Future Shape of Europe*, London: Foreign Policy Centre, 2000, pp. 69–76.

[21] Jan Zielonka, 'Should Europe become a state?', in Mark Leonard (ed), *The Future Shape of Europe*, London: Foreign Policy Centre, 2000, pp. 101–11.

[22] Anthony Forster, *Euro-scepticism in Contemporary British Politics: Opposition to Europe in the British Conservative and Labour parties since 1945*, London: Routledge, 2002.

[23] Louis Hartz, *The Liberal Tradition in America: An interpretation of American political thought since the Revolution*, New York: Harcourt Brace, 1955.

[24] Mario Telo, *European Union and New Regionalism: Regional actors and global governance in a post-hegemonic era*, London: Ashgate, 2001; Ian Bache and Matthew Flinders (eds), *Multilateral Governance*, Oxford: OUP, 2004.

[25] Mark Leonard, *Network Europe: The new case for Europe*.

[26] Jim Buller, *National Statecraft and European Integration: The Conservative Government and the European Union 1979–1997*, London: Pinter, 2000.

[27] Michael Heseltine, *The Challenge of Europe*, London: Weidenfeld & Nicolson, 1989.

[28] Will Hutton, *The World We're In*, London: Little, Brown, 2002.

[29] John Redwood, *Stars and Strife: The coming conflicts between the USA and the European Union*, London: Palgrave-Macmillan, 2001; John Redwood, *Just Say No: 100 arguments against the euro*, London: Politicos, 2001; Michael Spicer, *Treaty Too Far: A new policy for Europe*, London: Fourth Estate, 1992.

[30] Martin Holmes (ed), *The Euro-sceptical Reader*, London: Macmillan, 1996; Martin Holmes (ed), *The Euro-sceptical Reader 2*, London: Palgrave-Macmillan, 2002.

[31] David Baker, Andrew Gamble and David Seawright, 'Sovereign nations and global markets: modern British Conservatism and hyperglobalism', *British Journal of Politics and International Relations*, 4:3, (2002), pp. 399–428.

[32] Andrew Shonfield, *Modern Capitalism: The changing balance of private and public power*, Oxford: OUP, 1965; Michel Albert, *Capitalism against Capitalism*, London: Whurr, 1993; David Coates, *Models of Capitalism*, Cambridge: Polity, 2000.

[33] Peter Hall and David Soskice (eds), *Varieties of Capitalism: The institutional foundations of comparative advantage*, Oxford: OUP, 2001.

34   Michael Howard, Speech to the *News Corporation Conference in Cancun*, Mexico 19 March 2004.

35   Philip Bobbitt, *The Shield of Achilles: War, peace, and the course of history*, London: Allen Lane, 2002; Phil Cerny, *The Changing Architecture of Politics: Structure, agency and the future of the state*, London: Pinter, 1989.

Chapter 4

1   This essay was first published in Ben Wellings and Andrew Mycock (eds), *The Anglosphere: Continuity, dissonance, and location*, Proceedings of the British Academy, Oxford: OUP, 2019, pp. 175–190.

2   Charles Dilke, *Greater Britain,* pp. 226, 318.

3   Michael Kenny and Nicholas Pearce, *Shadows of Empire*, Cambridge: Polity, 2018.

4   Benedict Anderson, *Imagined Communities*, London: Verso, 1991.

5   Duncan Bell, *Building Greater Britain: Empire and identity in Victorian political thought, 1860–1900*, Princeton: Princeton University Press, 2007; Donald Watt, *Succeeding John Bull: America in Britain's place 1900–1975*, Cambridge: Cambridge University Press, 2008; James Bennett, *The Anglosphere Challenge: Why the English-speaking nations will lead the way in the twenty-first century*, Lanham, MD: Rowman & Littlefield, 2004; Srdjan Vucetic, *The Anglosphere: A genealogy of a racialised identity in international relations*, Stanford: Stanford University Press, 2011.

6   Anthony Payne, 'The study of governance in a global political economy', in Nicola Phillips (ed), *Globalizing International Political Economy*, London: Palgrave-Macmillan, 2005.

7   Daniel Archibugi and David Held (eds), *Cosmopolitan Democracy: An agenda for a new world order*, Cambridge: Polity, 1995.

8   Immanuel Wallerstein, *The Modern World System*, New York: Academic Press, 1974.

9   Robert Cox, *Production, Power and World Order: Social forces in the making of history*, New York: Columbia University Press, 1987.

10   David Held et al, *Global Transformations: Politics, economics and culture*, Cambridge: Polity, 1999.

11   Colin Hay and David Marsh (eds), *Demystifying Globalization*, London: Palgrave-Macmillan, 2000.

12   Peter Katzenstein, *Small States in World Markets*, Cornell: Cornell University Press, 1985.

13   Robert Gilpin, *The Political Economy of International Relations*, Princeton: Princeton University Press, 1987.

14   John Williamson, *Latin American Adjustment: How much has happened?*, Washington: Institute for International Economics 1990.

15   Linda Weiss, *The Myth of the Powerless State*, Cambridge: Polity, 1998; Ronald Dore, *Stock Market Capitalism, Welfare Capitalism: Japan, Germany and the Anglo-Saxons*, Oxford: Oxford University Press, 2000.

16   Edward Lincoln, *Japan's New Global Role*, Washington: Brookings Institution, 1993.

17   John Keane, *Tom Paine: A political life*, London: Bloomsbury, 1995.

18   David Dimbleby and David Reynolds, *An Ocean Apart*.

19   Aaron Friedberg, *The Weary Titan: Britain and the experience of relative decline 1895–1905*, Princeton: Princeton University Press, 1988.

20   Barnett, *The Collapse of British Power*.

21   Christopher Hitchens, *Blood, Class, and Nostalgia*, London: Vintage, 1991.

22   Watt, *Succeeding John Bull*.

[23] Charles Kindelberger, *The World in Depression, 1929–1939*, London: Allen Lane, 1973; Robert Gilpin, *The Political Economy of International Relations*, Princeton: Princeton University Press, 1987.

[24] Iestyn Adams, *Brothers Across the Ocean: British foreign policy and the origins of the Anglo–American special relationship, 1900–1905*, London: Tauris, 2005.

[25] Bell, *Building Greater Britain*.

[26] A.P. Thornton, *The Imperial Idea and its Enemies: A study in British power*, London: Macmillan, 1985.

[27] Dimbleby and Reynolds, *An Ocean Apart*.

[28] Lloyd Gardner, *A Covenant with Power: America and world order from Wilson to Reagan*, London: Macmillan, 1984.

[29] James Cronin, *Global Rules: America, Britain and a disordered world*, New Haven: Yale University Press, 2014; Watt, *Succeeding John Bull*; John Dumbrell, *A Special Relationship: Anglo–American relations from the cold war to Iraq*, London: Palgrave-Macmillan, 2006.

[30] David Reynolds, *Britannia Unchained*, p. 360.

[31] John Ikenberry, 'Liberalism and Empire: Logics of order in the American unipolar age', *Review of International Studies*, 30, (2004), pp. 609–630.

[32] Eric Hobsbawm, *Industry and Empire: An economic history of Britain since 1750*, London: Weidenfeld, 1999.

[33] Joseph Nye, *The Paradox of American Power: Why the world's only superpower cant go it alone*, New York: OUP, 2002.

[34] Bennett, *The Anglosphere Challenge*.

[35] Kenny and Pearce, *Shadows of Empire*.

[36] Alan Macfarlane, *The Riddle of the Modern World*, London: Macmillan, 2000.

[37] Bennett, *The Anglosphere Challenge*.

[38] Claudio Veliz, *The New World of the Gothic Fox: Culture and economy in English and Spanish America*, Berkeley: University of California Press, 1994; Walter Russell Mead, *God and Gold: Britain, America and the making of the modern world*, New York: Vintage Books, 2008.

[39] Robert Conquest, *Reflections on a Ravaged Century*, London: John Murray, 1999.

[40] Samuel Huntington, *Who Are We?*, New York: Simon & Schuster, 2004; Russell Kirk, *America's British Culture*, New Brunswick, NJ: Transaction Publishers, 1993.

[41] Alan Cafruny and Magnus Ryner, *Europe at Bay: American hegemony and the crisis of European Union*, London: Lynne Rienner, 2007; Kees van der Pijl, *The Making of an Atlantic Ruling Class*, London: Verso, 1984.

Chapter 5

[1] This essay was first published in 1979, in *Socialist Register*, 1979, pp. 1–25.

[2] Typical products of the right-wing upsurge are recent collections such as: Patrick Cormack (ed), *Right Turn,* London: Leo Cooper, 1978; and *The Coming Confrontation* (IEA), London: IEA, 1978. The contributors range from Paul Johnson to Julius Gould, Reg Prentice, and the Duke of Edinburgh.

[3] I have examined in greater detail the changing Conservative party in two recent essays: 'The Conservative party', in Henry Drucker (ed), *Multi-Party Britain,* London: Macmillan, 1979; and 'Conservative economic policy', in Zig Layton-Henry (ed), *Conservative Party Politics,* London: Macmillan, 1979.

4   They are surveyed by C.J. Friedrich, 'The political ideas of neo-liberalism', *American Political Science Review,* 49 (1955), pp. 509–25.

5   The IEA was founded in 1957 and has produced a constant stream of pamphlets (over 250 publications). It recruits its writers mainly from academic economists. The Centre for Policy Studies was founded by Keith Joseph and Margaret Thatcher in 1974, and has produced a number of pamphlets, including the keynote, *Why Britain Needs a Social Market Economy,* London: CPS, 1975. It has also published collections of the speeches of its two founders as well as a range of pamphlets the intellectual level of which has been variable.

6   Apart from their journalism they have all written more extended studies, especially Brittan, who has written pamphlets for both the IEA and the CPS. See also his recent and important book, *The Economic Consequences of Democracy,* London: Temple Smith, 1977.

7   See Stuart Hall et al, *Policing the Crisis,* London: Macmillan, 1978.

8   See, for instance, Samuel Brittan, *Government and the Market Economy,* London: IEA, 1971, and *Participation Without Politics,* London: IEA, 1975.

9   Alexander Rüstow, one of the German neo-liberals, was the first to coin the term neo-liberalism and to use the phrase '*Freie Wirtschaft – Starker Staat'* (free economy, strong state).

10   See the onslaught contained, for example, in Trevor Russel, *The Tory Party: Its policies, divisions and future,* Harmondsworth: Penguin, 1978. Russel, a former Labour party member is an active member of the Tory Reform Group.

11   *The Road to Serfdom* (London, 1944) is the best known of Hayek's writings, but more important are his later writings, particularly *The Constitution of Liberty,* London: Routledge, 1960; *Law, Legislation, and Liberty* (3 volumes), London: Routledge, 1982; and *Studies in Philosophy, Politics, and Economics,* London: Routledge, 1967.

12   Hayek, *The Constitution of Liberty,* p. 11.

13   Moreau's assessment of Norman was as follows: 'in his view politicians and political institutions are in no fit state to direct with the necessary competence and continuity this task of organisation (economic and financial organisation of the world) which he would like to see undertaken by central banks, independent at once of governments and of private finance', quoted by Andrew Boyle, *Montagu Norman* London: Cassell, 1967, p. 205.

14   They make loyalty tests and the *Berufsverbot* much easier to impose.

15   Robert Moss, *The Collapse of Democracy,* London: Temple Smith, 1975.

16   Milton Friedman, 'The line we dare not cross', *Encounter,* November, 1976. See also Gordon Tullock, *The Vote Motive,* London: IEA, 1976.

17   A brief perusal of the social market literature reveals how profoundly these writers distrust the state. The IEA has taken to translating the term 'state' as politicians and bureaucrats, to strip away from it its aura of omniscience and omnipotence and reveal the fallible agents underneath.

18   Keith Joseph, *Conditions for Fuller Employment,* London: CPS, 1978, p. 20.

19   See, for example, Alan Walters, *Economists and the British Economy,* London: IEA, 1978. The bitterness of liberal economists against Keynesian economists is deeply felt. See W.H. Hutt, *Politically Impossible?,* London: IEA, 1971.

20   See, for example, Tim Congdon, *Monetarism,* London: CPS, 1978, and William Rees-Mogg, *Democracy and the Value of Money,* London: IEA, 1977.

21   J.M. Keynes, *The General Theory of Interest, Employment, and Money,* London: Macmillan, 1973, p. 322.

22 John Jewkes, *Delusions of Dominance*, London: IEA, 1977. See also the Centre for Policy Studies series on government intervention, 'The Way the Money Goes'.

23 See Samuel Brittan, *Government and the Market Economy*.

24 Hayek, *The Constitution of Liberty*, p. 264. This represents a considerable shift from the position he adopted in *The Road to Serfdom*.

25 Hayek's views on inflation and the consequences of Keynesianism are usefully collected in *A Tiger by the Tail*, London: IEA, 1972. See also his Nobel Lecture, *Full Employment at any Price?*, London: IEA, 1975.

26 J.E. Powell, *Freedom and Reality*, London: Elliot Right Way Books, 1969, ch. 10. When Powell first emerged as an exponent of economic liberalism in the 1960s he was dismissed as a crank and widely derided. But he pioneered the analysis which has now become orthodox.

27 This is not the same, however, as arguing that the idea of the social market economy must be attributed to this or that fraction of capital. I regard the evidence for this as slim and the underlying argument unsound.

28 For an exposition of it see Milton Friedman's Nobel Lecture, *Inflation and Employment*, London: IEA, 1977; and Samuel Brittan, *Second Thoughts on Full Employment Policy*, London: CPS, 1975.

29 See Hayek, *The Confusion of Language in Political Thought*, London: IEA, 1968.

30 See, in particular, Hayek, *Law, Legislation, and Liberty*, vol. 2, and Samuel Brittan and Peter Lilley, *The Delusions of Incomes Policy*, London: Temple Smith, 1976.

31 Friedman, 'The line we dare not cross'.

32 A very different way of looking at capitalism comes from those who analyse capitalism as a system of production rather than as a system of markets. W.W. Rostow's *The World Economy*, London: Macmillan, 1978, is an example of the former approach which assigns a very small role to monetary factors. Rostow, whose own allegiance to capitalism is hardly in question, argues that the present recession will only be overcome and capitalism placed on a stable basis again if there is a further massive extension of state powers and investment, particularly in the energy field.

33 This is of course recognised and the necessary measures fully discussed. See, for example, Keith Joseph, *Solving the Union Problem is the Key to Britain's Recovery*, London: CPS, 1979; and Samuel Brittan, *The Economic Consequences of Democracy*, ch. 19. One of the most drastic suggestions is for the creation of a professional specialised strike-breaking force, which would be available to man essential installations in the event of strikes, and would presumably allow lockouts to be threatened and implemented more easily in some sectors.

34 One recent major attempt to rethink socialist strategy, although from a different position from the one proposed here, is Anthony Cutler et al, *Marx's Capital and Capitalism Today*, London: Routledge, 1977.

Chapter 6

1 This essay was published in Stuart Hall and Martin Jacques (eds), *The Politics of Thatcherism*, London: Lawrence & Wishart, 1983, pp. 109–131. Earlier versions first appeared in *Marxism Today* in November 1979 and November 1980. My thanks are due to Martin Jacques for encouraging me to write the original articles.

2 See Michael Steed and John Curtice, 'An analysis of the voting', in David Butler and Dennis Kavanagh, *The British General Election of 1979*, London: Macmillan, 1980. The South East, South West, East and West Midlands all registered swings

of over 6 per cent. It is calculated that skilled workers swung 11½ per cent to the Conservatives, unskilled workers 9 per cent, and that as a result the Labour party attracted only 50 per cent of the trade-union vote and only 45 per cent of the working-class vote.

3   The term Thatcherism was first used by Stuart Hall in *Marxism Today*.

4   In Scotland the swing to the Tories was 0.7 per cent. In Greater Clydeside and Glasgow there was a small swing to Labour. Elsewhere in the North the swing to the Conservatives averaged 4 per cent. The Conservatives were also weakened because their long-standing alliance with Ulster Unionism, sundered in 1972 when direct rule was declared, had still not been restored by 1979. Steed and Curtice summarise the result of the election as follows; the swing 'gave the Conservatives as large a plurality of votes (7%) over the next largest party as any party had enjoyed since Labour's 1945 landslide … Yet Mrs Thatcher took office with a smaller share of the national vote than any Prime Minister enjoying a secure parliamentary majority since Bonar Law in 1922' (p. 393).

5   I have explored this doctrine at greater length in 'The free economy and the strong state', *Socialist Register 1979*, pp. 1–25.

6   Once the gold standard collapsed in 1931 the National Government, having purged itself of the few doctrinaire economic liberals like Philip Snowden in its ranks, imposed a measure of protection and encouraged the formation of cartels and a range of means for reducing competition in the home market because of the depressed state of world demand.

7   Hugh Clegg chaired the Standing Commission on Pay Comparability set up by James Callaghan in 1979 following the protests against the Government's incomes policy during the Winter of Discontent.

8   An alliance between the SDP and the Liberals was subsequently arranged and the impact of this and of the 1981 Cabinet reshuffle were discussed in a later article in *Marxism Today*, November 1981.

Chapter 7

1   This essay was first published in Adrian Ellis and Krishan Kumar (eds), *Dilemmas of Liberal Democracies*, London: Tavistock, 1983, pp. 80–97.

2   Charles Lindblom, *Politics and Markets*, New York: Basic Books, 1977, p. 351.

3   Fred Hirsch, *Social Limits to Growth*, London: Routledge and Kegan Paul, 1977; Fred Hirsch, 'The ideological underlay of inflation', in Fred Hirsch and John Goldthorpe (eds), *The Political Economy of Inflation*, Oxford: Martin Robertson, 1978.

4   Seymour Martin Lipset, *Political Man*, London: Mercury, 1963, p. 406.

5   Robert Skidelsky, *Politicians and the Slump*, London: Macmillan, 1967.

6   Liberal Party, *Britain's Industrial Future*, London: Benn, 1928; Liberal Party, *We Can Conquer Unemployment*, London: Cassell, 1929; R.J. Mcleod, *The Development of Full Employment Policy, 1939–45*, Oxford: unpublished D. Phil. Thesis, 1978.

7   J.M. Keynes, *The Economic Consequences of the Peace*, London: Macmillan, 1971.

8   R.H. Tawney, *The Acquisitive Society*, London: Collins, 1961.

9   Joseph Schumpeter, *Capitalism, Socialism, and Democracy*, London: Allen and Unwin, 1954; F.A. Hayek, *The Road to Serfdom*, London: Routledge and Kegan Paul, 1944.

10   John Strachey, *The Nature of Capitalist Crisis*, London: Gollancz, 1934.

11   Andrew Gamble, *The Conservative Nation*, London: Routledge and Kegan Paul, 1974.

12 Fred Hirsch, 'The ideological underlay of inflation', p. 281.
13 Nigel Fisher, *Harold Macmillan*, London: Macmillan, 1981, p. 29.
14 David Eccles, 'Popular Capitalism', *Objective* 20, (1955), p. 5.
15 John Strachey, *Contemporary Capitalism*, London: Gollancz, 1956.
16 Tony Crosland, *The Future of Socialism*, London: Cape, 1956; Tony Crosland, *Socialism Now*, London: Cape, 1974.
17 James Alt, *The Politics of Economic Decline*, Cambridge: Cambridge University Press, 1979.
18 Tom Nairn, *The Breakup of Britain*, London: New Left Books, 1977.
19 Tony Crosland, *Socialism Now*, London: Cape, 1974, p. 26.
20 Tony Crosland, *Socialism Now*, p. 27.
21 Peter Clarke, *The New Liberalism*, Cambridge: Cambridge University Press, 1978.
22 F.A. Hayek, *A Tiger by the Tail*, London: Institute of Economic Affairs, 1972.
23 Andrew Gamble, 'The free economy and the strong state', in Ralph Miliband and John Saville (eds), *Socialist Register*, London: Merlin, 1979.
24 Samuel Brittan, *The Economic Consequences of Democracy*, London: Temple Smith, 1977.
25 Brendon Sewill and Ralph Harris, *British Economic Policy*, London: Institute of Economic Affairs, 1975.
26 Fred Hirsch, 'The ideological underlay of inflation', p. 279.
27 Samuel Brittan and Peter Lilley, *The Delusion of Incomes Policy*, London: Temple Smith, 1977.
28 James Douglas, 'The overloaded crown', *British Journal of Political Science*, 6:4, (1976), pp. 483–506.
29 Eric Hobsbawm, *The Forward March of Labour Halted*, London: Verso, 1981.
30 Ian Bradley, *Breaking the Mould*, Oxford: Martin Robertson, 1981.
31 Milton Friedman, *Inflation and Unemployment*, London: Institute of Economic Affairs, 1977.
32 Andrew Friend and Andy Metcalfe, *Slump City: The politics of mass unemployment*, London: Pluto, 1981.
33 Andrew Gamble, 'Liberals and the economy', in Vernon Bogdanor (ed), *Liberal Party Politics*, Oxford: Oxford University Press.
34 Peter Jay, *Inflation, Employment, and Politics*, London: Institute of Economic Affairs, 1976.
35 Alt, *The Politics of Economic Decline*.

Chapter 8

1 This essay was first published in *New Left Review*, 214 (1995), pp. 3–25.
2 Anthony Seldon and Stuart Ball (eds), *Conservative Century: The Conservative party since 1900*, Oxford: OUP, 1994.
3 Many of its key features were classically caught by Tom Nairn in his essay, 'The twilight of the British state', in *The Breakup of Britain*, London: Verso, 1981, and by Perry Anderson, 'The figures of descent', in *English Questions*, London: Verso, 1992.
4 Paul Whitely, Patrick Seyd and Jeremy Richardson, *True Blues: The politics of Conservative party membership*, Oxford: OUP, 1994. They estimate (p. 222) that the party has been losing 64,000 members annually since 1960 which, if the trend continues, would leave it with less than 100,000 members by the end of the century. They estimate the membership of the party in 1995 to be 756,000.

Their survey showed that the average age of its members was sixty-two. One effect of the declining membership is that it has reduced the party's funding base. The party has been running a deficit since 1992 which, although reducing, still stood at £11 million in 1995.

5 Ivor Crewe, 'Voting and the electorate', in Patrick Dunleavy, Andrew Gamble, Ian Holliday and Gillian Peele (eds), *Developments in British Politics 4*, London: Macmillan, 1993, pp. 2–122.

6 Dennis Kavanagh and Anthony Seldon (eds), *The Major Effect*, London: Macmillan, 1994, analyses different aspects of Major's premiership, now one of the longest in the twentieth century.

7 The history of previous splits in the party is reviewed in David Baker, Andrew Gamble and Steve Ludlam, '1846 ... 1906 ... 1996? Conservative splits and European integration', *Political Quarterly*, 64:4, (1993), pp. 420–34.

8 The details of the factional revolt against the leadership can be found in David Baker, Andrew Gamble and Steve Ludlam, 'Whips or scorpions? Conservative MPs and the Maastricht Paving Motion Vote', *Parliamentary Affairs*, 45:4, (1992), pp. 656–88, and 'The parliamentary siege of Maastricht 1993: Conservative divisions and British ratification', *Parliamentary Affairs*, 47:1, (1994), pp. 37–60.

9 Margaret Thatcher contributes a telling commentary on these events in *The Path to Power*, London: Harper Collins, 1995, ch. 13. See also Bernard Connolly, *The Rotten Heart of Europe: The dirty war for Europe's money*, London: Faber, 1995. Connolly argues that the increase of rates to 15 per cent was not serious but was designed to provide an excuse for the exit of sterling from the ERM.

10 Connolly argues that the situation might have been worse under Labour because Labour's tactic would have been to attempt to devalue while remaining within the ERM. This would have led to an intensification of the crisis.

11 This is one of the central implications of the model developed by *The British Election Study*. See Anthony Heath, Roger Jowell and John Curtice, *How Britain Votes*, Oxford: OUP, 1985.

12 Stuart Hall and Bill Schwarz, 'State and society, 1880–1930', in Mary Langan and Bill Schwarz (eds), *Crises in the British State*, London: Hutchinson, 1985.

13 Jim Bulpitt, 'The discipline of the new democracy: Mrs Thatcher's domestic statecraft', *Political Studies*, 34:1, (1985), p. 21.

14 Bernard Semmel, *Imperialism and Tariff Reform*, Cambridge, Mass: Harvard University Press, 1960.

15 F.A. Hayek, *The Constitution of Liberty*, London: Routledge, 1960, p. 398.

16 Keith Joseph, *Stranded on the Middle Ground*, London: Centre for Policy Studies, 1976.

17 Ian Gilmour, *Dancing with Dogma: Britain under Thatcherism*, London: Simon & Schuster, 1992. See also the statements by Alan Howarth who, on the eve of the Conservative conference in October 1995, became the first Conservative MP ever to cross the floor and join Labour.

18 Two very different perspectives can be found in Gilmour's *Dancing with Dogma*, and Shirley Letwin, *The Anatomy of Thatcherism*, London: Fontana, 1992. See Andrew Gamble, 'The entrails of Thatcherism', *New Left Review*, 198, March-April 1993, pp. 117–28.

19 John Gray, *The Undoing of Conservatism*, London: Social Market Foundation, 1994.

20 Nairn, 'The twilight of the British state'; Ferdinand Mount, *The British Constitution Now*, London: Heinemann, 1992; J.H. Grainger, 'Mrs Thatcher's last stand', *Quadrant*, no. 4, 1980.

21 Rod Rhodes and David Marsh (eds), *Implementing Thatcherism*, Colchester: University of Essex, 1992.

22 Jim Bulpitt, *Territory and Power in the UK*, Manchester: Manchester University Press, 1983.

23 For Scotland see the account in Arthur Midwinter, Michael Keating and James Mitchell, *Politics and Public Policy in Scotland*, London: Macmillan, 1991.

24 An immediate consequence was that the Conservatives, although polling more votes than any other party, had fewer parliamentary seats than Labour. If they had still been able to count on the Ulster Unionists, they would have been the largest single party and Heath might have been able to continue at the head of a minority administration.

25 For an account of the devolution debate see Andrew Marr, *The Battle for Scotland*, London: Penguin, 1992.

26 Buchanan-Smith and Rifkind both resigned. The tactic of opposing devolution paid short-term dividends because the collapse of Labour's devolution plans destroyed the party's fragile parliamentary position. The nationalists would no longer vote for the government and it duly lost a vote of confidence by one vote, precipitating an election at a very favourable time for the Conservatives.

27 James Cooper, 'The Scottish problem: English Conservatism and the Union with Scotland' in Joni Lovenduski and Jeffrey Stanyer (eds), *Contemporary Political Studies 1995*, London: Political Studies Association, 1995, pp. 1384–93.

28 Nigel Harris, *Competition and the Corporate Society*, London: Methuen, 1972; Keith Middlemas, *Politics in Industrial Society*, London: Deutsch, 1979.

29 Harold Macmillan played an important part in introducing Keynesian thinking into the party. See *The Middle Way*, London: Macmillan, 1938.

30 See the Conservative manifesto in 1987; also Geoffrey Maynard, *The Economy Under Mrs Thatcher*, Oxford: OUP, 1988; Alan Walters, *Britain's Economic Renaissance*, Oxford: OUP, 1986.

31 A large literature is developing on the claims and counter-claims about economic performance in the Thatcher decade. For Thatcher's own claims see *The Path to Power*, ch. 16; also Nicholas Crafts, 'Reversing relative economic decline? The 1980s in historical perspective', *Oxford Review of Economic Policy*, 7:3 (1991), pp. 81–98; Ken Coutts and Wyn Godley, 'The British Economy under Mrs Thatcher', *Political Quarterly*, 60:2 (1989), pp. 137–51; Jonathan Michie (ed), *The Economic Legacy 1979–1992*, London: Academic Press, 1992; Nigel Healey (ed), *Britain's Economic Miracle: Myth or Reality?*, London: Routledge, 1993; and Francis Green (ed), *The Restructuring of the UK Economy*, London: Harvester Wheatsheaf, 1989.

32 Peter Walker became Welsh Secretary in 1987, and pursued an active industrial strategy of the kind which had been ruled out in the rest of the country.

33 Maurice Cowling, *The Impact of Hitler: British politics and British policy 1933–1940*, Cambridge: CUP, 1975; John Charmley, *Chamberlain and the Lost Peace*, London: Hodder & Stoughton, 1989.

34 Thirty-nine Conservative MPS voted against. Twenty other Labour MPs abstained. Many of the Labour MPs who voted against joined the SDP in 1981.

35 Tom Nairn, *The Left Against Europe*, Harmondsworth: Penguin, 1973.

36 The speech was mostly unexceptional, but contained some ringing declarations which made the headlines, such as 'We have not successfully rolled back the frontiers of the state in Britain only to see them reimposed at the European level'.

37 To counter the activities of high-profile anti-European organisations like the European Foundation, a number of pro-European organisations have been

established. One of the most important of these, Action Centre on Europe, has the support of leading British banks and companies, and is chaired by Sir Geoffrey Howe.

38 Thatcher's views are set out in *The Path to Power*, ch. 13. The same position is put forward by Connolly in *The Rotten Heart of Europe*.

39 See Colin Leys' review of Will Hutton, *The State We're In*, in *New Left Review*, 212, pp. 3–13.

40 The strength and confidence of the right was in evidence at the 1995 Brighton conference, particularly in the warmth of the conference reception for the anti-European speech made by Michael Portillo, and the unwillingness of any of the leadership to directly counter the tide of anti-European feeling.

41 If the Conservatives lose the next election, the size of the swing against them may be crucial in determining the future of the party since in a much smaller parliamentary party, this will decide the composition of the electorate in the next leadership election.

Chapter 9

1 This essay was first published in *British Politics*, 10:1 (2015), pp. 3–15.

2 Margaret Thatcher, *Statecraft*, London: Harper Collins, 2002, p. 320.

Chapter 10

1 This essay was first published in *Political Studies*, 38:3, (1990), pp. 404–20.

2 Edmund Burke, *The Writings and Speeches of Edmund Burke*, Oxford: Clarendon Press, 1981, p. 274.

3 Current textbooks include: Richard Rose, *Politics in England*, London: Macmillan, 1989; Max Beloff and Gillian Peele, *The Government and Politics of the United Kingdom*, London: Weidenfeld, 1990; Colin Leys, *Politics in Britain*, London: Verso, 1989; Dennis Kavanagh, *British Politics: Continuities and Change*, Oxford: Oxford University, Press 1985; John Dearlove and Peter Saunders, *An Introduction to British Politics*, Cambridge: Polity, 1984; Philip Norton, *The British Polity*, London: Longman, 1984; and Patrick Dunleavy, Andrew Gamble and Gillian Peele (eds), *Developments in British Politics* 3, London: Macmillan, 1990.

4 W.H. Greenleaf, *The British Political Tradition Volume One: The Rise of Collectivism*, London: Methuen, 1983.

5 Greenleaf, *The British Political Tradition*, p. 7.

6 The shared assumptions of American political science in its early phases of development were noted by Bernard Crick, *The American Science of Politics*, London: RKP, 1959.

7 Jean Blondel, *The Discipline of Politics*, London: Butterworth, 1981.

8 A.V. Dicey, *Introduction to the Study of Law and the Constitution*, London: Macmillan, 1885.

9 Fred Ridley, *The Study of Government*, London: George Allen & Unwin, 1975; Rodney Barker, 'The rise and eclipse of the social democratic state', in Robert Borthwick and Jack Spence (eds), *British Politics in Perspective*, Leicester: Leicester University Press, 1984.

10 A.H. Birch, *Representative and Responsible Government*, London: George Allen & Unwin, 1964.

11 John Mackintosh, *The Government and Politics of Britain*, London: Hutchinson, 1970.

[12] Stefan Collini, Donald Winch and John Burrow, *That Noble Science of Politics*, Cambridge: Cambridge University Press, 1983.

[13] Jack Hayward, *Political Science in Britain,* mimeo, 1989.

[14] For a mainstream Labour view on the importance of the doctrine of parliamentary sovereignty, see Aneurin Bevan, *In Place of Fear*, London: McGibbon & Kee, 1952, p. 100.

[15] Michael Oakeshott, *Rationalism in Politics*, London: Methuen, 1962.

[16] See for example, Nevil Johnson, *In Search of the Constitution*, London: Methuen, 1976.

[17] Samuel Beer, *Modern British Politics*, London: Faber, 1965.

[18] A.V. Dicey, *Law and Public Opinion in England*, London: Macmillan, 1926; Harold Laski, *The Grammar of Politics*, London: Allen & Unwin, 1925; Beer, *Modern British Politics*; Greenleaf, *The British Political Tradition*.

[19] Keith Middlemas, *Politics in Industrial Society*, London: Andre Deutsch, 1979; Jim Bulpitt, 'The discipline of the new democracy: Mrs Thatcher's domestic statecraft', *Political Studies*, 34:1, (1985), pp. 19–39.

[20] Ralph Miliband, *Parliamentary Socialism*, London: George Allen & Unwin, 1961, and *The State in Capitalist Society*, London: Weidenfeld & Nicholson, 1967; Harold Laski, *Parliamentary Government in England*, London: George Allen & Unwin, 1938. See also Leys, *Politics in Britain*.

[21] Ralph Miliband, *Capitalist Democracy in Britain*, Oxford: Oxford University Press, 1982.

[22] Barker, 'The rise and eclipse of the social democratic state', p. 4.

[23] Dearlove and Saunders, *An Introduction to British Politics*, especially ch. 1.

[24] Blondel, *The Discipline of Politics*.

[25] See, for example, Richard Rose, *Influencing Voters*, London: Macmillan, 1967, and David Butler and Donald Stokes, *Political Change in Britain*, London: Macmillan, 1974.

[26] Philip Norton, *Dissension in the House of Commons, 1974–1979*, Oxford: Oxford University Press, 1980, and *The Commons in Perspective*, Oxford: Martin Robertson, 1981.

[27] Richard Rose, *Politics in England*, London: Macmillan, 1989, 5th edn; Kavanagh, *British Politics*.

[28] Dearlove and Saunders, *An Introduction to British Politics*; D. Coates, *The Context of British Politics*, London: Hutchinson, 1984; Vicky Randall, *Women in Politics*, London: Macmillan, 2nd edn, 1987.

[29] David Easton, *A Systems Analysis of Political Life*, New York: Wiley, 1965.

[30] Patrick Dunleavy and Brendan O'Leary, *Theories of the State*, London: Macmillan, 1987; Patrick Dunleavy, 'Theories of the state in British politics', in Henry Drucker et al (ed), *Developments in British Politics 2*, London: Macmillan, 1986.

[31] David Green, *The New Right*, Brighton: Wheatsheaf, 1987.

[32] See, for example, Charles Lindblom, *Politics and Markets*, New York: Basic Books, 1977, and Miliband, *The State in Capitalist Society*.

[33] Alan Cawson, *Corporatism and Political Theory*, Oxford: Basil Blackwell, 1986.

[34] Rod Rhodes, *Beyond Westminster and Whitehall*, London: Unwin Hyman, 1988.

[35] E.A. Brett, *The World Economy Since the War*, London: Macmillan, 1985.

[36] S.E. Finer (ed), *Adversary Politics and Electoral Reform*, London: Anthony Wigram, 1975; Stuart Walkland, 'The politics of parliamentary reform', *Parliamentary Affairs,* XXIX: 2 (1976); Johnson, *In Search of the Constitution*.

[37] Stuart Hall and Bill Schwarz, 'State and society, 1880–1930', in Mary Langan and Bill Schwarz (eds), *Crises in the British State*, London: Hutchinson, 1985.

38 Tom Nairn, *The Breakup of Britain*, London: New Left Books, 1977; Jim Bulpitt, *Territory and Power in the United Kingdom*, Manchester: Manchester University Press, 1983.

39 Arend Lijphart, 'The Northern Ireland problem: cases, theories and solutions', *British Journal of Political Science*, 5:1 (1975), pp. 83–106. See also Brendan O'Leary, 'The limits to coercive consociationalism in Northern Ireland', *Political Studies*, 37:4 (1989), pp. 562–588.

40 Michael Hechter, *Internal Colonialism*, London: Routledge, 1975.

41 For a fuller exploration of these three problems, see Andrew Gamble, 'The Thatcher decade in perspective', in Patrick Dunleavy, Andrew Gamble and Gillian Peele (eds), *Developments in British Politics 3*, London: Macmillan, 1990.

42 Greenleaf, *The British Political Tradition*.

43 Samuel Beer, *Britain against Itself*, London: Faber, 1982.

44 Ron Inglehart, *The Silent Revolution: Changing values and political styles among western publics*, Princeton: Princeton University Press, 1977.

45 Stuart Hall, *The Hard Road to Renewal*, London: Verso, 1989.

46 Norton, *The British Polity*.

47 Bob Jessop, Keith Bonnett, Simon Bromley and Trevor Ling, *Thatcherism*, Cambridge, Polity, 1989.

48 Martin Wiener, *English Culture and the Decline of the Industrial Spirit*, Cambridge: Cambridge University Press, 1981; Correlli Barnett, *The Audit of War*, London:, Macmillan, 1986; Nairn, *The Breakup of Britain*.

49 Antony Birch, 'Overload, ungovernability and delegitimation: the theories and the British case', *British Journal of Political Science*, 14:2 (1984), pp. 135–160.

50 Richard Holme and Michael Elliott (eds), *1688–1988: Time for a New Constitution*, London: Macmillan, 1988.

51 V. Bogdanor, *Devolution*, Oxford: Oxford University Press, 1979.

52 Bulpitt, 'The discipline of the new democracy'.

53 For attempts in this direction, see: Norman Lewis and Ian Harden, *The Noble Lie*, London: Hutchinson, 1986; Cosmo Graham and Tony Prosser (eds), *Waiving the Rules*, Milton Keynes: Open University Press, 1988; Andrew Gamble and Celia Wells (eds), *Thatcher's Law*, Cardiff: University of Wales Press, 1988.

54 Gerry Stoker, *The Politics of Local Government*, London: Macmillan, 1988.

55 Middlemas, *Politics in Industrial Society*. See also Cawson, *Corporatism and Political Theory*, and Rhodes, *Government Beyond Westminster and Whitehall*. The theory of policy networks is set out by Maurice Wright, 'Policy community, policy network and comparative industrial policies', *Political Studies,* 36:4, (1988), pp. 593–612. For pluralist theory of the policy-making process, see Jeremy Richardson and Grant Jordan, *Governing under Pressure*, Oxford: Martin Robertson, 1979.

56 See the special issue of *Public Administration,* 68:1, (1990), devoted to the core executive.

57 See the discussion of New Right and neo-pluralist theories in Dunleavy and O'Leary, *Theories of the State*.

58 Mancur Olson, *The Rise and Decline of Nations*, New Haven: Yale University Press, 1982.

59 David Marquand, *The Unprincipled Society*, London: Cape, 1988; Wyn Grant (ed), *The Political Economy of Corporatism*, London: Macmillan, 1985; Peter Hall, *Governing the Economy*, Cambridge: Polity Press, 1986; Bob Jessop, *Essays in the Theory of the State*, Cambridge: Polity, 1990.

60 Geoffrey Ingham, *Capitalism Divided*, London: Macmillan, 1984. See also Perry Anderson, 'The figures of descent', *New Left Review*, 161, (1987), pp. 20–77.

61 William Miller, 'Voting and the electorate', in Patrick Dunleavy, Andrew Gamble and Gillian Peele (eds), *Developments in British Politics 3*, London: Macmillan, 1990.

62 Ron Johnston, Charles Pattie and J.G. Allsopp, *A Nation Dividing?*, London: Longman, 1988.

63 See Norman Barry, *The New Right*, London: Croom Helm, 1987, and Dunleavy and O'Leary, *Theories of the State*.

64 See, for example, John Mohan (ed), *The Political Geography of Contemporary Britain*, London: Macmillan, 1989.

Chapter 11

1 This essay was first published in *Publius*, 36:1, (2006), pp. 19–35.

2 Robert Hazell, 'Reforming the constitution', *Political Quarterly*, 72:1, (2001), pp. 39–49.

3 Tom Nairn, *After Britain: New Labour and the return of Scotland*, London: Granta, 1999.

4 John Redwood, *The Death of Britain?*, London: Palgrave-Macmillan, 1999.

5 Peter Hitchens, *The Abolition of Britain*, London: Quartet, 1999.

6 Anthony Barnett, *This Time: Our constitutional revolution*, London: Vintage, 1997.

7 Tom Nairn, *Breakup of Britain: Crisis and neo-nationalism*, London: Verso, 1977; Nevil Johnson, *Reshaping the British Constitution: Essays in political interpretation*, London: Palgrave-Macmillan 2004; Ferdinand Mount, *The British Constitution Now: Recovery or decline?*, London: Heinemann, 1992; Philip Corrigan and Derek Sayer, *The Great Arch: English state formation as cultural revolution*, Oxford: Blackwell, 1985.

8 Linda Colley, *Britons: Forging the Nation 1707–1837*, New Haven: Yale University Press, 1992; Norman Davies, *The Isles: A history*, London: Palgrave-Macmillan, 1999; Christopher Harvie, *Scotland and Nationalism: Scottish society and politics 1707–present*, London: Routledge, 1998; Roger Scruton, *England: An elegy*, London: Pimlico, 2001; Robert Colls, *Identity of England*, Oxford: Oxford University Press, 2002; Richard Weight, *Patriots: National identity in Britain*, London: Palgrave-Macmillan, 2002.

9 Arend Lijphart, *Patterns of Democracy: Government forms and performance in thirty six countries*, New Haven: Yale University Press, 1999; R.L. Watts, *Comparing Federal Systems*, 2nd edn, Montreal: McGill-Queens University Press, 1999; Daniel Elazar, *Exploring Federalism*, Tuscaloosa: University of Alabama Press, 1987; Stuart Weir and David Beetham, *Political Power and Democratic Control in Britain: The democratic audit of the United Kingdom*, London: Routledge, 1999; Kenneth Wheare, *Federal Government*, Oxford: Oxford University Press, 1946; Michel Moran, *The British Regulatory State: High modernism and hyper innovation*, Oxford: Oxford University Press, 2003.

10 Andrew Gamble, *Between Europe and America: The future of British politics*, London: Palgrave-Macmillan, 2003.

11 Lijphart, *Patterns of Democracy*.

12 Jim Bulpitt, *Territory and Power in the United Kingdom*, Manchester: Manchester University Press, 1983.

13 David Judge, *The Parliamentary State*, London: Sage, 1993.

14 Leo Amery, *Thoughts on the Constitution*, Oxford: OUP, 1947.

15 Watts, *Comparing Federal Systems*; Elazar, *Exploring Federalism*.

16 Peter Madgwick and Richard Rose (eds), *The Territorial Dimension in United Kingdom Politics*, London: Macmillan, 1982; James Mitchell, *Governing Scotland: The invention of administrative devolution*, London: Palgrave-Macmillan, 2003.

17 John Kendle, *The Round Table Movement and Imperial Union*, Toronto: Toronto University Press, 1975.

18 Dylan Griffiths, *Thatcherism and Territorial Politics: A Welsh case-study*, Aldershot: Avebury, 1996.

19 David Stewart, *Challenging the Consensus: Scotland under Margaret Thatcher 1979–1990*, Glasgow University Ph.D thesis, 2004. Published as *The Path to Devolution and Change: A political history of Scotland under Margaret Thatcher*, London: Palgrave-Macmillan, 2009.

20 Paddy Ashdown, *The Ashdown Diaries*, London: Allen Lane, 2000.

21 Tam Dalyell, 'Devolution: The end of Britain', in *The Rape of the Constitution?*, Keith Sutherland (ed), London: Imprint Academic, 2000, pp. 213–8.

22 Douglas Carswell, *Direct Democracy: An agenda for a new model party*, London: direct-democracy.co.uk, 2005.

23 Robert Hazell (ed), *The State and the Nations: The first year of devolution in the United Kingdom*, London: Academic, 2000.

24 Evans, Mark (1995), *Charter 88: A successful challenge to the British political tradition?*, Aldershot: Dartmouth.

25 Geoffrey Evans and Brendan O'Leary, 'Northern Irish voters and the British-Irish agreement: foundations of a stable consociational settlement', *Political Quarterly*, 71:1, (2000), pp. 78–101.

26 R.A. Young, *The Secession of Quebec and the Future of Canada*, Montreal: McGill-Queens University Press, 1996.

27 A version of English votes for English laws was introduced by the Conservative Government in 2015.

28 Simon Heffer, *Nor Shall My Sword: The reinvention of England*, London: Weidenfeld & Nicholson, 1999.

29 Vernon Bogdanor, *Devolution in the UK*, Oxford: Oxford University Press, 2001; Vernon Bogdanor, 'Asymmetric devolution: Toward a quasi-federal constitution', in *Development in British Politics 7*, Patrick Dunleavy et al (eds), London: Palgrave-Macmillan, 2003, pp. 222–241. See also Archie Brown, 'Asymmetrical devolution: The Scottish case', *Political Quarterly*, 69:3, (1998), pp. 215–223.

30 Moran, *The British Regulatory State*.

31 Mark Evans, *Constitution-Making and the Labour Party*, London: Palgrave-Macmillan, 2003.

Chapter 12

1 This essay was first published in Richard Heffernan, Colin Hay, Meg Russell and Philip Cowley (eds), *Developments in British Politics 10*, London: Palgrave-Macmillan, 2016, pp. 1–19.

2 Robert Ford and Matthew Goodwin, *Revolt on the Right: Explaining support for the radical right in Britain*, London: Routledge, 2014.

3 *http://ec.europa.eu/public_opinion/index_en.htm*

4 Andrew Gamble, *Politics and Fate*, Cambridge: Polity, 2000.

5 James Mitchell, *Devolution in the United Kingdom*, Manchester: Manchester University Press, 2009.

[6] Norman Davies, *The Isles: A history*, London: Macmillan, 1999.

[7] Linda Colley, *Britons: Forging the nation 1707–1837*, New Haven: Yale University Press, 1992.

[8] Claudio Veliz, *The New World of the Gothic Fox: Culture and economy in English and Spanish America*, Berkeley: University of California Press, 1994.

[9] Duncan Bell, *The Idea of Greater Britain: Empire and the future of world order, 1860–1900*, Princeton: Princeton University Press, 2007.

[10] Michael Kenny, *The Politics of English Nationhood*, Oxford: Oxford University Press, 2014.

[11] British Social Attitudes Report – Trends in National Identity. www.bsa.natcen.ac.uk/latest-report/british-social-attitudes-30/devolution/trends-in-national-identity.aspx

[12] Richard Jones, Guy Lodge, Charlie Jeffery, Glenn Gottfried, Roger Scully, Ailsa Henderson and Daniel Wincott, *England and its Two Unions: The anatomy of a nation and its discontents*, London: IPPR, 2013.

[13] Gösta Esping-Andersen, *The Three Worlds of Welfare Capitalism*, Cambridge: Polity, 1990.

[14] Colin Hay and Daniel Wincott, *The Political Economy of European Welfare Capitalism*, London: Palgrave, 2012.

[15] Anthony King, *Who Governs Britain?*, London: Pelican, 2015.

[16] Arend Lijphart, *Patterns of Democracy*, London: Sage, 1999.

[17] Vernon Bogdanor, *The New British Constitution*, Oxford: Hart, 2009.

[18] Meg Russell, *The Contemporary House of Lords: Western bicameralism revived*, Oxford: Oxford University Press, 2013.

[19] Samuel Beer, *Modern British Politics*, London: Faber, 1965.

[20] Nevil Johnson, *Reshaping the British Constitution: Essays in interpretation*, London: Palgrave-Macmillan, 2004.

[21] David Whyte (ed), *How Corrupt is Britain?*, London: Pluto, 2015.

[22] Andrew Gamble, *Between Europe and America: The future of British politics*, London: Palgrave-Macmillan, 2003.

[23] David Dimbleby and David Reynolds, *An Ocean Apart: The relationship between Britain and America in the twentieth century*, New York: Vintage Books, 1989.

[24] John Dumbrell, *A Special Relationship: Anglo–American relations in the cold war and after*, London: Palgrave-Macmillan, 2001; Christopher Hitchens, *Blood, Class, and Empire: The enduring Anglo–American relationship*, New York: Nation Books, 2004.

[25] James Bennett, *The Anglosphere Challenge: Why the English-speaking countries will lead the way in the twenty-first century*, Lanham: MD, Rowman & Littlefield, 2004.

[26] Stephen Bell and Andrew Hindmoor, *Masters of the Universe but Slaves of the Market: Bankers and the great financial meltdown*, Cambridge: Harvard University Press, 2015.

[27] Colin Hay, *The Failure of Anglo–liberal Capitalism*, London: Palgrave-Macmillan, 2013.

[28] Peter Hall and David Soskice, *Varieties of Capitalism: The institutional foundations of comparative advantage*, Oxford: Oxford University Press, 2013.

Epilogue

[1] David Baker, Andrew Gamble and Steve Ludlam, '1846 … 1906 … 1996? Conservative splits and European integration', *Political Quarterly*, 64:4, (1993), pp. 420–34.

[2] David Olusoga, *Black and British: A forgotten history*, London: Pan, 2017.

3   Perry Anderson, 'The intransigent right'; in Perry Anderson, *Spectrum: From right to left in the world of ideas*, London: Verso, 2005, pp. 3–28.

4   David Olusoga, *Black and British: a forgotten history*, London: Pan, 2017, p. 32.

Acknowledgements

The author and publisher wish to thank the publishers of the following essays for permission to reproduce them, with minor changes, in this volume:

'After Brexit' from Colin Hay and Daniel Bailey (eds), *Diverging Capitalisms: Britain, the City of London, and Europe* (2019), pp. 17–42, reproduced with permission of Palgrave Macmillan.

'Explanations of British decline' originally published as 'Theories and Explanations of British Decline', in Richard English and Michael Kenny (eds), *Rethinking British Decline* (1999), pp. 1–22. Published by Macmillan and reproduced with permission of Springer Nature through PLSclear.

'The European disunion' from the *British Journal of Politics and International Relations* 8:1 (2006), pp. 34–49, reproduced with permission of SAGE. https://doi.org/10.1111/j.1467-856X.2006.00224.x

'The Anglo–American world view and the question of world order' from Ben Wellings and Andrew Mycock (eds), *The Anglosphere: Continuity, dissonance, and location. Proceedings of the British Academy* (2019), pp. 175–190, reproduced by permission of Oxford University Press. https://global.oup.com/academic/product/the-anglosphere-9780197266618

'The free economy and the strong state' from the *Socialist Register* (1979), pp. 1–25, reproduced with permission of the Merlin Press. www.merlinpress.co.uk

'Thatcherism and Conservative politics' from Stuart Hall and Martin Jacques (eds), *The Politics of Thatcherism* (1983), pp. 109–131, reproduced with permission of Lawrence & Wishart through PLSclear.

'The crisis of Conservatism' from *New Left Review* 214 (1995), pp. 3–25, reproduced with permission of *New Left Review*.

'The Thatcher myth' from *British Politics* 10: 1 (2015), pp. 3–15, reproduced with permission of Palgrave Macmillan.

'Theories of British politics' from *Political Studies*, 38:3 (1990), pp. 404–20, reproduced with permission of SAGE. https://doi.org/10.1111/j.1467–9248.1990.tb01078.x

'The constitutional revolution in the UK' from *Publius* 36:1 (2006), pp. 19–35, reproduced by permission of Oxford University Press.

'What's British about British politics?' from Richard Heffernan et al (eds), *Developments in British Politics 10* (2016), pp. 1–19. Published by Palgrave Macmillan and reproduced with permission of Springer Nature through PLSclear.

Index